SuperBo

Tom Stevenson has been writing on wine since the mid-1970s. He conceived the *Sunday Telegraph Good Wine Guide*, and his highly praised *Champagne*, winner of four awards, established him as one of the country's leading wine authors. His *Sotheby's World Wine Encyclopaedia*, published in 1988, won five more awards and *Wines of Alsace* (Faber and Faber, 1993) won the Veuve Clicquot Wine Book of the Year Award in the USA. In recent years Tom Stevenson has been voted both 'Wine Writer of the Year' and 'Wine Trade Writer of the Year'. *The New Sotheby's Wine Encyclopaedia* (Dorling Kindersley) is published this autumn. His first edition of *SuperBooze* was published by Faber in 1995.

OTHER BOOKS ON WINE FROM FABER

Bordeaux (new edition) by David Peppercorn
Burgundy (new edition) by Anthony Hanson
French Country Wines by Rosemary George
Haut-Brion by Asa Briggs
Sauternes by Stephen Brook
Sherry (new edition) by Julian Jeffs
The Wines of Alsace by Tom Stevenson
The Wines of Australia (new edition) by Oliver Mayo
The Wines of Greece by Miles Lambert-Gócs
The Wines of the Loire by Roger Voss
The Wines of New Zealand by Rosemary George
The Wines of the Rhône (new edition) by John Livingstone-Learmonth
The Wines of South Africa by James Seely

SuperBooze 1998
The Definitive Guide to Supermarket Drink

TOM STEVENSON

faber and faber
LONDON · BOSTON

First published in 1997
by Faber and Faber Limited
3 Queen Square London WC1N 3AU

Photoset by Parker Typesetting Service, Leicester
Printed in England by Mackays of Chatham plc, Chatham, Kent

All rights reserved

© Tom Stevenson, 1997

Tom Stevenson is hereby identified as author of this
work in accordance with Section 77 of the Copyright,
Designs and Patents Act 1988

*This book is sold subject to the condition that it shall not, by way of trade
or otherwise, be lent, resold, hired out or otherwise circulated without the
publisher's prior consent in any form of binding or cover other than that in
which it is published and without a similar condition including this
condition being imposed on the subsequent purchaser*

A CIP record for this book
is available from the British Library

ISBN 0–571–19277–7

CONTENTS

Introduction viii
    Acknowledgements xv
    The 1998 SuperBooze Awards xvi
Supermarket Directory xx

This year's best buys on a supermarket-by-supermarket basis:

Asda 1
Booths 15
Budgens 29
Co-op 40
Co-operative 58
Crazy Prices 73
Cullens 74
Europa 75
Food Fair 81
Food Giant 82
Gateway 83
Good Neighbour 84
Harts 85
Kwik Save 86
Londis 96
Marks & Spencer 103
Morrisons 116
Plymco 129
Presto 130
Quinsworth 131
Safeway 132
Sainsbury's 145
Savacentre 156

SoLo 157
Somerfield 158
Stewarts 167
Tesco 168
Waitrose 185
Wellworths 199
The Wine & Beer Rankings 200
This year's best buys by type & style:
Red Wines 201
  Argentina 201
  Bordeaux 201
  Bulgaria 203
  Cabernet Sauvignon 203
  Cabernet-based blends 205
  Cabernet Franc 206
  Chianti (including other Sangiovese and Sangiovese-dominated blends) 207
  French Vins de Pays 208

Gamay 209
Italy (other than Chianti) 209
Malbec (pure and blended) 210
Merlot (pure and blended) 210
New Zealand 211
Pinotage 212
Pinot Noir 212
Portugal 213
Rhône 214
Rhône-Rangers 215
Rioja (including other Tempranillo and Tempranillo-dominated blends) 215
Spain (other than Rioja) 216
Syrah/Shiraz 217
Syrah/Shiraz-dominated blends 218
Zinfandel 219
White Wines 220
Argentina 220
Bordeaux (dry style) 220
Chardonnay (pure and blended) 221
Chenin Blanc (dry style) 224
French Vins de Pays 225
German style 227
Gewurztraminer 227
Italy 228
Medium dry 228
Muscadet 229
New Zealand 229
Pinot Blanc 230
Pinot Gris 230
Riesling 231
Riesling (medium-to-sweet style) 231
Sauvignon Blanc 231
Semillon (pure and blended) 233
Sweet or dessert wine style 234
Viognier 234
Rosé Wines 235
Dry and off-dry 235
Medium to medium-sweet 235
Sparkling Wines 236
Brut or dry sparkling wine 236
Sweet sparkling wine 238
Fortified Wines 239
Port: early-bottled styles 239
Port: late-bottled styles 240
Sherry 241
Liqueur Muscat 242
Beer
Bitter or traditional ale style (without widgets) 243

Bitter or traditional ale style (with widgets) 248
Dark beers (milds, stouts and porters; without widgets) 249
Dark beers (stouts; with widgets) 250
Lager and Pilsner styles (without widgets) 251
Lager and Pilsner styles (with widgets) 254
Pale Ale 255
Spirit Price Guide 257
Glossary of Technical and Tasting Terms 262
Index 281

INTRODUCTION

Can this really be the third edition of *SuperBooze*? Time must fly when I'm as high as a kite in my tasting room. But I'm not the only one enjoying myself; you must be too. Within twelve months of *SuperBooze* becoming the first shop-by-shop consumer guide to cover own-label beers, their sales soared by no less than 65 per cent. And since *SuperBooze* widened its scope to encompass branded beers too, premium beers have become one of the fastest-expanding sectors of the drinks market.

SuperBooze cannot take *all* the credit for increasing the sales of own-label beers by such a staggering percentage – it would have had to sell several million copies to achieve that – but it obviously played its part, which does at least verify that the guide has its finger on the pulse. It is premium beers, particularly British speciality beers, that are catching on, not the fruit beers of Belgium that some journalists still prattle on about. The real interest lies in regional ales, both traditional and innovative, but the current boom is just the tip of the iceberg. The range and availability of British beers are still at a very early, developmental stage. Beer today still falls a long way short of the sophistication that wine already possessed back in the early 1970s – but it won't take a quarter of a century to close the gap.

Trade education is just about zero: there's no formal training for beer buyers, or even courses on how to taste the product (an entirely different process from wine tasting). But things are beginning to move, and when the supermarket beer-buying departments are taken as seriously as the wine-buying departments, we'll see a revolution on the shelves.

Introduction

At the moment it is ridiculous that in 90 per cent of supermarkets, regional beers are either available on a local basis only or, because the buying and distribution are centralized, not at all. Can you imagine the same constraints on selling wine? By the Millennium, however, you can expect not only twenty times the range of beers to be available, but also that they be displayed in a similar format to wines, grouped by region and flavour. The presentation of the products will also be more evocative of their actual taste, with beers brewed from single varieties of hops (and malts) to give customers building blocks of basic aromas and flavours, just as Chardonnay, Cabernet *et al* have for wine drinkers. Beers and beer drinkers will move on, of course, just as wines and wine drinkers have, but however much the ABC (Anything But Chardonnay) consumers complain about the overkill of varieties, they must remain for future generations to be guided by, and so it will be for beer drinkers.

How to use this book

With wines and beers listed under each supermarket in ascending price order in just six sections (Red, White, Rosé, Sparkling, Fortified and Beers), *SuperBooze* is by far the easiest drinks guide to find your way around in. If you want to know what the best value products for a particular supermarket are, just look up its entry in the **Supermarket Directory**. If you want to know the best value product sold by all the supermarkets at a particular price point for a specific type or style (such as Chardonnay, Shiraz or Pilsner), look up that category in **The Wine & Beer Rankings**. All the products for each category are listed, not just the medal-winners. They are in price order, not medal order, making this section far more useful in discerning how the wines, beers and indeed supermarkets have performed in each tasting. Furthermore, they are listed in columns, making it far easier to run your finger down the products, retailers, supermarkets or prices to find exactly what you want.

Each category heading is now listed in the contents at the front of the book, making it easier still to find the type of product you're after. And – shock, horror – a *full index*! At long last, you can do that one thing so many people have tried to do when picking up a consumer drinks guide: check to see whether a particular product is in the book. It's not too much to ask, is it? Well, chop off my drinking arm for not giving you an index in the first place. It was inexcusable.

Each supermarket* has pledged that at least 80 per cent of all wines and beers submitted to *SuperBooze* will be available in at least 80 per cent of its branches. On the one hand, this guarantees that most recommendations will be available to most readers most of the time, while on the other it provides a certain flexibility, enabling supermarkets to show at least some products of a more limited production.

What if you want a product that turns out to be one of the 20 per cent and your store does not stock it? Or what about the old problem whereby the more a product is hyped up, the sooner it will sell out?

This is where the **Stock Me and Buy One** scheme comes in. In the past, no matter how confident a supermarket was about having sufficient stocks to last the duration of a guide's recommendations, it was impossible to predict what the surge in sales would be or where those who will want specific

*This does not apply to symbol groups or the Co-op, owing to the individual ownership of the former and the great variation in branch size of the latter.

Introduction xi

products live. The new *SuperBooze* scheme does not offer a complete answer – nothing could, short of supermarkets overstocking every line in all their branches and having to dump the leftovers – but **Stock Me and Buy One** comes as close as I can think to making every single recommendation available to every single reader.

If you want a recommended product from a supermarket logo, but cannot find it in your local branch, just ask the manager (or owner, in the case of a symbol group such as Londis). He or she will be authorized to order it in if it is still in stock within the company. Some supermarkets will even try to track down an out-of-stock item throughout the group to see if any branch has any left. You do not have to commit yourself to anything more than a single bottle or can (unless it happens to be a four-pack, six-pack etc). The manager (or owner) is not obliged to provide this service, but has the discretion to do so, and his or her group will possess the capability to respond, and must do so if requested by one of its managers and stocks remain.

What is the shelf-life of *SuperBooze*?
This was the question I was most often asked on my promotional tasting tour last year. As mentioned earlier, the more a product is recommended, the sooner it will sell out, so the purpose of any guide is in a very real sense self-defeating. That said, the UK has had sixteen years' experience of shop-by-shop, shelf-by-shelf wine guides, which makes British consumers the most sophisticated in the world when dealing with the realities of such publications. Most readers know the problems, accept that imperfect guides are better than no guides at all, and try to grab the best bargains as quickly as their finances and thirst allow.

No matter how hard a supermarket tries to ensure the

shelf-life of its products, absolute guarantees are a pipe dream; and although it is obviously in a supermarket's own interest to make sure that all the products I rave about will be available – which means extra money through the till – some supermarkets try harder to do this than others. Each supermarket has the opportunity to submit new lines and forthcoming vintages right up until two weeks before my copy deadline, but not all of them take advantage of this. Every year I hope to push, nudge and bully more supermarkets to help themselves by submitting more long-term future lines as late as possible – even if it does complicate the tastings and give my computer database a headache.

All blind-tasted by price point

SuperBooze is unique in tasting all products blind, which means that the bottles are covered to prevent my knowing their identity. *SuperBooze* is also unique in tasting like with like within the same price category. It is simply not possible to taste the same style and price category of wine in different places at different times and make accurate comparative judgements. This has nothing to do with any lack of skill in the taster; no supermarket buyer, however brilliant a taster he or she may be, would contemplate making a decision while going from cellar to cellar tasting. They bring home samples of all the most promising wines within a set budget and taste them together, sometimes blind, sometimes not, in order to decide which is best. If this method is good enough for supermarkets to buy their wines by, it's good enough for me to judge them by.

Because I taste everything blind, my notes relate to a number only and are entered on the computer in ignorance of the name of the actual wine or beer. There are two rounds

Introduction

of tastings, with all potential medal-winners subjected to a second test. This is necessary for two reasons. Firstly because, in the largest categories, there can be as many as forty wines or beers at roughly the same price, and as I taste in flights of twelve (usually eight flights a night), potential medal-winners can be tables apart. Secondly because, although potential medal-winners stand out from the rest of the field, it is a much tougher test when they are in each other's company; the second tasting makes it easier to distinguish the different medal levels. These notes are entered on the database together with the medal status, the computer performs the super-selection process – whereby the lowest *tranche* of wines and beers I thought worthy of recommendation are ruthlessly discarded – then feeds the data to my word processor. It is only at this point that I see the identity of the products; I often add comments on that particular wine, beer or appellation, but I do not materially alter my description, as can be seen from those notes where I freely admit guessing wrong. When late submissions of new lines and forthcoming vintages arrive after my main tastings have begun, they usually go straight into the potential medal winner tasting. If this has already finished, my tasting coordinator consults the database to identify a bronze medal product of the same style and price category. This is then purchased and put up as a yardstick against which to taste the late arrival.

I taste alone and in the seclusion of a professionally equipped tasting room where I cannot be disturbed. The wines are in this book because that's where I want them to be, not because I have arrived at any compromise with a partner, and not because I tasted the wine in a room full of other journalists whose vociferous support or rejection of a wine has swayed me (and if anyone suggests that two or more people can taste together and not have their opinion swayed from time to time, I suggest you do not believe them). The comments, medals and awards are therefore all my own. They have been arrived at through quiet deliberation, and if I think that tasting them again with food might affect how they perform, I take them back for supper. It's a hard life . . .

Acknowledgements

My thanks to numerous people at Faber and Faber, including Belinda Matthews, Joanna Mackle, Ian Bahrami, Ron Costley, Justine Willett, Alan Dingle, Tim Davies, Susan Law, Clare Lawler, Steve Blackburn and Rachel Alexander.

My gratitude for making the tastings possible and an unending supply of information must go to Nick Dymoke-Marr, Alastair Morrell and Illy Jaffar (Asda), Chris Dee and Dave Smith (Booths), Alan Crompton-Batt (British American), Tony Finnerty and Rod Alexander (Budgens), Angela Muir MW and Anna Betts (Cellarwood International), Arabella Woodrow (Co-op), Christine Sandys, Alex Payce-Drury, Angus Clark and Gary Pemberton (Co-operative), Annie Todd (DSA), Adrian Tallboys (Europa), Richard Graves and Justin Addison (Kwik Save), Gary Maloney (Londis), Chris Murphy and Angela Johnson (Marks & Spencer), Stuart Purdie (Morrisons), Elizabeth Robertson MW and Victoria Molyneux (Safeway), Allan Cheesman and Dorcas Jamieson (Sainsbury's), Angela Mount (Somerfield), Nicki Walden (Tesco), Julian Brind MW and Joe Wadsack (Waitrose), with apologies for anyone inadvertently missed out. To Martin and Mark at Zedcor for taking in deliveries during our absence, to all the Zedcor fork-lift drivers who keep an eye on things. Finally to Cherry Pattison and my wife Pat who between them receive, unpack, label and log on almost one-third of the amount of wines that it takes twenty-five people to process at the International Wine Challenge!

The 1998 Superbooze Awards

The supermarket awards are based entirely on the rankings found in the section after the awards. After last year's two-way split between Booths and Safeway, it looks as if Booth's wine and beer buyers, Chris Dee and Dave Smith, went gung-ho for a clear-cut decision; and they stormed home to victory in every way you want to interpret the medal statistics.

Undisputed Supermarket of the Year

Booths

I retasted fresh examples of all the gold medal wines and beers to decide on the following top awards:

Red Wines of the Year

☞ The Best Value Red Wine of the Year
Ⓖ **José Neiva 1994 Oak Aged**
Booths, £2.49

☞ The Best Quality Red Wine of the Year
Ⓖ **Church Road Reserve 1994 Cabernet Sauvignon Merlot**
Marks & Spencer, £11.99

White Wines of the Year

☞ The Best Value White Wine of the Year
Ⓖ **Chardonnay par Yves Grassa 1996 Barrel Fermented, Vin de Pays des Côtes-de-Gascogne**
Asda, £4.99

☞ The Best Quality White Wine of the Year

Belondrade y Lurton 1994 Rueda
Waitrose, £10.95

Rosé Wines of the Year

☞ The Best Value Rosé Wine of the Year
No award this year
☞ The Best Quality Rosé Wine of the Year
No award this year

Sparkling Wines of the Year

☞ The Best Value Sparkling Wine of the Year
Seaview Pinot Noir Chardonnay 1994 Brut
Somerfield, £8.49
☞ The Best Quality Sparkling Wine of the Year
Champagne Chartogne-Taillet NV Brut, Cuvée Sainte-Anne
Safeway, £15.99

Fortified Wines of the Year

☞ The Best Value Fortified Wine
Castillo de Liria NV Moscatel
Kwik Save, £2.99
☞ The Best Quality Fortified Wine of the Year
Lustau Solera Reserva Fine Sherry NV Pedro Ximénez San Emilio
Booths, £10.99

Beers of the Year

☞ Special Beer Award of the Year
For mastering the 'widget' technology and producing a

bottled bitter that true bitter drinkers can appreciate.

(G) Fuggles Imperial Strong Ale, Castle Eden Brewery
Budgens, Co-op, Co-operative, Kwik Save, Safeway
Per pint: £1.58–£1.81

☞ The Best Value Bitter of the Year
(G) Ward's Classic Yorkshire Ale
Booths
Per pint: £1.02

☞ The Best Quality Bitter of the Year
(G) Riggwelter Strong Yorkshire Ale, Black Sheep Brewery
Booths, Morrisons, Sainsbury's
Per pint: £1.76–£1.81

☞ The Best Value Light Beer of the Year
(G) Asda German Pilsener
Asda
Per pint: £1.29

☞ The Best Quality Light Beer of the Year
(G) Marston's Burton S.P.A.
Morrisons, Tesco
Per pint: £1.81

☞ The Best Value Dark Beer of the Year
(G) Murphy's Draught Stout (bottled)
Budgens, Co-operative, Morrisons, Safeway
Per pint: £1.69–£1.76

☞ The Best Quality Dark Beer of the Year
(G) Guinness Foreign Extra Stout
Booths
Per pint: £2.15

Introduction xix

Prices

Prices were correct at the time of tasting. You should expect some changes due to exchange-rate fluctuations, prices rising at source, possible increases in VAT and other variables, but these should be within reason, and the historical price in this book will help you to spot any excessive increases.

Please note that prices were not adjusted prior to publication because all the wines and beers were tasted within their own price category; to change that would be to make a mockery of the blind tasting, the notes made and the medals awarded.

Different Vintages

Wines recommended in this book are specific to the vintages indicated. Follow-on vintages *might* be of a similar quality and character, but are likely to be either better or worse. Wines of real interest are seldom exactly the same from one year to the next. Cheap fruity wines, whether white or red, are often better the younger they are, and the difference between vintages is generally less important for bulk wines produced in hotter countries, but even these will vary in some vintages. The difference in vintage is usually most noticeable for individually crafted wines produced the world over. Don't be put off a wine because it is of a different vintage, as you could be missing an even greater treat, but do try a bottle before laying out on a case or two.

Is a £3 Gold Medal as good as a £6 Gold Medal?

It is possible, but unlikely. It should be remembered that a medal is awarded for the category, which includes price as well as style. If this were not so, and medals were awarded purely on quality, regardless of price, then the world's most expensive wines would have to be the yardsticks, and a £20 wine would be hard pushed to qualify for a bronze, let alone a £3 wine earning a gold. The best-value £3 gold medal wine might match up to, say, a £4 gold medal wine, but you cannot realistically expect it to compare with a £6 gold medal wine.

SUPERMARKET DIRECTORY

The following supermarket entries encompass more than 10,000 superstore, supermarket and convenience store outlets in England, Scotland, Wales and Northern Ireland.

Under each category (Red Wine, White Wine, Rosé Wine, Sparkling Wine, Fortified Wine, Beer) products are listed in ascending order of price; thus the first medal-winner you find will be the best value, while the last will probably be the best quality, although things can never be as precise as that. Still, that's the fuzzy rationale, and it's easy to remember. Unless otherwise stated, the price of each wine is for a full 70cl bottle. If it is a half-bottle, litre, magnum or whatever, this will be indicated.

Beer prices are given at the end of each entry, just before the country of origin, as can and bottle sizes vary so much and many beers are priced for a multipack. For easy comparison, you will find the equivalent price per pint immediately following the name of the beer.

For every supermarket I have selected the Best Value red wines, white wines and beers, which are indicated by a pointing finger (☞), and this is also used to highlight the Wines of the Year and Beers of the Year.

ASDA

Number of stores *210*
  Opening hours *Monday–Saturday 9a.m.–8p.m., Sunday 10a.m.–4p.m.*
Maximum range *346 wines, 205 beers, 146 spirits*
  Alternative methods of payment *Cheque with card, Switch and Delta debit cards, Access, Visa*
Local delivery *Not provided, but will help carry goods to car if requested*
Discounts *Under review*
Refund policy? *No excuses guarantee – you return a faulty bottle and Asda will either replace it, exchange it for a bottle of the same value, or give you a full refund.*
Other services *Free loan of glasses, sale or return. In August 1997 Asda became the first supermarket to promise wine, beer and spirit tastings 'every Friday or Saturday in every store for ever'. Additionally, some 75 stores will run a series of tutored tasting evenings (check with your local store for details).*

Comment Asda is the fourth-largest supermarket, with 8 per cent of the market, having come a long way since it started out as Associated Dairies (hence its name), pioneering the superstore retailing concept in the UK as early as 1965. All Asda branches are now superstores. Although initially a northern-based group, with a strong presence in Scotland, Asda started moving south in the early 1980s, and it is probably no coincidence that this was when the group first began to take wine seriously.

Asda has fought price maintenance on pharmaceutical products and is seeking to remove VAT on sanitary items. Such controversial public stances grab the headlines, of course, but the company is genuinely price-competitive, which is probably why it has not gone the loyalty card route.

Asda has many brilliant wine and beer bargains, as this

year's better thought-out submissions have demonstrated with two and a half times as many gold medals as last year.

Red Wines

Claret NV Paul Barbe, Asda £2.99
(B) Only a penny more expensive than the cheapest claret recommended this year (see Tesco), this also rates a bronze medal, but is made in a softer, more Merlot-dominated style, for easier drinking on its own. [*Bordeaux, France*]

Montagne Noire Red NV Vin de Pays de l'Aude, Asda
£2.99
(B) A well-built, tasty young red, the flavours of which build in the mouth. Good with food. [*Southern France, France*]

Temple Ruins Greek Red Wine 1995 Asda £2.99
(S) Greek wines are not the oxidized horrors they used to be a decade ago, and this one, made in collaboration with Australian winemaker Ben Riggs, is an excellent example of how flavour-packed and substantial these wines can be. [*Greece*]

Pinot Noir 1995 River Route Selection £3.19
(B) The best-cheapest Pinot Noir tasted this year (all the cheaper wines either being oxidized or tasting of chemicals), this has real Pinot Noir varietal character, albeit of the red fruit-gum kind. Clean, light and fruity. Better than the Romanian Pinot Noir sold by Londis for 20p more, although it does not have the depth of fruit on the palate. [*Baratça, Romania*]

Red Wines

Marble Mountain 1995 St.-George Cabernet Sauvignon, Asda £3.49

Ⓑ Toasty nose, long and rich on the palate, with nice, mouth-tingling grippy tannins on the finish. Made in collaboration with Australian winemaker Ben Riggs. [*Peloponnese, Greece*]

Tramontane 1996 Syrah, Vin de Pays d'Oc, Asda £3.49

Soft and tasty, this is much better than the Grenache in the same range. [*Southern France, France*]

Bright Brothers 1994 Old Vines £3.70

Ⓑ Characteristically Australian idea of what an inexpensive red wine from this country should be, with a touch of residual sweetness to enhance the fruit, yet retaining the spicy-peppery typicity of its Portuguese origins. [*Estremadura, Portugal*]

Chilean Cabernet Merlot 1995 Vinicola Las Taguas, Asda £3.79

Ⓑ Fresh, sappy fruit. [*Mataquito, Chile*]

Côtes-du-Rhône 1996 Aged in Oak, Roger Bernoin

£3.99

Ⓖ An extremely intelligent use of *macération carbonique* and gentle oak-ageing has produced the most stylish Côtes-du-Rhône for under £4.99 – so why pay as much as that when you can have this for £3.99? [*Côtes-du-Rhône, France*]

Trentino Pinot Nero 1995 La Vis, Asda £3.99

Light and fresh, with more than a hint of varietal fruit, this is really not bad for a sub-£4 Italian Pinot Noir. [*Trentino, Italy*]

**Domaine de Grangeneuve 1995 Coteaux-du-Tricastin,
Cuvée Tradition** £4.49
> This soft, chocolaty red goes well with bangers and
> beans. [*Coteaux-du-Tricastin, Rhône, France*]

Jennsberg 1996 Pinot Noir, Asda £4.49
> (G) Firm and dry, with classic redcurrant–strawberry
> varietal character on nose and palate, this great bargain
> makes an excellent food wine. [*Paarl, South Africa*]

La Rural 1996 Malbec £4.49
> (B) Attractive, rustic richness of fruit with firm
> structure and less rustic, more violet-smooth on the
> finish. [*Mendoza, Argentina*]

Mount Hurtle 1995 Grenache Shiraz £4.49
> (S) Very stylish fruit for the price. [*South Australia,
> Australia*]

**La Domeque, Tête de Cuvée 1995 Vieilles Vignes
Syrah, Vin de Pays d'Oc** £4.99
> (B) Age this twelve months for a real treat. [*Southern
> France, France*]

**Rowan Brook Cabernet Sauvignon 1994 Winemaker's
Reserve Oak Aged, Asda** £4.99
> (G) A stunningly fresh bouquet of fresh-picked
> blackberries followed by tangy summer-pudding fruits
> on the palate. This would be a brilliant gold medal
> winner at £7.99, let alone at £4.99! [*Mataquito, Chile*]

Rozzano 1995 Villa Pigna £4.99
> (S) Rich forest fruits supported by smooth oak on the
> finish. [*Marches, Italy*]

Red Wines

Valdivieso 1996 Malbec £4.99

Ⓢ A dark, almost opaque purple-hued colour, with very rich smoky-violety fruit. More finesse than any of the other Malbec wines. [*Lontue, Chile*]

Château de Parenchère 1995 Bordeaux Supérieur £5.25

Ⓢ Big, dark, expansive red with excellent acidity and tannin, this is much finer than the inky, ungainly 1994 also sold by Asda. [*Bordeaux, France*]

Bankside Shiraz 1994 Hardys £5.99

The huge fruit and oak flavour here would normally deserve a silver medal, but is spoilt by a distinct *pétillance*. If you take a sip, keep the mouth closed and stick your tongue through the middle of the wine, you should feel the prickly sensation of carbonic gas – not enough to make the wine sparkling, but sufficient for it to loose its smoothness. Solution? Pump the gas out with a Vacu-vin (the only use I have for the implement!) See how much gas there is and taste how much smoother and better focused the fruit is. [*Padthaway & Clare Valley, South Australia, Australia*]

Baron de Ley 1991 Rioja Reserva £6.79

Ⓢ Very soft, with gentle fruit that assumes a liquorice intensity on the finish. Has finesse. [*Rioja, Spain*]

Fleurie 1995 Clos de la Chapelle des Bois £6.85

Deep-flavoured for Beaujolais, but nice, tasty fruit and some elegance. If this was the basic £4.99 Beaujolais, everyone would be singing its praises, but at £6.85 it is lucky to scrape in. [*Fleurie, Beaujolais, Burgundy, France*]

**Château Reynella 1994 Basket Pressed Cabernet
Merlot** £7.99
Ⓢ A stylish red with elegant fruit, cedary oak and
nice tannins. [*McLaren Vale, South Australia,
Australia*]

Penfolds Kalimna Bin 28 1993 Shiraz £8.99
Ⓖ This stunning wine tastes younger and fruitier
than the 1994 Kalimna Bin 28 and provides a
marvellous array of fresh-picked blackberry–
blackcurrant flavours. [*South Australia, Australia*]

White Wines

Vin de Pays des Côtes-de-Gascogne 1996 Asda £2.99
Ⓑ A zippy, zingy wine with lots of ripe apple and
pear fruit flavours. [*South Western France, France*]

**Hungarian Chardonnay 1996 Private Reserve,
Neszmély Winery** £3.29
Ⓑ A very fresh and clean dry white with easy-
drinking floral fruit. [*Mecsekalja, Hungary*]

**Hungarian Sauvignon Blanc 1995 Private Reserve,
Neszmély Winery** £3.29
Ⓑ Fresh, dry, floral fruit with a nice crisp finish and
no greenness. [*Sopron, Hungary*]

**Chilean Sauvignon Blanc 1996 Vinicola Las Taguas,
Asda** £3.49
Ⓑ Fresh, dry and crisp with good fruit, hinting of
apricots and gooseberries. [*Mataquito, Chile*]

White Wines

Montagne Noire 1996 Sauvignon Blanc, Vin de Pays d'Oc, Asda £3.49

S The fresh, crisp, tasty intensity of fruit in this wine is not out-and-out Sauvignon in character, but knocked the spots off lots that were. [*Southern France, France*]

Colli di Catone 1995 Frascati Superiore, Asda £3.99

If you're looking for supermarket Frascati (which is at least fresher than Frascati purchased elsewhere), this was the best tasted this year. [*Frascati, Italy*]

Fairview 1996 Gewürztraminer £3.99

Dry with correctly low acidity, this should develop some spice over the next 1–2 years. [*Paarl, South Africa*]

Montagne Noire Chardonnay 1996 Vin de Pays d'Oc, Asda £3.99

B Very fresh, as might be expected from a 1996 vintage, this wine will develop some toastiness in bottle, but promises to remain elegant in the process. [*Southern France, France*]

Penfolds Rawson's Retreat Bin 202 1996 Riesling £3.99

B Lime-fruit aroma, crisp, creamy fruit with a spritz and a very dry finish. [*South Australia, Australia*]

South Australia Chardonnay 1995 W1226, Asda £3.99

A standard oaked Oz Chardonnay that is well worth £3.99. [*South Australia, Australia*]

Trentino Chardonnay 1996 La Vis, Asda £3.99

B Authentic Chardonnay fruit and good Italian typicity in the same bottle! [*Trentino, Italy*]

**Muscadet de Sèvre-et-Maine Sur Lie 1995 Domaine
Gautron** £4.49
> This wine has the fatter, apricoty fruit of much riper
> grapes than are the norm for Muscadet, yet it still has
> the correct, crisp structure and narrowly missed a
> bronze medal. [*Muscadet de Sèvre-et-Maine, Loire,
> France*]

**Rowan Brook Chardonnay 1996 Winemaker's Reserve
Oak Aged, Asda** £4.49
> ⓖ Big, big flavour wrapped up in lemony oak.
> [*Casablanca, Chile*]

**Chardonnay par Yves Grassa 1996 Barrel Fermented,
Vin de Pays des Côtes-de-Gascogne** £4.99
> ⓖ For a Chardonnay that costs less than a fiver, this
> is very classy indeed. Beautifully focused, clean, ripe
> fruit and lovely understated oak make this a very
> elegant wine to drink on its own. Food only detracts.
> [*South Western France, France*]
> ☞ THE BEST VALUE WHITE WINE OF THE YEAR

Cuckoo Hill Viognier NV Vin de Pays d'Oc £4.99
> ⓢ The 1995 was the first vintage of this wine made
> under the auspices of Australian winemaker Nick
> Butler. That vintage is still nice, but fatter than last
> year and definitely reaching its peak. The 1996,
> however, tastes rather green compared with how the
> 1995 tasted one year ago, and I reckon it has been
> harvested too early. At Asda's press tasting this non-
> vintage version was proclaimed as 1996, but tasted
> against that vintage under blind conditions, this wine
> tastes nothing like it. Indeed, the 1996 did not even
> squeeze into *SuperBooze* as a basic recommendation,

White Wines

whereas the 1995 (*see* Co-operative) picked up a bronze once again, and this made silver. It tastes like a 1995/1996 blend, although I could not replicate this by mixing the two vintages together. [*Southern France, France*]

La Domeque, Tête de Cuvée 1996 Vieilles Vignes Blanc, Vin de Pays d'Oc £4.99
Fat and fruity, dry white lifted by a touch of Muscat. [*Southern France, France*]

Peter Lehmann 1996 Semillon £4.99
(ℬ) Knocking the spots off the normally excellent Lindemans Hunters Valley Semillon, this has a real, limey richness. [*Barossa, South Australia, Australia*]

Valdivieso 1996 Chardonnay £4.99
(ℬ) This wine has enough sweet, ripe, upfront fruit to warrant a silver medal, but for a lack of acidity which makes it a tad too fat. [*Andes foothills, Chile*]

Vouvray 1996 Hand Picked, Denis Marchais £4.99
(𝒮) This medium-sweet Vouvray is the only Chenin Blanc that was clean and fresh enough to be recommended from this year's *SuperBooze* tastings, and its tangy fruit is delicious enough for a silver medal. Best now if you prefer freshness, but will become honeyed over the next two years. [*Vouvray, Loire, France*]

Penfolds Barossa Valley 1996 Semillon-Chardonnay
£5.99
(ℬ) A serious wine that deserves a little ageing. [*Barossa, South Australia, Australia*]

Rosemount Estate 1996 Semillon Chardonnay £6.49
Ⓑ Rich and luscious, this would be a silver at £5.49 and a gold at £4.49. [*South Eastern Australia, Australia*]

Saint-Véran 1996 Domaine des Deux Roches £6.49
Ⓢ Full, fresh, crisp, lemony fruit of some intensity and class for a Saint-Véran. [*St-Véran, Burgundy, France*]

Chablis NV Guy Mothe, Asda £6.99
Ⓑ Very fresh and mouthwatering. [*Chablis, Burgundy, France*]

Château Reynella 1995 Chardonnay £7.99
Ⓢ Lemony-oak aroma, very rich fruit with a big, toasty finish. A complete wine that does not benefit from partnering food. [*McLaren Vale, South Australia, Australia*]

Chablis Premier Cru Fourchaume 1995 Domaine du Colombier £10.99
Ⓢ Very fresh, tasty and elegant, this wine knocked the spots off other supermarket *premier cru* Chablis, and was in a much higher class than a Puligny-Montrachet *premier cru* selling at twice the price. [*Chablis, Burgundy, France*]

Chablis Premier Cru Fourchaume 1994 Domaine du Colombier £11.99
Although rich and tasty, this wine is between the first flush of freshness and the bottle-matured stage, so it does not deserve a medal for current drinking (go for the 1995 instead), although anyone who enjoys more mature, complex white Burgundy should keep this a couple of years, when they will be greatly rewarded. [*Chablis, Burgundy, France*]

Sparkling Wines

Seaview Rosé NV Brut £6.49
Creamy strawberry and lavender fruit with a soft
mousse. [*McLaren Vale, South Australia, Australia*]

Cranswick Pinot Chardonnay NV Brut £6.99
(S) This very creamy, almost oaky, zesty-lemony fizz
is quite impressive for the price. [*Riverina, NSW,
Australia*]

Scharffenberger NV Brut £9.49
(S) Fine, elegant, rich and smooth, with a lovely
creamy-biscuity complexity beginning to build. Over
the years Asda has proved to be Scharffenberger's most
loyal fan in the UK – so why don't they sell
Scharffenberger's best wine, the Blanc de Blancs?
[*Mendocino, USA*]

Asda Champagne NV Brut Réserve, Cuvée Speciale
£11.99
(S) Creamy-biscuity richness and a fine structure
make this an excellent bargain. [*Champagne, France*]

Fortified Wines

Muscat de Frontignan Blanc 1996 Danie de Wet £4.99
(G) Orange-flower aroma, extremely floral Muscat
fruit. Elegant and stylish. [*Robertson, South Africa*]

Ruby Port NV Smith Woodhouse, Asda £4.99
Fresh, peppery fruit with an elegant finish. [*Douro,
Portugal*]

Vintage Character Port NV Smith Woodhouse, Asda
£5.49

S You certainly get a lot of richness for the price, and it is smoother and sweeter than most Ports at this price point. [*Douro, Portugal*]

LBV Port 1990 Smith Woodhouse, Asda £6.49

G Looking for as much power for your money as possible? Well, this has so much oomph and flavour that it's like buying a Dual Pentium II for the price of a 386! [*Douro, Portugal*]

Cockburn's Special Reserve Port NV £8.99

B Very smooth and satisfying, this is one of the most consistent ruby Ports made, but there are too many superior Ports at this price for it to warrant anything more than a bronze. [*Douro, Portugal*]

Graham's Late Bottled Vintage Port 1991 £9.99

G Powerful, intense and complete, with a satisfying balance of richness and sweetness. [*Douro, Portugal*]

Southbrook Farms NV Canadian Cassis
£7.99 (half-bottle)

S Stunning blackcurrant liqueur to rival the very best French Cassis. [*Ontario, Canada*]

Beers

Flanders Bier, Asda Per pint: £1.02

B Nice hoppy aromas, some real flavour and a clean, crisp finish. What more can you expect at this price point? £4.49 per 10x25cl bottles. [*5%, Belgium*]

Holland Bier, Asda Per pint: £1.02

B Deeper and fatter than most lagers or lager-style brews at this price point. £4.49 per 10x25cl bottles. [*5%, Breda, Holland*]

Asda German Pilsener Per pint: £1.29

G This lovely, assertively-flavoured brew is indeed the very best Pilsner on the market. £2.99 per 4x33cl bottles. [*5%, Dortmund, Germany*]

☞ THE BEST VALUE LIGHT BEER OF THE YEAR

Italian Birra, Export Premium Lager, Asda
Per pint: £1.29

Light, easy and refreshing. £2.99 per 4x33cl bottles. [*5%, Veneto, Italy*]

Gentleman Jack Strong Ale, Shepherd Neame, Asda
Per pint: £1.47

S Lovely hoppy aromas, almost Saaz Pilsner perfume, but with a genuine ale structure, finishing with a gentle mellowness and only a hint of bitterness. An unusual beer, thus completely befitting the real Gentleman Jack, who is profiled on the back label. £1.29 per 50cl bottle. [*5%, Kent, England*]

Rusty Rivet, Authentic Brown Ale, Shepherd Neame, Asda Per pint: £1.47

B The peppery hop aroma lifts this above all other milds tasted this year. £1.29 per 50cl bottle. [*4.7%, Kent, England*]

Whitechapel Porter, Shepherd Neame, Asda
Per pint: £1.47

B Compared with Shepherd Neame's Original Porter, this has the same depth of colour but a more ruddy hue, is less smoky but has more sherry notes, and is a touch sweeter. £1.29 per 50cl bottle. [*5.2%, Kent, England*]

BOOTHS

Number of stores *24*
Opening hours *Vary from store to store, but the majority open Monday–Tuesday and Saturday 8.30a.m.–6p.m., Wednesday and Thursday 8.30a.m.–7p.m., Friday 8.30a.m.–8p.m., Sunday 10a.m.–4p.m. (16 stores only)*
Maximum range *600 wines, 200 beers, 300 spirits*
Alternative methods of payment *Cash, cheque with card, Switch and Delta debit cards, Access, Visa*
Delivery *No comment*
Discounts *5% off six bottles, 15% off wine purchases in excess of £150*
Refund policy? *Yes*
Other services *Sale or return on party purchases, free loan of glasses, free tasting every weekend (10 stores)*

Comment Booths' wine buyer is Chris Dee, a man who could recite all the Port vintages off the top of his head when he was just fifteen. By comparison, excelling in *SuperBooze* two years running must be a doddle. Still, seventeen gold medals and no fewer than five Wine or Beer of the Year Awards is pretty impressive by the standards of a mere mortal. As a child, Dee read about the subject for an entire year before tasting his first wine. He was head-hunted by Booths after setting up his own wine retailing business in Yorkshire, where he established something of a reputation for himself. Dave Smith, his opposite number in the beer department, submitted an equally stunning range.

For details of 'Stock Me and Buy One' see pages xi–xii.

Red Wines

José Neiva 1994 Oak Aged £2.49
(G) This wine stands out in its price category on all fronts. On appearance alone it is striking, with a deep, dark, purple-hued colour that has an intensity not normally seen at this price level. This promises so much that it could easily disappoint – but it does not. You cannot buy class at this price, fair enough, but this wine does provide masses of rich, smooth berry fruits wrapped up in the coconut and vanilla of American oak. The cheapest gold medal red wine in this year's *SuperBooze* by £1.50! [*Estremadura, Portugal*]
☞ THE BEST VALUE RED WINE OF THE YEAR

Vinha Nova NV Vinho de Mesa Tinto £2.99
(B) Full of juicy fruit that should be drunk straight away. [*Mesa, Portugal*]

Viña Alarba 1995 Calatayud £2.99
(S) The only reservation I have in giving this such a high score is that its fresh, sherbetty fruit is really so delicious for summertime drinking, but it will be autumn before *SuperBooze* is published. I'll keep my fingers crossed for an Indian summer, however – and you should check out the 1996 before *next* summer. [*Calatayud, Spain*]

Côtes-du-Ventoux 1995 La Falaise £3.49
Plummy fruit with a hint of spice and very gluggy to drink. [*Côtes-du-Ventoux, Rhône, France*]

Floral Vinho Tinto Reserva 1994 Caves Aliança £3.49
(B) A full-bodied yet easy-drinking red that makes an

Red Wines

interesting food wine now, but should develop over the next 12 months. [*Douro, Portugal*]

Côtes-du-Brulhois 1990 Cave de Donzac £3.69

ⓑ A distinctive wine for the price, with full, smoky-chocolaty fruit. [*France*]

Espiga 1995 Vinho Tinto £3.89

Dominated by spicy-resinous coconutty oak, the fruit seems quite nervous at the moment, but should settle down by Christmas. [*Estremadura, Portugal*]

Valle de Vistalba 1995 Barbera, Casa Nieto & Senetiner £3.99

ⓑ A Barbera with sweet fruit for less than £4 just has to snatch a medal. [*Mendoza, Argentina*]

Château la Brunette 1995 Bordeaux £4.15

ⓢ A *petit château* of amazingly individual style and character for such an inexpensive price. [*Bordeaux, France*]

Palmeras Estate 1995 Oak Aged Cabernet Sauvignon £4.49

ⓢ Stylish red with summer-pudding fruits on nose and palate, supported by grippy tannins. An elegant food wine. [*Nancagua, Chile*]

Virginie 1994 Cabernet Sauvignon, Vin de Pays d'Oc £4.49

Firm fruit with fine menthol after-aromas and tingly grippy tannins. [*Southern France, France*]

Booths Oak Aged Vintage Claret 1994 Bordeaux Supérieur £4.99

ⓑ Sweet, ripe, Merlot-dominated fruit on the nose,

with oak coming through strongly on palate and finish.
[*Bordeaux, France*]

Guelbenzu 1995 Jardin £4.99
Deep and dark with toasted-roasted, inky fruit aroma and full-bodied, full-flavoured fruit on the palate. A wine of some finesse and complexity, characteristics that will only increase over the next few years. [*Navarra, Spain*]

Mont-Marçal 1991 Cabernet Sauvignon Reserva £5.49
Elegant structure supporting perfumed fruit and silky tannins. [*Penedés, Spain*]

Domaine de l'Hortus 1994 Classique £5.99
Fine, rich and flavourful wine with the finesse, complexity and class of fruit you would have to pay at least twice as much for in Bordeaux. [*Coteaux-du-Languedoc, Southern France, France*]

Artadi 1994 Viñas de Gain, Rioja £6.49
Pure Tempranillo exclusively from Rioja Alavesa, and the finesse shows in the spicy fruit with good grippy tannins. [*Rioja, Spain*]

Carmen 1995 Grande Vidure Cabernet Reserve £6.99
Blackcurranty aroma followed by creamy fruit. [*Maipo, Chile*]

Faugères 1994 Gilbert Alquier £6.99
I nearly motored past this but was glad I gave it a second chance; because when the wraps came off I saw it was a Faugères, which are normally quite chunky, whereas this is silky smooth with sweet, ripe fruit of some finesse. [*Faugères, Southern France, France*]

Fleurie 1995 Paul Boutinot £7.99
(S) Exceptionally well structured for Beaujolais, but has deep, powerful flavour and extract to match. [*Fleurie, Beaujolais, Burgundy, France*]

Pago de Carraovejas 1994 Ribera del Duero £9.75
(S) I loved this wine and the only thing preventing it from being a gold medal winner was the indication it gave that its blackcurranty character would soon become overblown. At the moment, however, the wine shows considerable complexity with multilayered fruit, oak and spice. Keep the odd bottle to see if I'm wrong, by all means, but if you like it in its current state, you should drink it all up by Christmas 1997 – which shouldn't be too difficult. [*Ribera del Duero, Spain*]

Plantagenet 1994 Shiraz £10.75
(S) Stylish, elegant wine with deliciously peppery-spicy fruit. [*Mount Barker, Western Australia, Australia*]

White Wines

José Neiva 1994 Oak Aged £2.49
(B) A fresh, light-bodied, dry white wine with coconutty American oak dominating both the nose and palate. A good match with cold, creamy chicken dishes. [*Estremadura, Portugal*]

Santa Lucia 1995 Lightly Oaked Viura £3.29
(S) This wine is exactly what the label says it is – a lightly oaked Viura – and very elegant it is too. [*Tierra Manchuela, Spain*]

Santara 1995 Chardonnay £3.99
(S) Australian-trained British winemaker Hugh Ryman made this delightfully fruity wine, with its tropical fruit notes on the nose and tangy-pineapple flavour on the palate. [*Conca de Barberà, Spain*]

Château Lamothe Vincent 1996 Sauvignon £4.19
This fresh, crisp wine would have been a bronze at this price, but for its hint of green. [*Bordeaux, France*]

Barramundi NV Semillon/Colombard/Chardonnay £4.29
(S) Preferred this to the Barramundi wine-box, though that's very good too. This has more intensity, however, perhaps because of the addition of Colombard, which is responsible for the tangy fruitiness found in many Vins de Pays des Côtes de Gascogne. [*South Eastern Australia, Australia*]

Sauvignon Blanc 1996 Welmoed Winery £4.39
The back label states 'asparagus and lemon fruit', but although this wine is lemony in a fresh, crisp way, it does not have the aroma or flavour of asparagus, and won't have – thank goodness – unless you age it for a couple of years. [*Stellenbosch, South Africa*]

Virginie 1995 Vermentino, Vin de Pays d'Oc £4.69
(B) A rich and interesting dry white with a touch of spritz on the finish. [*Southern France, France*]

Villa Maria Private Bin 1996 Sauvignon Blanc £6.49
(G) Soft and ripe, yet crisp, gooseberry fruit with a slight spritz. [*Marlborough, New Zealand*]

Riddoch 1994 Chardonnay £6.99
⒮ Ripe, toasty, tropical fruits. [*Coonawarra, South Australia, Australia*]

Ninth Island 1996 Chardonnay £7.99
Crisp, lemony fruit, rounding off on the finish. [*Tasmania, Australia*]

Katnook Estate 1996 Sauvignon Blanc £8.99
⒢ Amazingly fresh, crisp and zingy for an Australian Sauvignon. Lovely tropical fruits and a brilliantly fresh, dry aftertaste. [*Coonawarra, South Australia, Australia*]

Mas de Daumas Gassac 1995 Vin de Pays de l'Hérault
£15.49
⒮ Sweet, ripe fruit that goes well with a blue cheese salad starter. There's no doubt this is silver medal quality, but only if you've got the dosh and have tasted everything else up to this price point! [*Southern France, France*]

Sparkling Wines

Yaldara Rosé NV Reserve Brut £5.75
⒝ Simple but very fresh strawberry fruit with good length. [*South Australia, Australia*]

Chapel Down Epoch NV Brut £6.99
⒝ Ripe apricot fruit makes this a good challenge to New World fizz. [*Kent, England*]

Lindauer NV Brut £7.49
A reliably fresh and zesty fizz. [*Auckland, New Zealand*]

Booths Champagne NV Brut £12.69
ⓢ Very fresh, fruity, soft and seductive. Ideal for drinking on its own. [*Champagne, France*]

Fortified Wines

Booths Finest Reserve Port NV Quinta da Rosa £8.15
Ⓖ Here's a supposedly 'basic' blended ruby that really should be laid down for ten years. How extraordinary. Still dominated by wine and fruit, it has a lovely finesse and with further ageing this will develop a profound spicy-complexity on the finish. [*Douro, Portugal*]

Churchill's White Port NV £8.99
Ⓑ Better on the palate than the nose, this has the pepperiness of a ruby port to keep it young. [*Douro, Portugal*]

Lustau Solera Reserva Fine Sherry NV Pedro Ximénez San Emilio £10.99
Ⓖ Liquid Christmas pudding! This has the same oil-like viscosity and intense sweetness as Sainsbury's Pedro Ximénez, but with a more focused intensity and much better acidity. Absolutely divine! [*Jerez, Spain*]

☞ THE BEST QUALITY FORTIFIED WINE OF THE YEAR

Beers

Ward's Classic Yorkshire Ale Per pint: £1.02
(G) An unbelievable price for a beer of this distinction. It has an elegant smoky-bitter flavour, with a delicately perfumed aroma that comes from three hops: Challenger, Fuggles and Progress. £0.99 per 55cl bottle. [*5%, Sheffield, England*]
☞ THE BEST VALUE BITTER OF THE YEAR

Budweiser Budvar Per pint: £1.35
(G) Elegant, refreshing and perfectly hopped, this classic really is the business. £1.19 per 50cl bottle. [*5%, Czech Republic*]

Black Douglas, Broughton Ales Per pint: £1.42
(B) An unusual beer with a dark brown colour, a very malty taste and a tangy-dry finish. £1.25 per 50cl bottle. [*5.2%, Peeblesshire, Scotland*]

Bishops Finger Kentish Strong Ale, Shepherd Neame
Per pint: £1.42
(S) This knocks spots off the canned version: beautifully fresh and crisp with a powerful true-bitter flavour and long, hoppy aftertaste. £1.25 per 50cl bottle. [*5.4%, Kent, England*]

Two Pints Bitter, Cropton Brewery Per pint: £1.42
(B) In by no means a typical bitter style, this brew has perfumed-peppery hops and a dry finish. £1.25 per 50cl bottle. [*4%, North Yorkshire, England*]

Waggle Dance Traditional Honey Beer, Vaux
Per pint: £1.44

(S) This soft, full, luscious ale with perfumed-hop aromas, clean, off-dry malty taste and a crisp finish is apparently named after the dance honey bees execute when they have located nectar. £1.39 per 55cl bottle. [5%, *Sunderland, England*]

Marston's Pedigree Bitter
Per pint: £1.45

(B) Very fresh and clean, almost sweet. £1.45 per 56.8cl bottle. [*4.5%, Burton-on-Trent, England*]

Landlord, Timothy Taylor's Strong Pale Ale
Per pint: £1.47

(S) A delicate brew with a mild, hoppy flavour and a long, mellow-bitter finish. £1.29 per 50cl bottle. [*4.1%, Keighley, Yorkshire, England*]

Bombardier Premium Bitter, Charles Wells
Per pint: £1.47

Although this has a good bitter finish, some will find its strangely liquorous texture rather incongruous. £1.29 per 50cl bottle. [*4.3%, Bedford, England*]

Booth & Co. Ltd Anniversary Ale, 1847–1997
Per pint: £1.47

(G) A lovely balance between smoothness, genuine bitterness and a clean, thirst-quenching taste. A truly distinctive beer. £1.29 per 50cl bottle. [*4.1%, England*]

Pendle Witches Brew, Strong Lancashire Ale, Moorhouse's
Per pint: £1.47

(B) Not for bitter drinkers, but good for those who prefer a softer, more mellow brew. £1.29 per 50cl bottle. [*5.1%, Lancashire, England*]

Bass, Our Finest Ale Per pint: £1.49

S Very smooth, elegant and stylish with an almost perfumed hoppy aroma. £1.49 per 56.8cl bottle. [4.4%, Burton-on-Trent, England]

Theakston Lightfoot, Traditional Pale Beer
Per pint: £1.50

S Fragrant hopped aroma followed by crisp, floral-hopped, lightly malty flavour. £1.45 per 55cl bottle. [5.2%, North Yorkshire, England]

Cocker Hoop Golden Bitter, Jennings Brothers
Per pint: £1.53

B This very rich, malty brew is not as sweet as last year and more toffee than creamy. £1.35 per 50cl bottle. [4.8%, Cumbria, England]

Uncle Sams Bitter, Cropton Brewery Per pint: £1.53

A cross between perfumed hops and lavender polish – be warned! £1.35 per 50cl bottle. [4.4%, North Yorkshire, England]

Hürlimann Premium Swiss Lager, Shepherd Neame
Per pint: £1.58

S This 'Swiss' beer is brewed under licence in England. It's sharp and assertively fizzy to the bottom of the glass. £1.39 per 50cl bottle. [5%, Kent, England]

Black Sheep Ale, Paul Theakston's Black Sheep Brewery Per pint: £1.58

G Mellow, full and stylish, with a good bitter flavour and some nutty-smoky complexity on the finish. A delight to drink. £1.39 per 50cl bottle. [4.4%, North Yorkshire, England]

Fuller's London Pride, Premium Ale — Per pint: £1.58

(G) This fresh, intense, hoppy-malty brew is particularly well suited to the bottling process and always hits home for those who prefer genuinely dry, authentically bitter beers. £1.39 per 50cl bottle. [*4.7%, London, England*]

Spitfire Bottle Conditioned Ale, Shepherd Neame
Per pint: £1.58

(S) Distinctive pear-hoppy aroma and flavour, nicely dry, well-hopped finish. Not quite up to last year's standard, but an excellent beer nevertheless. £1.39 per 50cl bottle. [*4.7%, Kent, England*]

Formidable Ale, Cains — Per pint: £1.58

(B) A light-coloured ale with delicate aromas when tasted against bitters, but a definitely beery taste when compared to lagers. £1.39 per 50cl bottle. [*5%, Liverpool, England*]

Bob's Gold, Ruddles Character Ales — Per pint: £1.58

(G) Blind tastings have taught me that I'm not too fond of Ruddles' brews, so I was pleasantly gobsmacked to find I had awarded this one a gold. It is a pure hop varietal brew and the name refers to the Gold variety of hops used by Ruddles for this mellow, aromatic, flavoursome and most satisfying ale. £1.39 per 50cl bottle. [*4.7%, Rutland, England*]

Backwoods Bitter, Cropton Brewery — Per pint: £1.58

(S) This most unusual brew has rich, attractive, malty aromas, with bitter-sweet, toffee-malty and liquorice flavours, and a hint of peppery hops on the finish. £1.39 per 50cl bottle. [*5.1%, North Yorkshire, England*]

Monkmans Slaughter Bitter, Cropton Brewery
Per pint: £1.58

(S) Very rich, liquorice-flavoured brew with a sharp, tangy-bitter finish. £1.39 per 50cl bottle. [*6%, North Yorkshire, England*]

Marston's Oyster Stout, Bottle Conditioned
Per pint: £1.69

(S) Although very smooth and easy drinking, this brew lacks the intensity, bitterness and complexity of a great stout when it hits the shelf, but having kept a few bottles over the last year, I have noted how the flavour deepens and mellows after six months' cellaring. £1.49 per 50cl bottle. [*4.5%, Burton-on-Trent, England*]

Riggwelter Strong Yorkshire Ale, Black Sheep Brewery
Per pint: £1.76

(G) A great but most unusual beer, its aromatics are closer to fortified wine than ale, and the intensely flavoured, smooth palate with distinctive wood-smoke complexity is more for sipping than supping. £1.55 per 50cl bottle. [*5.7%, Yorkshire, England*]

☞ THE BEST QUALITY BITTER OF THE YEAR

Worthington's White Shield, Fine Strong Ale
Per pint: £1.84

(G) Hugely improved in recent years, White Shield is almost back to the form it held until twenty years ago, but although it still lacks that ripe, yeasty-fruity bloom that regular White Shield drinkers will remember, and therefore has some way to go, this fresh, fruity and very smooth beer still rates a gold. A case of 'great but could do better'. £0.89 per 27cl bottle. [*5.6%, Burton-on-Trent, England*]

Guinness Foreign Extra Stout Per pint: £2.15

Extra Stout is a very apt name for this exceptionally extracted brew, the complex flavours of which are remarkably concentrated and build on the palate to a rousing crescendo of bitter-coffee, burnt-toffee, black treacle and liquorice intensity. Not many draught stout drinkers go for it, though. £1.25 per 33cl bottle. [*7.5%, Dublin, Ireland*]

☞ THE BEST QUALITY DARK BEER OF THE YEAR

BUDGENS

STOCK ME AND BUY ONE

Number of stores *116*
Opening hours *Vary too widely to generalize*
Maximum range *450 wines, 150 beers, 120 spirits*
Alternative methods of payment *Cheque with card, Switch and Delta debit cards, Access, Visa*
Local delivery *Not provided, but will help carry goods to car if requested*
Discounts *5 per cent on mixed cases of wine*
Refund policy? *No comment*
Other services *Free loan of glasses in trial stores only, no sale or return (full case returns only), but ice can be purchased from 50 of the larger stores, and ready-chilled wines available in trial stores*

Comment A supermarket chain pure and simple, with no outlets that could in any way be described as superstores – although Budgens' aggressive pricing policy is certainly competitive with that of the big chains, and the range of wines and beers submitted by Tony Finnerty, the group's buyer, has beaten some of the more famous supermarkets this year. Finnerty is a one-man show, his duties extending from buying wines, beers and spirits to changing the photocopy paper. Despite this, his selection this year has greatly improved Budgens' performance.

Red Wines

Baron d'Arignac 1996 Vin de Pays de l'Aude £2.55
A light, fresh quaffing red with a touch of sweetness to emphasize the fruit. [*Southern France, France*]

Diego de Almagro 1993 Felix Solis £3.19
This light red with its easy-drinking, coconutty fruit

For details of 'Stock Me and Buy One' see pages xi–xii.

was a contender for bronze, but lost out in the super-
selection process due to its rustic character – although
some may find that is part of its charm. [*Valdepeñas,
Spain*]

**Young Vatted Cabernet Sauvignon 1995 Pietroasa
Vineyards** £3.49

Ⓢ A deliciously ripe and fruity red of some elegance
and marginal oak influence. Made by Australian
Graham Dixon. [*Dealul Mare, Romania*]

Dornfelder 1994 Gustav Adolf Schmitt £3.99
The ultimate Liebfraumilch-lover's red wine. I defy
anyone to taste this – literally – blind and say in all
honesty that it's red! [*Rheinhessen, Germany*]

Pepperwood Grove 1995 Cabernet Franc £3.99
Nice enough, but this wine does not have the richness
of the vintage, and the fruit is thinner, more grassy and
less succulent, although it does have a touch of
sweetness. [*California, USA*]

South African Pinotage NV Clear Mountain £3.99
Not the best at this price point, but the cedary-tangy
fruit and lack of bubblegum is better than we're used to
from a sub-£4 Pinotage. [*Western Cape, South Africa*]

Sutter Home 1994 Zinfandel £4.29
Soft, brambly fruit. [*Napa, California, USA*]

Waimanu NV Premium Dry Red Wine £4.49
Ⓑ Light to medium-bodied with juicy, blackcurrant
fruit and a long finish. [*New Zealand*]

Château Malijay 1995 Fontanilles, Côtes-du-Rhône
£4.59

Good depth and nice tannins, but needs another 12 months to show at its best. [*Côtes-du-Rhône, France*]

Crozes-Hermitage 1994 Quinson £4.75
ⓑ Tasty, elegant, easy-drinking fruit. [*Crozes-Hermitage, Rhône, France*]

Cadet Claret 1995 Baron Philippe de Rothschild £4.99
There was a time when Mouton Cadet was sold at this price point, but it got a lot of stick from critics, and has been shoved upmarket (£8.99!) to make room for this son of Mouton with its all-too-predictable alliteration for a name. [*Bordeaux, France*]

Palacio de la Vega 1993 Navarra £4.99
ⓑ Soft cedary fruit, but with a nice firm finish making it accessible with or without food. [*Navarra, Spain*]

Bourgogne Pinot Noir 1995 Charles Viénot £5.99
Good grippy tannins for food now, but the fruit has yet to develop; will repay keeping for 18 months. [*Burgundy, France*]

Nexus 1994 San Simone £7.99
ⓑ Very tangy-spicy fruit with nice tannin structure. Well suited to food. [*North-east Italy, Italy*]

Mouton Cadet Réserve 1994 Baron Philippe de Rothschild £8.99
Not a bad wine, with its nice cool fruit, hints of menthol and good tannin structure. Mouton Cadet has certainly cleaned up its act, but what worldly-wise wine drinker pays £9 for a branded blend? [*Médoc, Bordeaux, France*]

Avignonesi 1993 Vino Nobile di Montepulciano £9.99
(G) A classy food wine with elegant, creamy fruit and fine tannins. Lovely length. Will age gracefully. [*Tuscany, Italy*]

White Wines

Valblanc 1995 Colombard, Vin de Pays du Gers £2.79
Fresh, crisp dry white with an interesting apricot fruitiness. [*South Western France, France*]

Bulgarian Vintage Blend 1995 Chardonnay & Sauvignon Blanc, Domaine Boyar £2.99
(S) A Mâcon style but with even juicier fruit, this is quite superb value for money, especially when Bulgarian Chardonnay or Chardonnay-based blends were awful until just a few years ago. [*Preslav, Bulgaria*]

Domaine L'Argentier 1995 Terret, Vin de Pays des Côtes-de-Thau £3.49
(B) If this was a Tesco wine, they'd label it 'Great With Starters' as it really shows at its best with food, and is able to stand up to various flavours, yet would not overwhelm the most delicate that might follow it. [*Southern France, France*]

Domaine Villeroy-Castellas 1996 Sauvignon Blanc, Vin de Pays des Sables du Golfe du Lion £3.99
Fresh and gentle fruit with suck-a-stone finish. [*Southern France, France*]

Waimanu NV Premium Dry White Wine £3.99
Always reliable for its fresh, lightly fruity, easy drinking off-dry white wine style. [*New Zealand*]

White Wines

Chardonnay 1995 Jidvei Winery £4.49
ℬ Distinctive for the price, this wine has tons of flavour and more than a hint of apricot in the fruit.
[*Tirnave Valley, Romania*]

Bourgogne Chardonnay 1996 Charles Viénot £4.99
There are a few cheaper Burgundies than this, but none that I would drink, let alone recommend. This is fresh, clean and best for early drinking, but will take another 12 months ageing without difficulty.
[*Burgundy, France*]

Grande Cuvée Chardonnay 1995 Laroche, Vin de Pays d'Oc £4.99
𝒢 This wine gets a gold – despite the misleading claim that it comes from the 'prime chalk vineyards of Languedoc' (there is plenty of limestone in Languedoc, but no chalk whatsoever) – because, quite simply, you would have to pay two to three times the price for this elegantly oaky Chardonnay if it came from a Burgundian appellation, whatever soil it was grown on!
[*Southern France, France*]

Mâcon-Igé 1996 Les Vignerons d'Igé £4.99
Good freshness and fruit of some intensity with a hint of pineapple. [*Mâcon, Burgundy, France*]

Rosemount Estate 1996 Chardonnay £6.99
𝒮 Big, mellow and toasty on top, with juicy-fleshy fruit underneath. [*Hunter Valley, NSW, Australia*]

Sparkling wines

Champagne Taittinger NV Brut Réserve £22.99
Ⓢ Taittinger's non-vintage is certainly on form, with young, fresh, delightfully elegant fruit and a fine mousse. Drink now or age a year or two. [*Champagne, France*]

Fortified Wines

Rozès 1992 Late Bottled Vintage Port £7.99
Ⓑ Rich, tasty, mellow and long. [*Douro, Portugal*]

Beers

Blonderbraü Pils Per pint: £0.68
Recommended because, with the exception of Sainsbury's Bière des Flandres, there's nothing else worth recommending at this price point! Inoffensive telly beer. £2.99 per 10x25cl bottles. [*4.6%, St.-Omer, France*]

IPA Draught Bitter, Greene King
Per pint: £0.85
Ⓑ Some hoppy aromas and although not very bitter as such, it does have a nice mellow taste. £2.99 per 4x50cl cans. [*3.6%, Suffolk, England*]

Ruddles Draught Best Bitter, Rutland Brewery
Per pint: £1.29
Flowery-hop aromas on the nose and a smidgen of bitterness creeping through creamy head. £3.99 per 4x44cl widgetized cans. [*3.7%, Rutland, England*]

Guinness Original Stout
Per pint: £1.37

Ⓑ Dense, dark, bitter chocolate, coffee and liquorice. Quite stern, but great with a Stilton ploughman. £3.19 per 4x33cl bottles. [*4.3%, Dublin & London, Ireland & England*]

Murphy's Draught Irish Stout
Per pint: £1.45

Ⓑ Very soft, mild and sweet, but there is a cardboardy aftertaste to this brew this year (detected in samples from all outlets) which demotes Murphy's from silver to bronze. £4.49 per 4x44cl widgetized cans. [*4%, Ireland & UK*]

Kilkenny Irish Beer Draught, St Francis Abbey Brewery, Guinness
Per pint: £1.45

Ⓑ Sweet and creamy. £4.49 per 4x44cl widgetized cans. [*5%, Kilkenny & Dublin, Ireland*]

Budweiser Budvar
Per pint: £1.47

Ⓖ Elegant, refreshing and perfectly hopped, this classic really is the business. £1.35 per 50cl bottle. [*5%, Czech Republic*]

Draught Guinness
Per pint: £1.57

Ⓖ Draught Guinness stands out from other draught stout sold in cans because of the intensity of its smoky-toasty-malty aroma. It is every bit as smoky as Beamish, but has such a greater depth of other top-quality ingredients that this smokiness is not

immediately apparent. What is more easily perceived is
the lovely roasted barley tones that give Guinness the
satisfying edge other stouts lack. £4.85 per 4x44cl
widgetized cans. [*4.1%, Dublin, Ireland, and London,
England*]

Spitfire Bottle Conditioned Ale, Shepherd Neame
Per pint: £1.69

⑤ Distinctive pear-hoppy aroma and flavour, nicely
dry, well-hopped finish. Not quite up to last year's
standard, but an excellent beer nevertheless. £1.49 per
50cl bottle. [*4.7%, Kent, England*]

Bishops Finger Kentish Strong Ale, Shepherd Neame
Per pint: £1.69

⑤ This knocks spots off the canned version:
beautifully fresh and crisp with a powerful true-bitter
flavour and long, hoppy aftertaste. £1.49 per 50cl
bottle. [*5.4%, Kent, England*]

Murphy's Draught Irish Stout Per pint: £1.69

⑨ Widgetized Murphy's in a bottle is vastly
superior to the canned version because it has an edge
and wisp of smoke. There is also no cardboard taint.
£1.49 per 50cl widgetized bottle. [*4%, Ireland and
UK*]

☞ THE BEST VALUE DARK BEER OF THE YEAR

Bud Ice, Anheuser-Busch Inc. Per pint: £1.70
Not recommended as such, just included so that I can
put in print that I honestly wonder if Anheuser-Busch
could be sued for making the following claim about this
watery beer: 'Our exclusive ice brewing process
produces a rich, smooth taste that's remarkably easy to
drink.' £0.99 per 33cl bottle. [*5.2%, St Louis, USA*]

Caffrey's Draught Irish Ale   Per pint: £1.74

(B) Sweet and creamy. £5.39 per 4x44cl widgetized cans. [*4.8%, Co. Antrim, UK*]

Fuller's London Pride, Premium Ale   Per pint: £1.81

(G) This fresh, intense, hoppy-malty brew is particularly well suited to the bottling process and always hits home for those who prefer genuinely dry, authentically bitter beers. £1.59 per 50cl bottle. [*4.7%, London, England*]

6X Export, Wadworth   Per pint: £1.81

(S) Tasty and smooth, with refined, malty bitter notes and none of the sour sultana-malty character that blighted this brew last year. £1.59 per 50cl bottle. [*5%, Devizes, England*]

Fuggles Imperial Strong Ale, Castle Eden Brewery
    Per pint: £1.81

(G) A widgetized bitter for hardened bitter drinkers! The wonderful aroma of Fuggles hops comes streaming through the creamy head, with an assertive, hoppy bitterness dominating the finish. £1.59 per 50cl widgetized bottle. [*5.5%, Co. Durham, England*]

☞ SPECIAL BEER AWARD OF THE YEAR

Foster's Ice Beer, Courage Limited   Per pint: £1.81

This 'Aussie' beer is brewed in England and has more flavour than last year. £1.05 per 33cl bottle. [*5%, England*]

Fuller's ESB Export, Extra Special Bitter
    Per pint: £1.92

(B) Not my sort of beer, but its powerful, malty-rich

flavour is adored by many. £1.69 per 50cl bottle.
[*5.9%, London, England*]

Fuller's Old Winter Ale Per pint: £1.92
This rich, mellow ale with its smoky complexity is more reminiscent of Yorkshire than London. £1.69 per 50cl bottle. [*5.3%, London, England*]

Old Hooky Premium Ale, Hook Norton Brewery
Per pint: £1.92
Elegant, flowery-hopped aroma with a fresh, well-hopped bitterness on the palate. A distinctive brew. £1.69 per 50cl bottle. [*4.6%, Oxfordshire, England*]

Old Speckled Hen, Strong Fine Ale, Morland
Per pint: £1.99
A refreshing and tasty beer with a characterful maltiness in both the aroma and on the palate, and the barest hint of smoke. £1.75 per 50cl bottle. [*5.2%, Oxfordshire, England*]

Fuller's 1845, Bottle Conditioned Celebration Strong Ale Per pint: £2.03
Deep, full, bitter-toffee, malty flavour with an intense liquorice finish and smoky-peppery hops on the aftertaste. £1.79 per 50cl bottle. [*6.3%, London, England*]

Beck's Per pint: £2.12
Too popular for its own good; the clean, fresh taste of this beer is nice enough, but outclassed at this price point by so many other brews. £2.39 per 64cl bottle. [*5%, Bremen, Germany*]

Grolsch Premium Lager   Per pint: £2.21
Ⓖ Very fruity, crisp and deep flavoured. A classic.
£1.75 per 45cl bottle. [*5%, Groenlo, Holland*]

CO-OP

STOCK ME AND BUY ONE

Number of stores *2,446*
Opening hours *Vary too widely to generalize*
Maximum range *550 wines, 250 beers, 260 spirits*
Alternative methods of payment *Cheque with card, but which credit cards are acceptable varies so much according to store and region that generalization is not possible*
Local delivery *Not provided, but 'selected stores' will help carry goods to car if requested*
Discounts *None*
Refund policy? *Refund and replacement, followed up by an investigation; if requested, customers are advised of the outcome*
Other services *Ice can be purchased*

Comment Having fought off the attempted take-over by City maverick Andrew Regan, the Co-op's on–off merger with the Co-operative (i.e. the Co-operative Retail Service, formerly called Co-operative Pioneer; *see* entry on page 58) is definitely off for the foreseeable future – although it is bound to happen at some time or other, and the focus on Co-operative as its trading name will make the task easier when it happens.

The biggest problem any drinks guide faces when contemplating coverage of the Co-op is the very nature of the beast, for its 2,446 outlets are owned by 30 totally independent societies. In the last few years, however, Co-op trading has polarized into a handful of buying groups. The Manchester-based CWS (Co-operative Wholesale Society) now controls about 70 per cent of all Co-op turnover and sources all Co-op own labels. The wine department has been run since 1986 by Arabella Woodrow, a Master of Wine and Doctor of Microchemistry, who has done so much to improve the image, choice and value of Co-op wines. About 2,300 of

For details of 'Stock Me and Buy One' see pages xi–xii.

Red Wines

Tempranillo Oak Aged NV Co-op £3.29
Ⓢ All-American coconutty oak on nose with succulent, creamy-coconutty oak on the palate and a long mellow finish. A great silver for coconut-lovers, but for those who are not into that particular nut, the Stowells Tempranillo wine box (*see* Co-operative) is another silver medal wine that works out at 17p a bottle cheaper. [*Utiel-Requena, Spain*]

Chapel Hill NV Cabernet Sauvignon £3.49
A peppery-capsicum touch adds an interesting dimension to the light, fresh blackcurrant fruit, which has a dash of sweetness on the finish. [*Balatonboglár, Hungary*]

Chilean Long Slim Red 1994 Cabernet Merlot, Co-op
£3.49
Ⓑ Fresh, vibrantly fruity red with nice grippy tannins. [*Central Valley, Chile*]

Claret Bordeaux NV Co-op £3.49
Good mouthful of soft fruit, with a blackcurrant note and some grippy tannins, making the wine equally good with or without food. [*Bordeaux, France*]

Côtes-du-Rhône NV Co-op £3.49
Soft, easygoing red wine with creamy fruit. [*Côtes-du-Rhône, France*]

Dão 1994 Co-op £3.59
A medium to full-bodied red with good Portuguese peppery-spice typicity of fruit. [*Dão, Portugal*]

Chianti 1995 Piccini, Co-op £3.99
Although there were plenty of Chiantis up to £1 cheaper, this was the best cheapest tasted this year. [*Tuscany, Italy*]

Four Rivers 1995 Cabernet Sauvignon £3.99
ⓑ So much like blackcurrant juice that you might not even notice it's alcoholic! [*Maipo, Chile*]

Kingston 1996 Shiraz Mataro £3.99
Ⓢ Rich and tasty with nice grippy tannins. [*Murray Valley, Victoria, Australia*]

Marqués de Monistrol 1993 Merlot £3.99
This firm, oak-driven wine with a big coconutty aroma and aftertaste is not my idea of heaven, but it deserves a bronze medal for those who like the style. Open one hour beforehand and decant back and forth to aerate. [*Penedés, Spain*]

Robertson 1996 Merlot £4.29
A good guzzle that's jammy and grassy at the same time. Flexible with or without food. [*Robertson, South Africa*]

Cabernet Sauvignon 1995 Angove's, Co-op £4.49
Tasty blackcurrant fruit with grippy tannins to make the palate tingle. [*South Australia, Australia*]

Château Pierrousselle 1995 Bordeaux, Co-op £4.59
Ⓖ A big mouthful of Cabernet flavour with firm, food wine structure and a long aftertaste. [*Bordeaux, France*]

Red Wines

Cape Afrika 1992 Pinotage £4.99
ℬ Very rich, with a blackcurranty taste that set it apart from all the other Pinotage tasted this year – which could easily persuade me that there is some Cabernet or Merlot here. From South Africa's 'first black controlled wine negotiant' (sic). [*Stellenbosch, South Africa*]

Le Canne 1995 Boscaini Bardolino Classico Riserva
£4.99
ℬ Italy's answer to unpretentious Beaujolais, only better. [*Bardolino, Veneto, Italy*]

Duque de Viseu 1992 Dão £5.49
𝒮 Pristine, focused and packed with sweet, ripe fruit. [*Dão, Portugal*]

Vacqueyras 1995 Cuvée du Marquis de Fonseguille
£5.49
Peppery fruit of some weight. [*Vacqueyras, Rhône, France*]

Gigondas 1995 Fleuron des Vignes £6.29
Relatively slow-maturing wine for a supermarket cuvée, and needs two to three years to show true potential. [*Gigondas, Rhône, France*]

Château Fourtanet 1993 Côtes-de-Castillon £6.49
𝒮 A classy wine that builds in the mouth to a liquorice intensity, and makes a good partner to leek-dominated dishes. [*Côtes-de-Castillon, Bordeaux, France*]

Côte-de-Beaune-Villages 1995 Jules Vignon, Co-op
£6.49
𝒮 Excellent Pinot Noir fruit for the price. Great

with food now, but keep 2–3 years for a real treat.
[*Côte-de-Beaune, Burgundy, France*]

Gran Condal 1990 Rioja Reserva £6.49

(S) Gran Condal used to be a great classic Rioja, but it went through a dodgy patch with recent vintages. It now seems to be back on form with this modern rendition of the traditional style, which is expressed through its balance of oak to acidity. Available in the Co-operative Retailers Vintage Selection. [*Rioja, Spain*]

Shiraz 1994 Baileys £6.49

(S) Elegant and fruity and well worth the price.
[*Victoria, Australia*]

Fixin 1994 Les Vins Pierre Leduc £6.99

(B) Big, thick, rustic and rich, this wine gets a bronze through sheer character. [*Fixin, Burgundy, France*]

Leasingham Domain 1994 Cabernet Sauvignon Malbec £6.99

(B) Rich, deep, inky fruit and cedary oak. [*Clare Valley, South Australia, Australia*]

Morgon, Les Charmes 1994 Domaine Brisson £6.99

Quite deep and smooth. Good with food. Available in the Co-operative Retailers Vintage Selection. [*Morgon, Beaujolais, Burgundy, France*]

Barolo 1992 Cantina Terre del Barolo £7.99

(B) Open at least one hour before drinking to get the most from this classic, orange-hued Barolo. Available in the Co-operative Retailers Vintage Selection. [*Barolo, Piedmont, Italy*]

Château Monlot Capet 1993 St.-Emilion Grand Cru
£8.49

Ⓢ Soft, tasty, chocolaty fruit flavours that build in the mouth, finishing with smooth, oak tannins. [*St.-Emilion, Bordeaux, France*]

Châteauneuf-du-Pape 1994 Cellier des Princes £8.99

Ⓑ Nice tannic grip for food. [*Châteauneuf-du-Pape, Rhône, France*]

White Wines

Romanian Country Wine NV Vinvico £2.49

Soft and easy, this wine has an off-dry flavour with a subtle aromatic twang. [*Oltina, Romania*]

Mosel Deutscher Tafelwein NV St.-Urbanus Weinkellerei, Co-op £2.99

Ⓢ Deeper-flavoured and with richer fruit than most German wines at this price. Very fresh, with nice Muscaty aromas. [*Mosel, Germany*]

Chilean Long Slim White 1996 Chardonnay Semillon, Co-op £3.49

A good flavoursome, clean, fresh, off-dry white wine. [*Lontue, Chile*]

Sauvignon Blanc NV Bordeaux, Co-op £3.49

Ⓑ Crisp yet rich, with some apricot in the fruit to denote the Bordeaux ripeness. [*Bordeaux, France*]

Barramundi NV Semillon/Chardonnay
£9.49 (2–litre wine box)

Ⓑ Very gluggy, easy-drinking fruit, enhanced by a

touch of sweetness on the finish, which may offend the
purists, but is welcome at this price point. [*South
Eastern Australia, Australia*]

**Frascati Superiore 1995 Tuscolana Esportazioni,
Co-op** £3.69

If you thought it was impossible to find a light, dry
Italian white wine that is not only clean but also offers
real fruit flavour, try this. [*Frascati, Italy*]

Cape Afrika 1996 Rhine Riesling £3.99

ℬ For those who want a medium-style wine that is
fatter and more suited to food than Liebfraumilch and
other similarly inexpensive German wines, this is very
fresh, clean and lightly aromatic. From 'South Africa's
first black controlled wine negotiant' (sic). [*Robertson,
South Africa*]

Château Pierrousselle 1995 Entre-Deux-Mers, Co-op
£3.99

This crisp, spritzy dry white is a good match for
asparagus. [*Entre-Deux-Mers, Bordeaux, France*]

Fiuza 1995 Sauvignon £3.99

ℬ Normally, any hint of green disqualifies a wine
from my tasting, but in this case it is just a hint on mid-
palate, and the fresh, lemony aroma with silky-lemony
fruit on the finish is so good that not only did the wine
get through, it thoroughly deserved a bronze medal.
Made by Australian Peter Bright. [*Ribatejo, Portugal*]

Santara 1995 Chardonnay £3.99

𝒮 Australian-trained British winemaker Hugh
Ryman made this delightfully fruity wine with its
tropical fruit notes on the nose and tangy-pineapple

White Wines

flavour on the palate. [*Conca de Barberà, Spain*]

Sauvignon Blanc 1996 Welmoed Winery £3.99
The back label states 'asparagus and lemon fruit', but although this wine is lemony in a fresh, crisp way, it does not have the aroma or flavour of asparagus, and won't have – thank goodness – unless you age it for a couple of years. [*Stellenbosch, South Africa*]

Sauvignon Blanc Vin de Pays d'Oc NV Foncalieu, Co-op £3.99
A tasty, dryish white that most will find easy to drink. [*Southern France, France*]

Muscadet de Sèvre-et-Maine Sur Lie 1995 Domaine de la Haute Maillardière £4.39
(B) The delicate fruit, correctly lean structure and gentle spritz of this wine really deserve a silver medal, but it should have been consumed during the summer, before this guide was published, to show at its silver-medal best. Available in the Co-operative Retailers Vintage Selection. [*Muscadet de Sèvre-et-Maine, Loire, France*]

Casablanca 1996 Sauvignon Blanc £4.99
(B) Very fresh, lemony fruit; not at all green, more succulent-fruity in fact. It's also not very Sauvignonish, but makes a refreshing dry white wine in its own right. [*Curico, Chile*]

Fiuza 1995 Chardonnay £4.99
(S) Australian winemaker Peter Bright has used lots of lemony-coconutty oak, but there is plenty of rich, focused fruit too. [*Ribatejo, Portugal*]

Leasingham Domaine 1993 Semillon £6.49
Ⓢ Lovely, crisp lime fruit with mellowing toasty aromas. [*Clare Valley, South Australia, Australia*]

Kirchheimer Schwarzerde Beerenauslese 1994 Zimmermann-Graeff £3.99 (half-bottle)
Ⓑ Rich apricot jam sweetness underpinned with very good acidity. [*Pfalz, Germany*]

Monbazillac Cuvée Prestige 1994 Domaine du Haut-Rauly £3.99 (half-bottle)
Ⓑ The style is more fruit-driven than Co-operative's Monbazillac, which relies more on liquorice intensity, but this wine tastes younger and is at least as good. Available in the Co-operative Retailers Vintage Selection. [*South Western France, France*]

Rosé Wines

Rosé d'Anjou NV Co-op £3.19
Ⓑ I was going to say that this is the best own-label Rosé d'Anjou tasted this year, but this fresh, fruity, medium-sweet wine was in fact the *only* Rosé d'Anjou, own-label or domaine-bottled, that was clean enough to recommend. [*Rosé d'Anjou, Loire, France*]

Balbi Vineyard 1996 Syrah Rosé £3.69
Quite deep coloured; like a jammy red wine without the tannin. [*Mendoza, Argentina*]

Sparkling Wines

Barramundi NV Brut £5.49
This must be the same shipment as last year, only the jamminess so evident then has now developed into a sweet, creamy, toffee-like complexity. [*Australia*]

Fortified Wines

Fine Vintage Character Port NV Smith Woodhouse, Co-op £6.59
(B) Tasty, well blended and very sweet for its price and category. [*Douro, Portugal*]

Late Bottled Vintage Port 1991 Smith Woodhouse, Co-op £6.99
(S) Still tastes of fruit and wood, indicating that it would benefit from another year or two in bottle, but it has a very gentle, juicy sweetness for the price. [*Douro, Portugal*]

Rothbury NV Museum Reserve Liqueur Muscat
£5.49 (half-bottle)
(B) Fabulously rich and even more oil-like than Mick Morris's Liqueur Muscat (*see* Sainsbury's), with massive, barley-sugar sweetness. [*NSW, Australia*]

Beers

Ceres Royal Export Per pint: £1.01
(B) Not that special straight off the shelf, but you'll

notice a big difference if you keep these cans six
months (but not much longer). £3.55 per 4x50cl cans.
[*5.8%, Aarhus, Denmark*]

Cains Formidable Ale Per pint: £1.13

(B) Looks like lager but tastes more beery, with a
persistent, nicely hopped flavour. £1.99 per 100cl can.
[*5%, Liverpool, England*]

Saaz Pils, French Premium Lager Beer Per pint: £1.13

(B) Elegant, flowery Saaz hop aroma, with a sweet
and delicate flavour. £4.99 per 10x25cl bottles. [*5%,
Douai, France*]

**Drewrys Genuine Imported American Beer, Private
Liquor Brands UK** Per pint: £1.20

(B) One of only two American beers that didn't taste
like fizzy water! £2.99 per 4x35.5cl cans. [*5%, Indiana,
USA*]

Double Maxim Premium, Vaux Per pint: £1.26

(B) A textbook example of a bottled beer being so
superior to the canned version of the same brew that
they are chalk and cheese, and demonstrating how
essential it is to pay the premium asked for bottles over
cans. This is much fresher, crisper and cleaner than
Double Maxim in a can. £1.22 per 55cl bottle. [*4.7%,
Sunderland, England*]

Caledonian 70/- Amber Ale, Caledonian Brewery
Per pint: £1.35

(B) A bronze medal for those with a sweet tooth; this
has a nice, clean, malty taste dominated by peppery-
hop aromas and a touch of Mediterranean herbal scrub.
£1.19 per 50cl bottle. [*3.5%, Edinburgh, Scotland*]

Beers

DAB Original German Beer, Dortmunder Actien-Brauerei   Per pint: £1.40

S Pale, attractive, flowery-hopped aroma, fragrant and elegant on the palate, with a long, smooth, gently rich flavour, just a hint of bitterness, and lifted by a correctly crisp finish. A monster barrel. £12.29 per 5-litre can. [*5%, Germany*]

Ushers Founders Strong Ale   Per pint: £1.42

Strong and hoppy. £4.39 per 4x44cl cans. [*4.5%, Wiltshire, England*]

Master Brew Premium Ale, Bottle Conditioned, Shepherd Neame   Per pint: £1.47

B Not as full or well-defined as in previous years, but still a fine-flavoured beer with a light but distinctive bitter finish. £1.29 per 50cl bottle. [*4%, Kent, England*]

Greenmantle Ale, Broughton Ales   Per pint: £1.53

A dark-bitter colour with a fizzy, smoky-malt taste. £1.35 per 50cl bottle. [*3.9%, Peeblesshire, Scotland*]

Caledonian 80/- Export Ale, Caledonian Brewery
     Per pint: £1.53

B A classic as far as sweet-toothed beer lovers are concerned, Caledonian 80/- is marked by the perfumed-hop aromas that drift lazily through its clean, sweet-ripe, floral taste. £1.35 per 50cl bottle. [*4.1%, Edinburgh, Scotland*]

Black Sheep Ale, Paul Theakston's Black Sheep Brewery   Per pint: £1.53

G Mellow, full and stylish, with a good bitter flavour and some nutty-smoky complexity on the finish. A delight to drink. £1.35 per 50cl bottle. [*4.4%, North Yorkshire, England*]

Theakston Lightfoot, Traditional Pale Beer
Per pint: £1.54
(S) Fragrant hopped aroma followed by crisp, floral-hopped, lightly malty flavour. £1.49 per 55cl bottle. [*5.2%, North Yorkshire, England*]

Ward's Classic Yorkshire Ale Per pint: £1.54
(G) A beer of great distinction. It has an elegant smoky-bitter flavour, with a delicately perfumed aroma that comes from three hops: Challenger, Fuggles and Progress. £1.49 per 55cl bottle. [*5%, South Yorkshire, England*]

Waggle Dance Traditional Honey Beer, Vaux
Per pint: £1.54
(S) This soft, full, luscious ale with perfumed-hop aromas, clean, off-dry malty taste and a crisp finish is apparently named after the dance honey bees execute when they have located nectar. £1.49 per 55cl bottle. [*5%, Sunderland, England*]

Tennent's Robert Burns, Scottish Ale Per pint: £1.54
(B) Panders to those who prefer sweet, malty brews. £1.49 per 55cl bottle. [*4.2%, Glasgow, Scotland*]

Boston Beer, Whitbread Per pint: £1.55
This sweet and creamy 'American' beer is brewed under licence in the UK. £4.79 per 4x44cl widgetized cans. [*4.6%, England*]

Marston's Pedigree Bitter Per pint: £1.55
(B) Very fresh and clean, almost sweet. £1.55 per 56.8cl bottle. [*4.5%, Burton-on-Trent, England*]

Beers

Cumberland Ale, Jennings Brothers Per pint: £1.58
A sweetish, clean, fresh, easy-supping brew for non
beer drinkers! £1.39 per 50cl bottle. [*4.2%, Cumbria,
England*]

Wallace IPA, Maclay & Co. Thistle Brewery
Per pint: £1.58
(ℬ) Quite dark, with a peppery-spiced, hoppy aroma
and thick malty taste. Definitely Scottish, but is it IPA?
£1.39 per 50cl bottle. [*4.5%, Alloa, Scotland*]

White Rabbit Premium Beer, Mansfield Brewery
Per pint: £1.58
Supposedly hints of roasted oats, but more pear-like
cool-ferment odours to me. £1.39 per 50cl bottle.
[*4.3%, Nottinghamshire, England*]

Black Fort Premium Lager, Som's Per pint: £1.64
(𝒮) A smoky-tasting lager with Camp Coffee on the
finish. £0.95 per 33cl bottle. [*5%, India*]

Merlin's Ale, Broughton Ales Per pint: £1.65
(ℬ) A considerable improvement on last year's brew,
this now has a distinctive, smoky aroma, a light creamy
taste and a fruity tang and smokiness on the finish.
£1.45 per 50cl bottle. [*4.2%, Peeblesshire, Scotland*]

Old Jock Ale, Broughton Ales Per pint: £1.65
(ℬ) Rich and malty with a full, sweetish finish. £1.45
per 50cl bottle. [*6.7%, Peeblesshire, Scotland*]

Deuchars IPA, Export Strength, Caledonian Brewery
Per pint: £1.65
(ℬ) Deep, rich aromas with an assertively rich, malty
taste and a distinctive crisp, bitter finish. £1.45 per 50cl
bottle. [*4.4%, Edinburgh, Scotland*]

Cocker Hoop Golden Bitter, Jennings Brothers
Per pint: £1.69

(B) This very rich, malty brew is not as sweet as last year and more toffee than creamy. £1.49 per 50cl bottle. [*4.8%, Cumbria, England*]

Fuggles Imperial Strong Ale, Castle Eden Brewery
Per pint: £1.69

(G) A widgetized bitter for hardened bitter drinkers! The wonderful aroma of Fuggles hops comes streaming through the creamy head, with an assertive, hoppy bitterness dominating the finish. £1.49 per 50cl widgetized bottle. [*5.5%, Co. Durham, England*]

☞ SPECIAL BEER AWARD OF THE YEAR

Bombardier Premium Bitter, Charles Wells
Per pint: £1.69

Although this has a good bitter finish, some will find its strangely liquorous texture rather incongruous. £1.49 per 50cl bottle. [*4.3%, Bedford, England*]

Pendle Witches Brew, Strong Lancashire Ale, Moorhouse's
Per pint: £1.69

(B) Not for bitter drinkers, but good for those who prefer a softer, more mellow brew. £1.49 per 50cl bottle. [*5.1%, Lancashire, England*]

Marston's Oyster Stout, Bottle Conditioned
Per pint: £1.69

(S) Although very smooth and easy-drinking, this brew lacks the intensity, bitterness and complexity of a great stout when it hits the shelf, but having kept a few bottles over the last year, I have noted how the flavour deepens and mellows after 6 months' cellaring. £1.49 per 50cl bottle. [*4.5%, Burton-on-Trent, England*]

Samuel Smith's Old Brewery Pale Ale

Per pint: £1.70

(S) A firm and distinctive pale ale with good malty bitterness and a fine, well-hopped finish. £1.65 per 55cl bottle. [*5%, Yorkshire, England*]

The Famous Taddy Porter, Samuel Smith

Per pint: £1.70

(G) Extremely rich and intense, with coffee notes and a very dry, creamy finish. £1.65 per 55cl bottle. [*5%, Yorkshire, England*]

Hoegaarden White Beer, Bottle Conditioned

Per pint: £1.70

(B) This has a classic soapy-spicy aroma and stewed, spiced-apple flavour. £0.99 per 33cl bottle. [*5%, Brussels, Belgium*]

Sneck Lifter, Jennings Brothers   Per pint: £1.76

Less sweet and more smoky-peppery than last year. [*5.1%, Cumbria, England*]

Golden Promise Organic Ale, Caledonian Brewery

Per pint: £1.76

(B) Peppery-hoppy aromas followed by a crisp, malty taste and a very fresh finish. £1.55 per 50cl bottle. [*5%, Edinburgh, Scotland*]

Bishops Finger Kentish Strong Ale, Shepherd Neame

Per pint: £1.76

(S) This knocks spots off the canned version: beautifully fresh and crisp with a powerful true-bitter flavour and long, hoppy aftertaste. £1.55 per 50cl bottle. [*5.4%, Kent, England*]

Original Porter Strong Dark Ale, Shepherd Neame
Per pint: £1.76

⑤ An off-dry to off-sweet Porter with a rich flavour and smoky complexity. £1.55 per 50cl bottle. [*5.2%, Kent, England*]

India Pale Ale Original Export, Shepherd Neame
Per pint: £1.76

⑤ Beyond the fizz this has all the flavour of a true bottle bitter. £1.55 per 50cl bottle. [*4.5%, Kent, England*]

Spitfire Bottle Conditioned Ale, Shepherd Neame
Per pint: £1.76

⑤ Distinctive pear-hoppy aroma and flavour, nicely dry, well-hopped finish. Not quite up to last year's standard, but an excellent beer nevertheless. £1.55 per 50cl bottle. [*4.7%, Kent, England*]

Marston's India Export Pale Ale, Head Brewer's Choice
Per pint: £1.76

⑤ Citric notes heighten the palate while spicy-smoky aromas add complexity to the finish. £1.55 per 50cl bottle. [*5.5%, Burton-on-Trent, England*]

Fuller's London Pride, Premium Ale
Per pint: £1.76

Ⓖ This fresh, intense, hoppy-malty brew is particularly well suited to the bottling process and always hits home for those who prefer genuinely dry, authentically bitter beers. £1.55 per 50cl bottle. [*4.7%, London, England*]

Old Speckled Hen, Strong Fine Ale, Morland
Per pint: £1.81

⑤ A refreshing and tasty beer with a characterful

maltiness in both the aroma and on the palate, and the
barest hint of smoke. £1.59 per 50cl bottle. [*5.2%,
Oxfordshire, England*]

Daredevil, A Very Strong Traditional Ale, Everards
Per pint: £1.92
Very rich, mellow and malty, but with too much alcohol
showing to deserve a medal. £1.69 per 50cl bottle.
[*7.1%, Leicestershire, England*]

Staropramen, Prague Breweries   Per pint: £2.05
Light, perfumed and elegant. £1.19 per 33cl
bottle. [*5%, Prague, Czech Republic*]

Duvel, Brouwerij Moortgat   Per pint: £2.56
This classic is not for most bitter drinkers; its
fluffy head and smooth, unctuous, pungently fruity
flavour are alien to everything found in a pint at the
local. £1.49 per 33cl bottle. [*8.5%, Breendonk,
Belgium*]

CO-OPERATIVE

Number of stores *289*
Opening hours *Vary too widely to generalize*
Maximum range *383 wines, 150 beers, 160 spirits*
Alternative methods of payment *Cheque with card, Access, Visa*
Local delivery *Not provided*
Discounts *None*
Refund policy? *A full refund or an exchange. In exceptional cases both a refund and an exchange, followed by an investigation with the supplier concerned*
Other services *Ice can be purchased*

Comment Run by CRS (Co-operative Retail Service), which operates more than 500 outlets, including some 200 superstores, making it the largest society in the Co-operative movement – although not comparable to CWS, which services some 70 per cent of all the stores in the various regional societies (*see* the Co-op entry, page 40). CRS achieved its super-society status by virtue of its primary function, which is to rescue ailing societies; this is why CRS is not regionalized, but has stores located all over the country. Over the past 12 months its various trading facias of Leo's, LoCost and Co-operative have all been changed to Co-operative. Although Co-operative stocks a number of Co-op own-label and other CWS lines, it has its own range of Co-operative own-label products and purchases a large number of special lines.

Red Wines

Argentine Dry Red NV Bright Brothers £2.99
A soft, smooth, easy-drinking red with sufficient
structure to accompany food, but not the slightest bit
tannic. [*Mendoza, Argentina*]

Tempranillo NV Stowells of Chelsea
£12.49 (3-litre wine box)
Soft, strawberry-jam fruit; this is a super-value
silver medal winner for those who prefer the fruit-
driven style. Those who prefer to crunch through a
layer of coconut oak before reaching the fruit should
opt for the Co-op own-label Tempranillo Oak Aged in
a normal 75cl bottle at just 17p more per bottle
equivalent. [*La Mancha, Spain*]

Australian Dry Red Wine NV D.W.L.
£12.99 (3-litre wine box)
Toasty-coffee oak with dense, inky-berry fruit
and a long finish make this a distinctive wine at the
price – but some may find it too distinctive for their
liking. [*Australia*]

Kingston 1995 Grenache £3.79
Rich, ripe, creamy-jammy fruit – definitely for
swigging on its own. [*Murray Valley, Victoria,
Australia*]

Castel Pujol 1994 Tannat £3.99
There are not many interesting Uruguayan wines,
but this is one of the better examples. The Tannat, a
native grape of France's south-west, is Uruguay's best
red wine varietal, and this rendition has more depth

than most of its peers, with plenty of winter-warming fruit and accessible tannins on the finish. [*Las Violetas, Uruguay*]

Hoya de Cadenas 1989 Reserva £3.99

Ⓑ Very coconutty for a wine that claims to have been aged in oak for just 12 months. If it has had only a year in oak – which I find unlikely – it must have spent 7 years in bottle; who would keep a £3.99 in bottle for so long, and why? Coconut-lovers will feel at home with this wine, but others might prefer a fifty/fifty blend with Stowells Tempranillo wine box (see above). [*Utiel-Requena, Spain*]

La Baume Syrah Grenache 1995 Vin de Pays d'Oc

£3.99

Ⓑ An inky-rich, thick, tannic wine that will repay 12 months' ageing. [*Southern France, France*]

Pinotage 1995 Bovlei Winery £3.99

Ⓢ A piquant-fruity version of Pinotage with raspberry-acidity on the finish. Cheap, but no bubblegum. [*Wellington, South Africa*]

Valle de Vistalba 1995 Malbec, Casa Nieto & Senetiner

£4.49

Deep, dark and well-structured food wine. [*Mendoza, Argentina*]

Prestige Oak-Aged Claret 1994 Saint Vincent Baron

£4.69

A good mouthful of fruit supported by firm oak tannins. [*Bordeaux, France*]

Bisquertt 1995 Merlot £4.79

Ⓢ A deep, dark wine with a rich complexity of

Red Wines

flavours swirling in and out of each other and fine tannins on the finish. [*Colchagua, Chile*]

Vine Vale Shiraz 1995 Peter Lehmann £4.99
Toasty aromas with mellow fruit. [*Barossa, South Australia, Australia*]

Marqués de Cacérès 1992 Rioja £5.19
(S) Surprisingly rich fruit is sustained right through to the finish. Should be drinking like this for a year, then will gain in complexity and finesse for another two or three years. [*Rioja, Spain*]

Castelgreve 1995 Chianti Classico £5.49
(S) A really classy Chianti with heaps of fruit and great typicity. [*Tuscany, Italy*]

Cono Sur 1995 Cabernet Sauvignon, Selection Reserve
£5.59
(S) Full of elegant, stylish fruit that is reminiscent of fresh-picked blackberries, with nice tingly tannins on the finish. [*Chimbarongo, Chile*]

Lindemans Bin 50 1995 Shiraz £5.99
(S) Intense, inky-rich fruit, yet not without some elegance. [*South Australia, Australia*]

Rosemount Estate 1996 Shiraz Cabernet £5.99
(S) Fresh, soft and stylish red with creamy finish. [*South Eastern Australia, Australia*]

Gigondas 1995 Domaine de la Mourielle £6.89
(B) A stylish Gigondas that will improve further over the next two to three years. [*Gigondas, Rhône, France*]

Brouilly 1995 Georges Duboeuf £7.99
Real Gamay flavour – but so there should be for almost £8. [*Brouilly, Beaujolais, Burgundy, France*]

Siglo Reserva 1988 Rioja £7.99
Rich Rioja fruit with fine, prune-plum complexity and dry tannins. [*Rioja, Spain*]

Penfolds Kalimna Bin 28 1994 Shiraz £8.99
⑤ Fat and rich, with solid construction and complexity just beginning to build. [*Barossa, South Australia, Australia*]

White Wines

Classic Gewurztraminer 1995 Posta Romana £2.79
Although nothing like the 1993 – at least not yet – this has developed a touch of spice since it quickly replaced the two years older wine, which sold out after being nominated *SuperBooze* Best Value White Wine of the Year. Definitely sweet fruit, but it will be interesting to see if in a year's time the spice becomes as pungent as the 1993 was last year. [*Tarnave, Romania*]

Hungarian Country White NV Stowells of Chelsea
£11.49 (3-litre wine box)
More medium than the 'dry' which is claimed on the box, but this fresh, clean fruity wine with a tangy finish is certainly worth the asking price. [*Balatonboglár, Hungary*]

Badger Hill 1994 Chardonnay Oak Barrel Fermented
£2.99
This was the cheapest Chardonnay I could recommend, not as a Chardonnay *per se*, but simply as a young, fresh and fruity quaffing white. [*Szekszárd, Hungary*]

White Wines

Langenbach Kabinett 1995 Binger St.-Rochuskapelle
£2.99

B Piquant grapiness, surprisingly fresh for a 1995.
[*Rheinhessen, Germany*]

Muscat Ottonel 1995 Nagyréde Estate £2.99

S This is a definite silver medal for those who like
inexpensive German wines. Very fresh and grapy for a
1995; buy this if you can, but if the 1996 is as good it
should be even better – if you know what I mean . . .
[*Nagyréde, Hungary*]

Chapel Hill NV Irsai Oliver £3.19

Fat, clean, easy-drinking, slightly peachy fruit with an
aromatic touch. [*Balatonboglár, Hungary*]

Sauvignon Blanc NV Stowells of Chelsea
£14.59 (3-litre wine box)
Fresh, easy-drinking tap wine. [*Curico, Chile*]

Tamaioasa 1995 Pietroasa Estate £3.89

B Rich and raisiny, with more intensity of fruit than
any other sweet wine at this price point. Tamaioasa is
an ancient Romanian vine known as the 'Frankincense'
grape. [*Dealul Mare, Romania*]

Castel Pujol 1996 Sauvignon Blanc £3.99

Not really Sauvignon, but a good value off-dry white in
its own right, with fresh, clean fruit and a succulent
finish. [*Cerro Chapeu, Uruguay*]

Etchart 1996 Cafayate Torrontes £3.99

B Ultra-fresh Muscat-like dry white wine. Heaven
with fresh green asparagus and melted butter.
[*Cafayate, Argentina*]

CO-OPERATIVE

Kendermann 1995 Riesling Dry £3.99

S The cheapest dry Riesling recommended this year, and by far the best, earning its silver medal by having the freshest aroma and the most attractive, crisp, dry, apricot fruit. It also has the smartest label. [*Pfalz, Germany*]

Jacob's Creek 1996 Dry Riesling, Orlando £4.59

B Just as limey as Penfolds Rawson's Retreat (*see* Asda *and* Co-operative), but softer and without the spritz. [*South Eastern Australia, Australia*]

Cooks 1996 Sauvignon Blanc £4.99

B Fresh, gooseberry fruit with a crisp finish. Some supermarkets were still selling the 1995, but it had lost its zippiness. [*Gisborne, New Zealand*]

Cuckoo Hill Oak Barrel Chardonnay 1995 Vin de Pays d'Oc £4.99

B Fat and rich, yet maintaining an elegance, this wine was made by Australian Nick Butler. [*Southern France, France*]

Cuckoo Hill Viognier 1995 Vin de Pays d'Oc £4.99

B An extra 12 months in bottle has turned last year's fresh and juicy wine into a fatter, more succulent wine, but it really is peaking, and the 1996 vintage is too early picked for what is supposed to be an exotic variety. [*Southern France, France*]

Pinot Blanc 1995 Vin d'Alsace, Cave Vinicole d'Ingersheim £4.99

B This very fresh, clean, crisp, flavoursome wine was the best Pinot Blanc tasted this year. [*Alsace, France*]

Peter Lehmann 1996 Semillon £5.99
Ⓑ Knocked the spots off the normally excellent Lindemans Hunters Valley Semillon; this has a real limey richness. [*Barossa, South Australia, Australia*]

Château Tahbilk 1996 Marsanne Unwooded £6.29
Ⓑ Elegantly rich, crisp and dry, citrussy-spicy fruit. [*Victoria, Australia*]

Monbazillac 1995 Les Caves Saint-Romain £4.49
Ⓑ Rich liquorice intensity. Ideal with the plum pudding this Christmas, but will be even better at Christmas 1998 or even later. [*Monbazillac, Bordeaux, France*]

Rosé Wines

Hardys Grenache Shiraz 1996 Stamps of Australia
£4.49
Jammy fruit with a very crisp, dry finish. [*South Eastern Australia, Australia*]

Sparkling Wines

Asti NV Rialto £4.29
Ⓑ No Moscato Spumante was in the least bit recommendable, but this Asti, the cheapest submitted, was far and away the best tasted this year. Very fresh, sweet and fruity with a hint of peaches. [*Asti, Piedmont, Italy*]

Codorníu Première Cuvée NV Brut Chardonnay £6.49
Still a bit tight, but with better acidity than most
Cavas. It would be interesting to age this wine for 9–12
months, which is not something I would normally
recommend for a Cava. [*Cava, Spain*]

Seaview Rosé NV Brut £6.49
Creamy strawberry and lavender fruit with a soft
mousse. [*South Eastern Australia, Australia*]

Champagne Lanson NV Black Label Brut £18.49
(S) A classy non-vintage, but keep another 2–3 years
for the mellow, toasty bottle-aromas to develop.
[*Champagne, France*]

Fortified Wines

Yaldara Old Tawny NV Reserve £5.99
(G) This is Australian tawny 'Port' style, although it
can only mention tawny, not Port, of course. Tasted
blind with authentic Ports it tastes nothing like the real
stuff, but judged in its own right it is a lovely fortified
wine of quite stunning value for money. The style is
closer to a raisiny Moscatel, but lighter and creamier,
with prunes and custard on the finish. [*South Eastern
Australia, Australia*]

Dom Brial Muscat de Rivesaltes 1996
£3.99 (half-bottle)
(B) Very fresh and zesty, but very sweet rather than
intensely sweet. [*Languedoc-Roussillon, France*]

Porto Souza 1991 L.B.V. £8.99
Ⓢ Fat, juicy, plummy fruit. Keep five years. [*Douro, Portugal*]

Beers

Grolsch Premium Lager Per pint: £0.82
Ⓖ Very fruity, crisp and deep flavoured. A classic. £3.99 per 6x27.5cl bottles. [*5%, England*]

Banks's Draught, Smoothpour Per pint: £1.35
Ⓑ This hoppy-smoky creamed-up brew was the cheapest widgetized bitter to earn a medal. £4.19 per 4x44cl widgetized cans. [*3.5%, Wolverhampton, England*]

Beamish Draught Irish Stout Per pint: £1.38
Ⓑ It's amazing how the smoky-bitterness permeates this brew, despite the creamy widgetized effect. £4.29 per 4x44cl widgetized cans. [*4.2%, County Cork, Ireland*]

Boddingtons Draught Per pint: £1.38
Ⓑ The fruity-yeasty bloom in this brew makes it a superior bronze in the widgetized bitter category. £4.29 per 4x44cl widgetized cans. [*3.8%, Manchester, England*]

John Smith's Extra Smooth Bitter Per pint: £1.42
Ⓢ Some real bitter flavour putting its stamp on the creamy-widget effect makes this a true silver. £4.39 per 4x44cl widgetized cans. [*4%, Yorkshire, England*]

Guinness Original Stout Per pint: £1.42

B Dense, dark, bitter chocolate, coffee and liquorice. Quite stern, but great with a Stilton ploughmans. £1.25 per 50cl bottle. [*4.3%, Dublin, Ireland, and London, England*]

Draught Guinness Per pint: £1.48

G Draught Guinness stands out from other draught stout sold in cans because of the intensity of its smoky-toasty-malty aroma. It is every bit as smoky as Beamish, but has such a greater depth of other top-quality ingredients that this smokiness is not immediately apparent. What is more easily perceived is the lovely roasted-barley tones that give Guinness the satisfying edge other stouts lack. £4.59 per 4x44cl widgetized cans. [*4.1%, Dublin, Ireland, and London, England*]

Bass, Our Finest Ale Per pint: £1.59

S Very smooth, elegant and stylish with an almost perfumed hoppy aroma. £1.59 per 56.8cl bottle. [*4.4%, Burton-on-Trent, England*]

Marston's Pedigree Bitter Per pint: £1.59

B Very fresh and clean, almost sweet. £1.59 per 56.8cl bottle. [*4.5%, Burton-on-Trent, England*]

Kilkenny Irish Beer Draught, St Francis Abbey Brewery, Guinness Per pint: £1.61

B Sweet and creamy. £4.99 per 4x44cl widgetized cans. [*5%, Kilkenny and Dublin, Ireland*]

Boston Beer, Whitbread Per pint: £1.61

This sweet and creamy 'American' beer is brewed under licence in the UK. £4.99 per 4x44cl widgetized cans. [*4.6%, England*]

Amstel Bier   Per pint: £1.63
   Cleverly brewed to balance crispness and richness,
   Amstel has wide appeal and this year's brew is as good
   as it gets. £3.79 per 4x33cl bottles. [*5%, Amsterdam,
   Holland*]

Theakston Lightfoot, Traditional Pale Beer
                                                   Per pint: £1.64
   ⓢ Fragrant hopped aroma followed by crisp, floral-
   hopped, lightly malty flavour. £1.59 per 55cl bottle.
   [*5.2%, North Yorkshire, England*]

Waggle Dance Traditional Honey Beer, Vaux
                                                   Per pint: £1.64
   ⓢ This soft, full, luscious ale with perfumed-hop
   aromas, clean, off-dry malty taste and a crisp finish is
   apparently named after the dance honey bees execute
   when they have located nectar. £1.59 per 55cl bottle.
   [*5%, Sunderland, England*]

Budweiser Budvar   Per pint: £1.67
   ⓖ Elegant, refreshing and perfectly hopped, this
   classic really is the business. £3.89 per 4x33cl bottles.
   [*5%, Czech Republic*]

Stella Artois, Premium Lager Beer   Per pint: £1.69
   This really only gets in because I want Stella Artois
   drinkers to know I have tasted it and have found other
   better and cheaper beers of the same style. £5.89 per
   6x33cl bottles. [*5.2%, Leuven, Belgium*]

Fuller's London Pride, Premium Ale   Per pint: £1.69
   ⓖ This fresh, intense, hoppy-malty brew is
   particularly well suited to the bottling process and
   always hits home for those who prefer genuinely dry,

authentically bitter beers. £1.49 per 50cl bottle. [*4.7%, London, England*]

Fuggles Imperial Strong Ale, Castle Eden Brewery
Per pint: £1.69

⒢ A widgetized bitter for hardened bitter drinkers! The wonderful aroma of Fuggles hops comes streaming through the creamy head, with an assertive, hoppy bitterness dominating the finish. £1.49 per 50cl widgetized bottle. [*5.5%, Co. Durham, England*]

☞ SPECIAL BEER AWARD OF THE YEAR

6X Export, Wadworth　　　　　　　　Per pint: £1.69

Ⓢ Tasty and smooth, with refined, malty bitter notes and none of the sour sultana-malty character that blighted this brew last year. £1.49 per 50cl bottle. [*5%, Devizes, England*]

Murphy's Draught Irish Stout　　　Per pint: £1.69

⒢ Widgetized Murphy's in a bottle is vastly superior to the canned version because it has an edge and wisp of smoke. There is also no cardboard taint. £1.49 per 50cl widgetized bottle. [*4%, Ireland and the UK*]

☞ THE BEST VALUE DARK BEER OF THE YEAR

Caffrey's Draught Irish Ale　　　　Per pint: £1.71

Ⓑ Sweet and creamy. £5.29 per 4x44cl widgetized cans. [*4.8%, Co. Antrim, UK*]

San Miguel, Premium Export Lager　Per pint: £1.72

Clean and refreshing, but not quite the quality of previous years. £3.99 per 4x33cl bottles. [*5.4%, Madrid, Spain*]

The Celebrated Oatmeal Stout, Samuel Smith
Per pint: £1.75

Ⓢ Very dry, resinous and fruity with sherry notes.
£1.69 per 55cl bottle. [5%, *Yorkshire, England*]

Bud Ice, Anheuser-Busch Inc.   Per pint: £1.80

Not recommended as such, just included so that I can put in print that I honestly wonder if Anheuser-Busch could be sued for the following claim about this watery beer: 'Our exclusive ice brewing process produces a rich, smooth taste that's remarkably easy to drink.' £4.19 per 4x33cl bottles. [5.2%, *St. Louis, USA*]

Old Speckled Hen, Strong Fine Ale, Morland
Per pint: £1.81

Ⓢ A refreshing and tasty beer with a characterful maltiness in both the aroma and on the palate, and the barest hint of smoke. £1.59 per 50cl bottle. [5.2%, *Oxfordshire, England*]

Fuller's ESB Export, Extra Special Bitter
Per pint: £1.81

Ⓑ Not my sort of beer, but its powerful, malty-rich flavour is adored by many. £1.59 per 50cl bottle. [5.9%, *London, England*]

Fuller's 1845, Bottle Conditioned Celebration Strong Ale
Per pint: £1.92

Ⓢ Deep, full, bitter-toffee, malty flavour with an intense liquorice finish and smoky-peppery hops on the aftertaste. £1.69 per 50cl bottle. [6.3%, *London, England*]

Beck's   Per pint: £1.99

Too popular for its own good; the clean, fresh taste of

this beer is nice enough, but outclassed at this price point by so many other brews. £5.79 per 6x27.5cl bottles. [*5%, Bremen, Germany*]

Guinness Foreign Extra Stout   Per pint: £2.05

Extra Stout is a very apt name for this exceptionally extracted brew, the complex flavours of which are remarkably concentrated and build on the palate to a rousing crescendo of bitter-coffee, burnt-toffee, black treacle and liquorice intensity. Not many draught stout drinkers go for it, though. £1.19 per 33cl bottle. [*7.5%, Dublin, Ireland*]

Staropramen, Prague Breweries   Per pint: £2.05

Light, perfumed and elegant. £1.19 per 33cl bottle. [*5%, Prague, Czech Republic*]

Carlsberg Elephant, Strong Imported Beer

                                                         Per pint: £2.38

This strong, heady lager with an intense finish is a classic. £1.15 per 27cl bottle. [*7.2%, Copenhagen, Denmark*]

CRAZY PRICES

This supermarket group in Northern Ireland was purchased in early 1997 by Tesco, whose products could well be seen on its shelves in the near future. See **Tesco**.

CULLENS

Recently acquired by Europa, who paid £7.4 million for the 26-store chain. Cullens had a brilliant reputation for its eclectic wine range in the early 1980s, when it was one of the first retailers to go for New World wines in a big way. The Cullens name will not be changed, but there will eventually be an integration of wine, beer and spirit lines. See **Europa**.

EUROPA

Number of stores *42*
Opening hours *Vary widely; 8a.m.–10p.m. for most, but some are open 24 hours*
Maximum range *150 wines, 80 beers, 45 spirits*
Alternative methods of payment *Cheque with card, Switch, Access, Visa*
Local delivery *Not provided*
Discounts *None*
Refund policy? *No comment*
Other services *Coolers, fresh food and in some outlets a café service*

This edition welcomes Europa as a new participant in *SuperBooze*. I first had dealings with this family owned London-based group of convenience stores (which are closer to the original supermarket concept than superstores are), when I included its outlets in 1984 edition of the *Sunday Telegraph Good Wine Guide*. The relatively small range of wines and beers in a grocery-based convenience store will always be a limiting factor in its performance, but readers should not take too much notice of Europa's relatively few medal-winners, as this is its first year in *SuperBooze* and they have yet to learn the ropes.

Red Wines

Frontier Island Merlot 1994 Hungarian Country Wine
£3.59
Assertive peppery-raspberry fruit makes this a good match with food. [*Vaskeresztes, Hungary*]

Hidden River NV Ruby Cabernet £3.89
Deep-coloured red with *macération carbonique* lifting the nose and sappy fruit on the palate. [*Worcester, South Africa*]

Libertas 1994 Merlot £3.99
ⓑ A good swig of unpretentious, tangy brambly fruit. [*Coastal, South Africa*]

Merlot Vin de Pays d'Oc 1996 Baron Philippe de Rothschild £4.99
Fresh, easy-drinking, plummy fruit – good with food or without. [*France*]

Ochoa 1995 Tempranillo-Garnacha £5.19
Fruit gums on nose and palate, with nice grippy tannins on the finish. [*Navarra, Spain*]

Cune 1994 Rioja £6.19
Very soft with a creamy-coconutty aftertaste. [*Rioja, Spain*]

Rosemount Estate 1995 Cabernet Sauvignon £7.49
ⓖ Delicious, elegant, fruit-driven Cabernet with a seductive creamy finish. [*South Australia, Australia*]

Viñas del Vero 1994 Merlot £7.99
ⓢ A silver at £7.99 must mean very high quality and this is a serious wine indeed. Decant thirty minutes before drinking and serve to wine snobs who think all Spanish wines are plonk. The firm oak, fine tannins and classy fruit should change their minds – but don't tell them where the wine comes from until they've committed themselves! And don't worry about how it will age because it should improve significantly over the next 3–4 years. [*Somontano, Spain*]

White Wines

James Herrick 1995 Chardonnay, Vin de Pays d'Oc
£4.99

Ⓢ Fresh, succulent pineapple fruit. [*Southern France, France*]

Vionta 1995 Albariño £8.99
Not in the same class as the Pazo de Barrantes sold by Booths last year (and which I came to appreciate even more later in the year), this does, however, make a different and interesting dry white to serve with a starter course. [*Rias Baixas, Spain*]

Sparkling Wines

Monastrell Xarel-lo NV Cava Brut, Freixenet £8.99
Experimenting with non-traditional grapes – particularly black varieties like Monastrell, which are Spanish rather than French – must be the way to improve Cava while maintaining its authentic Spanish identity, but inevitably there will be a learning curve. This *cuvée* is a considerable improvement on the first shipment, which was very flabby, but it still lacks acidity; future *cuvées* should be even better, as Freixenet learns how to process black grapes for a white sparkling wine. [*Cava, Spain*]

Gloria Ferrer Blanc de Noirs NV Freixenet Sonoma Caves £9.49
A good example of basic, classic New World fizz, but is it worth £9.49? It definitely has the ability to age and

could prove to be well worth its asking price in a year's time. [*Sonoma, USA*]

Champagne Jacquart NV Brut Tradition £15.39
This fresh, easy-drinking Champagne is fair but not outstanding value, although the Jacquart 1990 is. Anyone who appreciates Champagne should snap up the 1990, which is the best-value *cuvée* I have tasted from that extraordinary vintage. [*Champagne, France*]

Beers

Beck's Per pint: £1.32
Too popular for its own good; the clean, fresh taste of this beer is nice enough, but outclassed at this price point by so many other brews. £1.49 per 64cl bottle. [*5%, Bremen, Germany*]

6X Export, Wadworth Per pint: £1.69
Tasty and smooth, with refined, malty bitter notes and none of the sour sultana-malty character that blighted this brew last year. £1.49 per 50cl bottle. [*5%, Devizes, UK*]

Bishops Finger Kentish Strong Ale, Shepherd Neame
Per pint: £1.70
This knocks spots off the canned version: beautifully fresh and crisp with a powerful true-bitter flavour and long, hoppy aftertaste. £0.99 per 33cl bottle. [*5.4%, Kent, England*]

König-Pilsener Per pint: £1.70
Stands out at its price point as a basic but good and tasty lager. £0.99 per 33cl bottle. [*4.9%, Duisburg, Germany*]

Spitfire Bottle Conditioned Ale, Shepherd Neame
Per pint: £1.70

(S) Distinctive pear-hoppy aroma and flavour, nicely dry, well-hopped finish. Not quite up to last year's standard, but an excellent beer nevertheless. £0.99 per 33cl bottle. [*4.7%, Kent, England*]

Draught Guinness Per pint: £1.74

(G) Draught Guinness stands out from other draught stout sold in cans because of the intensity of its smoky-toasty-malty aroma. It is every bit as smoky as Beamish, but has such a greater depth of other top-quality ingredients that this smokiness is not immediately apparent. What is more easily perceived is the lovely roasted-barley tones that give Guinness the satisfying edge other stouts lack. £1.35 per 44cl widgetized can. [*4.1%, Dublin, Ireland, and London, England*]

Old Speckled Hen, Morland Per pint: £1.81

(S) A refreshing and tasty beer with a characterful maltiness in both the aroma and on the palate, and the barest hint of smoke. £1.59 per 50cl bottle. [*5.2%, Oxfordshire, England*]

Cobra Indian Lager, Mysore Breweries Per pint: £1.88

(B) A good, tasty lager. This was infinitely superior to other Indian lagers submitted this year. £1.09 per 33cl bottle. [*5%, Bangalore, India*]

Carlsberg Elephant, Strong Imported Beer
Per pint: £2.41

(S) This strong, heady lager with an intense finish is a classic. £1.19 per 28cl bottle. [*7.2%, Copenhagen, Denmark*]

Grolsch Premium Lager Per pint: £2.46
Very fruity, crisp and deep flavoured. A classic.
£1.95 per 45cl bottle. [*5%, Groenlo, Holland*]

FOOD FAIR

A chain of 80 off-licensed supermarkets run by Yorkshire Co-operatives, Food Fair stores are similar in format to the Good Neighbour local supermarkets also operated by Yorkshire Co-operatives. Although the range varies according to the size of store (only one is a superstore), Food Fairs stock most of the wines and beers recommended in the main Co-op entry. Please use the recommendations under the main **Co-op** entry.

FOOD GIANT

A northern-based group of 28 superstores in which service has been reduced to a minimum in order to churn out the cheapest prices possible, because nothing is free and the management believe their approach is a more honest one. By making customers fork out for things like carrier bags, Food Giant manages to sell the very same wines and beers as its sister chain Somerfield at 5 to 15 per cent cheaper. Quite why there is such a large variation in the discount is hard to discern or justify, but SoLo is the most profitable company in the Somerfield group and SoLo customers enjoy a handsome discount. So why shop at Somerfield? For service perhaps, but if it's the price you're most interested in, there is no reason for shopping at Somerfield in preference to Food Giant. However, there are few circumstances in which they are in close proximity, so the choice seldom arises. Use the recommendations under the main **Somerfield** entry, but expect to pay 5 to 15 per cent less.

GATEWAY

Part of the Somerfield group, which also includes Food Giant and SoLo. The number of Gateway stores has dropped from 132 last year to 115, and although the business strategy remains the same – that the Gateway facia is due to disappear as the shops are either converted into Somerfield stores or sold off – the deadline of achieving this by the end of 1996 has obviously been missed. According to the chairman's report to shareholders, it will now be accomplished by late 1998. Most stores are being refurbished in the brighter, fresher Somerfield look in preparation for conversion. For the range of wines and beers recommended, use the main **Somerfield** entry.

GOOD NEIGHBOUR

Another small chain of supermarkets run by Yorkshire Co-operatives. Good Neighbour stores are similar in format to Food Fair supermarkets, but are only 25 in number. Although the range varies according to the size of store, Good Neighbour stocks most of the wines recommended in the main **Co-op** entry, to which readers are referred.

HARTS

These busy metropolitan shops are perceived as the more trendy and upmarket outlets of the Europa group. Please use the recommendations under the main **Europa** entry.

KWIK SAVE

Number of stores *950*
Opening hours *Monday–Wednesday and Saturday 9a.m.–5.30p.m., Thursday–Friday 9a.m.–8p.m., Sunday (selected stores only) 12 noon–4p.m.*
Maximum range *105 wines, 160 beers, 80 spirits*
Alternative methods of payment *Cheque with card, Switch and Delta debit cards*
Local delivery *None*
Discounts *None*
Refund policy? *Immediate exchange or full refund*
Other services *None*

Comment Kwik Save, which is currently downsizing the number of its shops, operates a typical discount store's 'no frills' service to minimize costs; this, with a significantly lower than average profit margin, helps to keep prices as low as possible. With such a low percentage profit, however, turnover has to be the priority, which is why Kwik Save's strategy has always been to target volume-selling products. Until relatively recently this meant a small range of cheap and rather dire wines, with Liebfraumilch and Lambrusco about as exciting as it got. Five years ago, however, Kwik Save realized that wine is different from baked beans and hired Angela Muir, a hard-headed Master of Wine, to reorganize things. Since then sales have gone from half-a-million cases to two million. Red wine sales alone went up 40 per cent last year – a phenomenon reported by other supermarkets, notably Safeway – and overall Kwik Save now claims three per cent of the total take-home wine market.

Although the performance of this supermarket has improved only very slightly in *SuperBooze* this year, it is at least heading in the right direction, and if and when the current phase of test-marketing a small range of wines between £4 and £9 is deployed throughout the group, we could see a radical change in the medal-winning fortunes of Kwik Save.

Red Wines

Les Oliviers NV Vin de Table Rouge £1.97
Nothing special, but this is the cheapest red to get a recommendation. It achieves this with some real, if rather basic, fruit that makes it soft and easy to drink, unlike most of the rough-and-ready plonk in this price bracket. [*France*]

Vin Rouge NV Vin de Table Français, Chantovent
£4.49 (1.5-litre plastic bottle)
Gutsy young red with good acidity that enables this cheap wine to improve in bottle for a few months and will keep it fresh for a year or more. Not a wine to lay down as such, but you don't have to worry about having to open it. [*France*]

Gabbia d'Oro NV Vino Rosso £2.39
(B) This is a definite bronze for those who find red wines too harsh. Gabbia d'Oro is exceptionally soft and easy to drink, with light, perfumed fruit and hardly any acidity or tannin. If you find even this wine too harsh, you will at least know not to bother looking for a red you *can* drink, because they do not come any softer than this! But if you do enjoy this wine, you will know there are red wines out there for you. Keep looking. [*Italy*]

Rouge de France NV Sélection Cuvée VE, Celliers de la Comtesse £4.99

Those who prefer the accent on mellowness rather than freshness will opt for the magnum over the bottle. Both are essentially the same wine, but the magnum has obviously had more time in bottle, and this has smoothed over the lighter, fresher, more fruit-driven characteristics. The bottle has a good hint of *macération carbonique*, but this merely lifts the fruit without producing the peardrop aroma that typifies Beaujolais. [*France*]

Flamenco NV Spanish Full Red £2.59

A cheap and cheerful red bursting with clean raspberry and blackcurrant jammy flavour. [*Cariñena, Spain*]

Bulgarian Country Wine NV Cabernet Sauvignon & Merlot, Domaine Boyar £5.19

Ⓑ Unpretentious Cabernet fruit for the price (less than £2.60 per bottle). The wine in this magnum is much better and marginally cheaper than the apparently same wine in a normal bottle size. Could easily age for a year or so. [*Suhindol, Bulgaria*]

Romanian Merlot 1996 Kwik Save £2.79

Ⓑ The thick and soupy fruit might not have much finesse, but it is substantial and tasty, and at £2.79 just has to be a medal winner. [*Recas, Romania*]

Bulgarian Merlot & Cabernet Sauvignon 1995 Domaine Boyar £2.89

Ⓑ The fruit might be thick and soupy, but who's looking for finesse at £2.89? It's soft and tasty. [*Liubimetz, Bulgaria*]

Red Wines

Pelican Bay NV Australian Red Wine, Kwik Save
£11.89 (3-litre wine box)
A definite hint of coconutty oak when tasted blind in a price category that has few oaked wines; but this coconut aroma is more subliminal when drinking this wine out of such a context, when it merely adds a certain creaminess to the fruit. I preferred the wine box to Pelican Bay in the bottle this year, as it's smoother. It's also marginally cheaper. [*South Eastern Australia, Australia*]

Côtes-du-Rhône NV F. Dubessy £2.99
A basic, fresh Rhône red with an easy-drinking, sweet and fruity flavour. [*Côtes-du-Rhône, France*]

Deep Pacific 1996 Merlot-Cabernet Sauvignon £2.99
ⓑ Attractive medley of raspberry and blackcurrant fruit. [*Rancagua, Chile*]

Skylark Hill Syrah 1995 Vin de Pays d'Oc £2.99
Tasty Syrah fruit for the price, with a juicy, refreshing finish. [*Southern France, France*]

Bulgarian Merlot Reserve 1992 Domaine Boyar £3.19
ⓑ Tasty fruit and smooth oak tannins. [*Liubimetz, Bulgaria*]

Elhovo 1992 Cabernet Sauvignon Reserve, Domaine Boyar £3.19
ⓑ The second cheapest Cabernet tasted, and it's a medal winner for its basic, yet eminently drinkable, blackcurrant fruit. Very fruity, medium bodied. The cheapest was from Kwik Save as well, a 1995 Vin de Pays d'Oc selling at £2.79 – a perfectly acceptable wine for the price that just failed to make it through the

Balbi Vineyard 1995 Malbec Syrah £3.29
Interesting bitter-chocolate fruit for such a cheap wine.
Best with food, especially beef casserole. [*Mendoza, Argentina*]

Domaine des Bruyères 1995 Côtes-de-Malepère £3.49
ⓈToasty-oak nose with well-structured fruit on the palate. This wine has some finesse for its price. [*Côtes-de-Malepère, Southern France, France*]

Paul Masson NV California Red Wine £3.49
Despite the hideous carafe, this is a deep purple-coloured wine with a good smack of sweetness in a soft, fresh, unchallenging style. [*California, USA*]

Pelican Bay NV Australian Shiraz-Cabernet £3.59
ⒷNice cheap, creamy-rich, ripe and spicy red. [*South Eastern Australia, Australia*]

Impala 1996 Pinotage £3.99
ⒷA fresh, zesty Pinotage with sherbetty-wine gum fruit but a hint of bubble gum. An unpretentious, easy-drinking version of this varietal from Australian-trained British winemaker Hugh Ryman. [*Western Cape, South Africa*]

White Wines

Les Oliviers NV Vin de Table Blanc £1.97
Clean and fresh, this was the cheapest drinkable 'dry' white I could find. It is actually more off-dry than dry, and the residual sugar enhances the fruit. [*France*]

White Wines

Hock NV Peter Bott £2.17
ℬ The cheapest in its category and it's fresh, clean and grapy – so it just has to be a medal winner. Definitely on the sweet side of medium-sweet. [*Rhein, Germany*]

Hock 1996 K. Linden, Kwik Save £4.35
ℬ Definitely medium-sweet, but equally definitely a touch drier than Kwik Save's Hock in the regular bottle size, this magnum is even fresher and works out to be just half a penny cheaper, so it too deserves a medal. [*Rhein, Germany*]

Flamenco NV Spanish Sweet White £2.59
Not much more than clean and medium-sweet to sweet, but that in itself is incredible for £2.59. [*Valencia, Spain*]

Soave NV Venier £2.67
Fresh, light-bodied and crisp with good acidity; as good as, if not better than, all the Soave except one of the most expensive. [*Veneto, Italy*]

Jade Peaks 1996 Chenin Blanc £2.79
S The fresh, ripe-pear fruit of pure, unadulterated, nicely ripened Chenin Blanc. If only inexpensive Loire Chenin could be like this! [*Coastal Region, South Africa*]

Muscadet 1996 Jean Michel £2.79
The cheapest Muscadet in the tasting turned out to be perfectly acceptable, with fresh appley fruit and, although correctly dry, in a rounder style than is normally found at the lower end of the Muscadet price spectrum. [*Muscadet, Loire, France*]

Kourtaki NV Retsina of Attica £2.89
Most Retsina is no longer dull, flabby or oxidized, but at the basic level it still smells of pine disinfectant, so if drinking this with moussaka does not quite rekindle the culinary excitement of your holiday in the Peloponnese, you can always use it to clean the loo. [*Attica, Greece*]

Piesporter Michelsberg 1996 K. Linden £2.97
(*B*) Fresh, sweet and tangy. [*MSR, Germany*]

Denbies 95 1995 £2.99
(*B*) Fresh, floral and aromatic, this wine tastes very dry in a medium-dry tasting, and this was heightened by a spritz on the finish. [*Surrey, England*]

Impala 1996 Cape White £2.99
(*B*) This soft, succulent and unthinkingly easy to drink wine is another Hugh Ryman production. [*Western Cape, South Africa*]

Skylark Hill Very Special White NV Vin de Pays d'Oc, Kwik Save £2.99
This crisp, young, fresh-flavoured *cuvée* has a touch of something more aromatic than I have found in previous blends – and it is definitely needed to balance what would otherwise be quite green. [*Southern France, France*]

St.-Laurens 1996 QbA Pfalz £2.99
(*G*) Very fresh indeed, with succulent, aromatic and grapy fruit. Another cheap German gold medal winner! This is much sweeter than Marks & Spencer's Kiwi-influenced Liebfraumilch, so it's a matter of horses for courses, but most drinkers of German wine

will agree that both deserve gold medals. [*Pfalz, Germany*]

Colombard Chardonnay NV £3.39

B Fresh and zippy fruit on the nose, crisp lemony fruit on the palate. [*South Eastern Australia, Australia*]

Pelican Bay NV Australian Chardonnay, Kwik Save

£3.59

Fresh and rich. Ideal for the odd glass, thus suits a wine box. [*South Eastern Australia, Australia*]

Sparkling Wines

Lambrusco 4 NV GI SpA £2.89

B Me recommending Lambrusco? Well, everything is relative, and this is of course a bronze medal wine for Lambrusco drinkers. If you do not care for Lambrusco, this will not turn you on to it, but my job is to look for the best wines of their type. For Lambrusco, the parameters of the search are not that much different than for Rosé d'Anjou, sweetish Chenin Blanc (Vouvray etc) or inexpensive German wines like Hock or Liebfraumilch. The wine has to be clean, with no off-putting aromas, after which there must be at least a rudimentary balance between sweetness and acidity. This wine scored well in these respects, but Lambrusco 4 in regular bottle size was a disaster, white or pink. Buy the bigger bottle! [*Emilia-Romagna, Italy*]

Cava Brunet NV Brut Reserva £4.99

Rich, mellow and distinctive, but I'm not sure I would enjoy drinking more than one glass, although Cava-lovers should check it out. [*Cava, Spain*]

Fortified Wines

Castillo de Liria NV Moscatel £2.99
G Very fresh, orange-peel zesty aroma with
intensely sweet, tremendously fresh, absolutely
delicious Muscat fruit and good, refreshing acidity.
This always has been fresh and a great bargain, but
every year it gets even fresher and even more of a
bargain. [*Valencia, Spain*]

Beers

Aston Manor Best Bitter Per pint: £0.47
B The cheapest bitter encountered this year. It has
a clean taste, with some hoppiness, when most cheap
bitters have no flavour at all. Must be a medal-winner.
£2.49 per 3-litre plastic bottle. [*3%, Birmingham, England*]

Brady's Original Irish Stout, Kwik Save Per pint: £0.90
B This smoky brew is closest to Beamish, but not
widgetized and with an added touch of coffee. £2.79
per 4x44cl cans. [*4%, Ireland*]

Gilde Pilsener Per pint: £1.14
S Refreshing, smooth taste with delicately
perfumed hop aromas. £3.99 per 6x33cl bottles. [*4.9%, Hannover, Germany*]

San Miguel Export, Cerveza Especial Per pint: £1.18
Really not bad, hence the recommendation, but
nowhere near as good as last year's silver medal-

winning canned San Miguel. £4.15 per 4x50cl cans.
[*5.4%, Madrid, Spain*]

Grolsch Premium Lager   Per pint: £1.22
This 'Dutch' beer is brewed in England, and the Brits
have done a better job with the canned Grolsch than
they did last year. There is, however, a touch of
cardboard – presumably from the filtering – which
prevents it from getting a medal. £4.29 per 4x50cl
cans. [*5%, England*]

Fuggles Imperial Strong Ale, Castle Eden Brewery
       Per pint: £1.58

(G) A widgetized bitter for hardened bitter drinkers!
The wonderful aroma of Fuggles hops comes
streaming through the creamy head, with an assertive,
hoppy bitterness dominating the finish. £1.39 per 50cl
widgetized bottle. [*5.5%, Co. Durham, England*]

☞ SPECIAL BEER AWARD OF THE YEAR

Fargo, Charles Wells   Per pint: £1.69
A smooth bitter that deserves recommendation. £1.49
per 50cl bottle. [*5%, Bedford, England*]

Dragon Stout, Desnoes & Geddes   Per pint: £2.18

(B) Very rich and sweet with sherry notes. £1.09 per
28cl bottle. [*7.5%, Jamaica, West Indies*].

LONDIS

Number of stores *1,700*
Opening hours *At least half the shops open for a minimum of fourteen hours a day, seven days a week*
Maximum range *250 wines, 100 beers, 100 spirits*
Alternative methods of payment *Cheque with card*
Local delivery *Most shops do, especially those in villages or rural locations*
Discounts *Most shops offer a discount for quantity, but it's up to the individual retailers, so try haggling*
Refund policy? *Will generally replace without any quibble*
Other services *Some shops offer sale-or-return terms and free loan of glasses*

Comment Having received the Symbol Group Award in 1991 and the Independent Grocer of the Year Award in 1994, Londis is obviously doing something right. But although wine buyer Gary Maloney is gradually vamping up the range with New World wines, symbol groups by their very nature tend to have a conservative customer base, and he is restricted by this. In any case, better for the more adventurous customers to have some medal-winning wines and beers to choose from than to ignore Londis altogether.

From a general trading point of view Londis has much to be pleased about, having seen the total number of its shops grow by 300 over the last two years, at a time when other symbol groups are shrinking – an increase that was double their own optimistic expectations. No Londis retailer is obliged to stock any Londis wines and spirits, but some 1,400 do, and there is a listing agreement whereby each retailer is committed to stock a minimum number of products and, more importantly, to sell all Londis products at the recommended price.

Red Wines

Classic Pinot Noir 1993 Posta Romana £3.39
Real Pinot Noir character. This wine has more depth of soft, succulent fruit than Asda's Romanian Pinot Noir at £3.19, although the latter has the better, fresher nose. [*Dealul Mare, Romania*]

Chapel Hill NV Cabernet Sauvignon £3.49
A peppery-capsicum touch adds an interesting dimension to the light, fresh blackcurrant fruit, which has a dash of sweetness on the finish. [*Balatonboglár, Hungary*]

Penfolds Rawson's Retreat Bin 35 1995 Cabernet Sauvignon-Shiraz-Ruby Cabernet £4.69
Thick, inky fruit dominated by cedary-oak. [*South Australia, Australia*]

Casa Porta 1995 Cabernet Sauvignon £4.99
Very youthful fruit on nose and palate, supported by firm tannins. Keep till Christmas 1998 or even 1999. [*Cachapoal, Chile*]

La Fortuna 1996 Merlot £4.99
Blackcurranty, with a touch of pepperiness on the finish. [*Lontue, Chile*]

Redwood Trail Pinot Noir 1995 Coastal Vintners £5.49
The best–cheapest (if £5.49 can be described as cheap) Pinot Noir, with good redcurrant varietal fruit and noticeable, but not overbearing, oak. Nice tannins for food too. [*California, USA*]

Wolf Blass Shiraz Cabernet Sauvignon 1995 Red Label
£6.49

(S) A classy wine that builds on the finish, and promises to develop well over the next couple of years. [*South Eastern Australia, Australia*]

Wolf Blass Cabernet Sauvignon 1995 Yellow Label
£6.99

(B) Closed on the nose, but nicely fresh, with elegant, creamy-coconutty fruit, on the palate. [*South Australia, Australia*]

Faustino V 1991 Rioja Reserva £7.49

(B) Quite deeply flavoured for a medium-bodied wine, this Rioja has fine acidity, giving it elegance and extra flexibility when accompanying food. [*Rioja, Spain*]

White Wines

Hock Deutscher Tafelwein NV Zeller Barl Kellerei, Londis £2.69

(B) Out of more than twenty German wines costing between £2.19 and £2.97, this was the only one that got through the *SuperBooze* tasting, where its very fresh, crisp, but definitely medium-sweet, grapy fruit stood out. [*Rhein, Germany*]

Niersteiner Gutes Domtal NV Zeller Barl Kellerei, Londis £2.99

(S) Definitely on the sweeter side of medium-sweet, but very succulent fruit and a nice tangy-grapy finish. [*Rheinhessen, Germany*]

Long Mountain 1995 Chenin Blanc £3.99
Ⓑ Fresh, clean Chenin fruit with a crisp finish.
   [*Western Cape, South Africa*]

**Redwood Trail Chardonnay 1994 By Sterling
Vineyards** £5.49
   Very soft fruit supported by lemony oak. For drinking
   on its own. [*California, USA*]

Wolf Blass Chardonnay Semillon 1996 £5.99
Ⓑ Rich succulent fruit supported by fresh, lemony
   oak. [*South Eastern Australia, Australia*]

Wolf Blass Chardonnay Barrel Fermented 1996 £6.99
Ⓑ Very fresh and tasty with broad strokes of creamy
   oak. [*South Australia, Australia*]

Chablis 1994 Les Maîtres Goustiers, SA L.R. £7.99
   Fresh, clean, lemony Chablis with a touch fatter finish
   than expected. [*Chablis, Burgundy, France*]

Rosé Wines

Blossom Hill Winery 1995 White Zinfandel £4.29
Ⓑ Fresh and perfumed with lively, medium-sweet
   fruit. [*California, USA*]

Sparkling Wines

Freixenet Cava NV Cordon Negro Brut £7.69
   Don't bother to buy this unless it bears the Lot
   Number L-6312; non-vintage Cordon Negro is usually
   boring, whereas this particular Lot Number (and

probably others, although I cannot confirm which) is crisp and zesty with more weight of fruit than usual. If you see any vintaged Cordon Negro, go for the excellent 1991. [*Cava, Spain*]

Champagne André Simon NV Brut £10.99

The NM number (243) at the bottom of the label tells me this was made by Marne et Champagne, and the lovely toasty aromas followed by firm, ripe, toasty fruit are in fact typical of how this firm's best Champagnes develop with a year or more of bottle-age. [*Champagne, France*]

Beers

John Smith's Bitter, Tadcaster Brewery Per pint: £1.01

Clean tasting with some real bitter flavour. £0.89 per 50cl can. [*4%, Yorkshire, England*]

Guinness Original Stout Per pint: £1.04

Dense, dark, bitter chocolate, coffee and liquorice. Quite stern, but great with a Stilton ploughmans. £0.89 per 48cl can. [*4.3%, Dublin, Ireland, and London, England*]

Kronenbourg 1664, Courage Ltd Per pint: £1.28

Its deep gold colour belies the fresh, hoppy aroma and crisp flavour beneath. Considering this is canned, not bottled, and brewed in the UK by Courage rather than in Strasbourg by Kronenbourg, it is surprisingly good, with a very authentic character. £0.99 per 44cl can. [*5%, Middlesex, England*]

Beers

**Master Brew Premium Ale, Bottle Conditioned,
Shepherd Neame**   Per pint: £1.53

B Not as full or well-defined as in previous years, but still a fine-flavoured beer with a light but distinctive bitter finish. £1.35 per 50cl bottle. [*4%, Kent, England*]

Draught Guinness   Per pint: £1.54

G Draught Guinness stands out from other draught stout sold in cans because of the intensity of its smoky-toasty-malty aroma. It is every bit as smoky as Beamish, but has such a greater depth of other top-quality ingredients that this smokiness is not immediately apparent. What is more easily perceived is the lovely roasted-barley tones that give Guinness the satisfying edge other stouts lack. £1.19 per 44cl widgetized can. [*4.1%, Dublin, Ireland, and London, England*]

Boddingtons Manchester Gold   Per pint: £1.54

S A superior silver in widgetized bitter terms, this brew is in a similar style to the basic Boddingtons Draught, but has more depth of bitter flavour. £1.19 per 44cl widgetized can. [*4.8%, Manchester, England*]

Foster's Ice Beer, Courage Limited   Per pint: £1.54

This 'Aussie' beer is brewed in England and has more flavour than last year. £3.59 per 4x33cl bottles. [*5%, England*]

Boston Beer, Whitbread   Per pint: £1.61

This sweet and creamy 'American' beer is brewed under licence in the UK. £1.25 per 44cl widgetized can. [*4.6%, England*]

**Kilkenny Irish Beer Draught, St Francis Abbey
Brewery, Guinness** Per pint: £1.67

ⓑ Sweet and creamy. £1.29 per 44cl widgetized can.
[*5%, Kilkenny, Ireland*]

Bud Ice, Anheuser-Busch Inc. Per pint: £1.72

Not recommended as such, just included so that I can
put in print that I honestly wonder if Anheuser-Busch
could be sued for the following claim about this watery
beer: 'Our exclusive ice brewing process produces a
rich, smooth taste that's remarkably easy to drink.'
£3.99 per 4x33cl bottles. [*5.2%, St Louis, USA*]

Spitfire Bottle Conditioned Ale, Shepherd Neame
Per pint: £1.81

ⓢ Distinctive pear-hoppy aroma and flavour, nicely
dry, well-hopped finish. Not quite up to last year's
standard, but an excellent beer nevertheless. £1.59 per
50cl bottle. [*4.7%, Kent, England*]

Bishops Finger Kentish Strong Ale, Shepherd Neame
Per pint: £1.81

ⓢ This knocks spots off the canned version:
beautifully fresh and crisp with a powerful true-bitter
flavour and long, hoppy aftertaste. £1.59 per 50cl
bottle. [*5.4%, Kent, England*]

MARKS & SPENCER

Number of stores *283*
Opening hours *Vary too widely to generalize*
Maximum range *200 wines, 20 beers, 10 spirits*
Alternative methods of payment *Cheque with card, M&S Charge Card, Switch and Delta debit cards*
Delivery *Not provided, although M&S Mail Order will deliver any of its special purchase wines (ask your local store to send you the list, which is updated every three months) and staff will help carry goods to car if requested*
Discounts *12 bottles for the price of 11*
Refund policy? *A no-quibble refund or replacement policy when customers return an open bottle they claim to be faulty*
Other services *None*

Comment M&S sell only own-label products, and every one has to justify its shelf space through turnover. Combine this fact with an extraordinary reputation for quality and value, and you can understand why this group is so successful. Its marketing formula ensures that customers mostly get what they want, together with a guarantee of consistency and quality. In the case of wine, however, this used to mean that while M&S was a safe place to shop, it was not a particularly exciting one. Newcomers to wine could confidently buy M&S wines, but the more experienced the wine drinker, the less inclined he was to browse through the group's rather rudimentary range. This changed several years ago, when the M&S wine team was given the freedom to build up the sort of range that can hold the interest of a more knowing shopper. In most cases, 'own-label' now means little more than inserting the M&S name on wines of truly individual character. As *SuperBooze* blind tastings have established, this has worked well for wine, but this year's scramble for gold medal-winning products by the top supermarkets has seen M&S struggle a bit. An analysis of this supermarket's performance indicates that the special treatment it gave to wines should now be given to beers. The relatively small range of M&S beers and in most cases their basic, if decent, quality has never helped the group's performance in *SuperBooze*; on top of that, the failure of Wethered's Draught Bitter to qualify this year, combined with the absence of its top-performing Traditional Yorkshire Ale, has allowed the group's position to sink even further. With regional and premium bottled beers about to experience the same boom as wine did twenty years ago, M&S really has to change its philosophy as far as this category is concerned if it is to have any chance of attracting the more sophisticated beer drinker. Perhaps someone should tell the board of directors that most beer drinkers today do not wear flat caps and mufflers, and would make lucrative potential customers for other M&S products.

Red Wines

La Falleras 1996 St Michael £2.99

⒝ Amazingly elegant, with fluffy-fresh fruit, for a red wine from Utiel-Requena in the baking hot Valencia region. [*Utiel-Requena, Spain*]

Parras Valley 1994 Cabernet Sauvignon-Merlot, St Michael £3.99

This Mexican wine has an unusual nose, but it is not off-putting and the fruit is clean, mellow and blackcurrenty. Made by John Worontschak, an Australian-trained but British-based flying winemaker. [*Parras Valley, Mexico*]

Syrah 1996 Vin de Pays d'Oc, Paul Sapin, St Michael
£3.99
Flowery aromas expressed as violets on the palate; the fruitiness in this wine will pick up by Christmas. [*Southern France, France*]

Domaine Jeune 1996 Cépage Counoise, Vin de Pays du Gard, St Michael £4.49
⑨ Soft, ripe, jammy fruit from one of the thirteen grape varieties occasionally used in Châteauneuf-du-Pape, but now an up-and-coming pure varietal wine. Not unlike a combination of the jamminess of Grenache with the richness and structure of Mourvèdre. [*Southern France, France*]

Tannat Matured in Oak 1996 Juanico, St Michael
£4.49
⑨ Typically rich Tannat, but atypically smooth for Uruguay, where this variety is usually quite chunky. Fine acidity. Oak does not dominate. [*Juanico, Uruguay*]

Casa Leona 1995 Reserve Cabernet Sauvignon, St Michael £4.99
⑨ Very fresh fruit-bush aromas belie the chocolaty fruit on the palate and the smooth, creamy-coffee oak that builds up on the finish. [*Rapel, Chile*]

Casa Leona 1996 Reserve Merlot, St Michael £4.99
⑨ A stylish wine dominated now by smooth, sweet vanilla-oak, but the fruit should deepen over the next year or two. [*Rapel, Chile*]

Rioja Tempranillo 1994 Bodegas Age, St Michael
£4.99

ⓑ Coconut and winegums! [*Rioja, Spain*]

Roseral 1994 Rioja, St Michael £4.99
Very fruity indeed. [*Rioja, Spain*]

Shiraz 1995 Oak Matured, St Michael £4.99
Uncomplicated, tangy-rich fruit. [*South Eastern Australia, Australia*]

Honey Tree Shiraz Cabernet 1996 Rosemount Estate, St Michael £5.50

ⓢ Elegant, fresh, soft and creamy red with a hint of cool mint on the finish. It's difficult to see any difference between this and the Rosemount Estate Shiraz Cabernet (*see* Co-operative), except that it is not in such a flashy bottle and it's 50p cheaper! [*South Eastern Australia, Australia*]

Canyon Road 1994 Cabernet Sauvignon, St Michael
£5.99

Light, soft, easy-drinking fruit with mellow, cedary-oak tones on the nose and finish. [*California, USA*]

Chianti Classico 1995 Basilica Cafaggio, St Michael
£6.99

This is not really a recommendation, but if you ever wanted to know what Chianti would be like if made in the Beaujolais style, this is the wine for you! [*Tuscany, Italy*]

Saints 1994 Cabernet Merlot, St Michael £6.99
Typically herbaceous Kiwi red with good richness on finish. [*Hawkes Bay, New Zealand*]

Red Wines

Canfera 1994 Single Vineyard, St Michael £8.99

Ⓖ To end up with a gold in *SuperBooze* a wine must be judged a gold-plus prior to the super-selection process, and to achieve that at £8.99 it has to be very special indeed. This is definitely new-wave Italian – although new-wave wines have been going twenty-odd years in Tuscany. This might have a flashy bottle and claim to be a 'super-Tuscan', but it is better than most Italian wines in flashy bottles and really deserves the 'super-Tuscan' tag. Gorgeously creamy fruit – pristine and focused, yet expressive varietally and of its *terroir* – it has beautifully integrated oak and fine tannins, making it superb on its own or with food, and a dead cert for ageing over the next 4–5 years. [*Tuscany, Italy*]

Shiraz 1995 Coonawarra Winegrowers, St Michael
£8.99

Ⓑ Rather obvious for a £9 wine, but there's no denying the gulpability of its rich, cedary-oaky fruit. [*Coonawarra, South Australia, Australia*]

The Ridge Wines 1995 Coonawarra Cabernet, St Michael £8.99

Ⓑ Rich, well-focused, blackcurranty fruit and some complexity on the finish. [*Coonawarra, South Australia, Australia*]

Rosemount 1993 Orange Vineyard Cabernet Sauvignon, St Michael £11.99

Ⓖ Seductively soft and smooth blackcurrant fruit of some elegance and finesse. [*Orange, NSW, Australia*]

White Wines

La Falleras 1996 St Michael £2.99
Very fresh, easy-drinking, gentle fruit with a satisfying, crisp finish. [*Utiel-Requena, Spain*]

Liebfraumilch 1996 Rheinhessen, St Michael £2.99
(G) A gold medal for Liebfraumilch? Well, I did give this a lot of thought and came to the conclusion that, although no one would ever claim Liebfraumilch to be a fine wine, if it is everything that one could reasonably demand from a Liebfraumilch, then it must be a gold-medal wine for Liebfraumilch drinkers. What other definition could there possibly be? Well, the deliciously fresh, clean and well-focused aromatic fruit in this wine, made in collaboration with New Zealander winemaker Jamie Marfell, is everything anyone could sanely expect from a medium-sweet Liebfraumilch, and more. [*Rheinhessen, Germany*]

Vin de Pays du Gers 1996 St Michael £2.99
A soft, fruity, amazingly easy to drink dry white wine. [*South Western France, France*]

Hock 1996 Deutscher Tafelwein Rhein, St Michael
£3.99
(S) Another wine made in collaboration with Kiwi Jamie Marfell, this is very similar to the Liebfraumilch, but I felt the latter has the edge. What I cannot understand, however, is how a Tafelwein from the same wine development programme can be fractionally more expensive than a Qualitätswein. [*Rhein, Germany*]

White Wines

Macabeo Chardonnay 1996 Concavins & Hugh Ryman, St Michael £3.49

(B) I would be hard pushed to guess that there is any Chardonnay in here – though I dare say its effect is designed more to plump out the Macabeo than to contribute any varietal flavour – but it is a satisfying, fresh dry white that is all too easy to drink. [*Conca de Barbera, Spain*]

Vin de Pays des Côtes-de-Gascogne 1996 Patrick Azcué, St Michael £3.49

Bramley apples. [*South Western France, France*]

Australian Medium Dry NV Southcorp Wines, St Michael £3.99

(B) The spritzy, lime-flavoured fruit has a good depth for the price, on the dry side of medium-dry. [*South Eastern Australia, Australia*]

Casa Leona 1996 Chardonnay, St Michael £3.99

Very lean for Chardonnay, but nice crisp, clean fruit. [*Rapel, Chile*]

Orvieto Classico 1996 Cantina del Coppiere, St Michael £3.99

Best cheapest dry Orvieto: clean, fresh and satisfying. What more do you want? [*Orvieto, Italy*]

Perdeberg Cellar 1996 Sauvignon Blanc, St Michael

£3.99

Fresh, dry and fruity; not terribly Sauvignon in style, but well worth a recommendation at this price. [*Paarl, South Africa*]

Sauvignon Blanc 1996 Viña San Pedro, St Michael
£3.99

B Fresh, soft and very clean, with a fat, succulently fruity finish. Made by flying French winemaker Jacques Lurton. [*Lontue, Chile*]

Domaine Mandeville Chardonnay 1996 Vin de Pays d'Oc, St Michael £4.49
Extraordinarily fresh. [*Southern France, France*]

Bianco di Custoza 1996 La Casella, St Michael £4.99
Although the super-selection process has denied this wine a gong, its crisp, zippy fruit does make it the best Bianco di Custoza I've encountered. [*Custoza, Veneto, Italy*]

Chardonnay Bin 65 1996 Lindemans, St Michael £4.99

S Better acidity than the 1995 vintage makes this a much livelier, more refreshing wine, with a nice dollop of oak. [*South Eastern Australia, Australia*]

Honey Tree Semillon Chardonnay 1996 Rosemount Estate, St Michael £5.50

B Rich and quite serious. You should keep this for 6–12 months. [*South Eastern Australia, Australia*]

Kaituna Hills 1996 Chardonnay, St Michael £5.50

S Beautifully fresh, succulent fruit with plenty of ripe acidity. [*Gisborne, New Zealand*]

Kaituna Hills 1996 Sauvignon Blanc, St Michael £5.50

S Deliciously ripe gooseberry fruit, really quite intense, and lifted on the finish by a definite spritz. Drink within months unless you like asparagus, because that is how it will go. [*Marlborough, New Zealand*]

White Wines

Chardonnay Viognier 1996 Juanico, St Michael £5.99
B Soft and rich with an aromatic fatness on the finish. [*Juanico, Uruguay*]

Montagny Premier Cru 1995 Les Vignes de la Croix, St Michael £6.99
Broad and toasty aromas with crisp Chardonnay fruit. Good food wine. [*Montagny, Burgundy, France*]

Petit Chablis 1996 C.V.C., St Michael £6.99
B Searingly dry, straight-as-a-die Chablis with acidity dominating the finish. To be consumed with food only! [*Chablis, Burgundy, France*]

Saints 1995 Chardonnay, St Michael £6.99
S Soft and peachy, this wine has lost the overt coconutty aromas that dominated last year, the fruit and oak having nicely knitted together in the bottle. [*Gisborne, New Zealand*]

Rosemount Estate 1995 Chardonnay, St Michael £7.50
S Crisp, toasty-lemony, oaky-fruit with a firm finish. Tastes drier than the 1996 (*see* Budgens). [*Hunter Valley, NSW, Australia*]

Chablis 1995 C.V.C., St Michael £7.99
B Very fresh indeed. Nice clean fruit. Straight. [*Chablis, Burgundy, France*]

Haan 1996 Barossa Valley Chardonnay, St Michael £7.99
B Some lemony fruit aromas, very pure fruit, with a smoky touch on the finish. [*Barossa, South Australia, Australia*]

Vine Vale Vineyard 1996 Chardonnay, St Michael £8.99
⟨ℬ⟩ Very fresh, dry and intense, fruit-driven wine that works well at the table. [*South Eastern Australia, Australia*]

Rosemount 1995 Orange Vineyard Chardonnay, St Michael £11.99
⟨𝒢⟩ Huge mouthful of ultra-fresh toasty fruit. [*Orange, NSW, Australia*]

Sparkling Wines

Asti NV Tosti, St Michael £5.99
Very fresh and very soft. [*Asti, Piedmont, Italy*]

Australian Chardonnay Blanc de Blancs 1994 Brut, Seppelt, St Michael £7.99
⟨𝒮⟩ Fresh, crisp, zesty-lemony fruit with a firm mousse of small bubbles. A satisfying wine now, this *cuvée* could take a further 18 months' ageing. [*South Eastern Australia, Australia*]

Champagne Veuve de Medts NV Brut Premier Cru, St Michael £13.99
Fresh, clean and crisp, this Champagne will plump out over the next 12 months. [*Champagne, France*]

Champagne Cuvée Orpale 1985 Blanc de Blancs Brut, St Michael £22.50
⟨𝒮⟩ Intensely rich fruit with delicious, slow-building finesse. A class act. [*Champagne, France*]

Fortified Wines

Cream Sherry NV Williams & Humbert, St Michael
£4.99

B Elegantly sweet with a Moscatel-raisiny hint to the richness on the finish, although I would be surprised to find that it contains any Moscatel. [*Jerez, Spain*]

Rich Cream Sherry NV Williams & Humbert, St Michael
£4.99

Enjoyably fresh and clean with a very sweet flavour, but lacks the balancing richness that would earn it a medal. [*Jerez, Spain*]

Tawny Port NV Morgan Brothers, St Michael £6.99

B Very smooth, yet has some fiery, peppery-spice on the finish. [*Douro, Portugal*]

Vintage Character Port NV Morgan Brothers, St Michael
£6.99

G When you get a Port that's more winey than porty, you know it will age and improve, even if it is only Vintage Character. Not really for those with a sweet tooth, but the fruit is concentrated and the finish intense, making it perfectly safe to lay down for 3–5 years. [*Douro, Portugal*]

Late Bottled Vintage Port 1988 Morgan Brothers, St Michael
£7.99

S Mature spicy-cedary bouquet, extraordinarily rich and powerful, but not quite classic – almost Australian! [*Douro, Portugal*]

10 Years Old Port NV Morgan Brothers, St Michael
£9.99

(S) There was a big gap in the price of Tawny Ports submitted, from £6.99 to this (and Tesco's Tawny) at £9.99, and there was an equally big step up in quality. Although this is distinctly paler than Tesco's 10 Year Old Tawny, it was sweeter. At first, it seemed to be simpler in taste, but the fire and spice built in the mouth to a tingly-grippy finish. The label reveals that this was bottled in 1995, which helps you discern whether I am writing about the same non-vintage blend. [*Douro, Portugal*]

Beers

York's Northern Bitter, St Michael   Per pint: £0.80
(B) A noticeably smoother, long-lasting head, and slightly pepper hop aroma stand out at this price point. £2.49 per 4x44cl cans. [*3.5%, England*]

Premium Original Pilsener Lager, St Michael
Per pint: £1.22
(S) Flowery-hopped aroma, with a mellow taste and crisp finish. £4.29 per 4x50cl cans. [*4.9%, Germany*]

Bière d'Alsace Premium French Lager, Fischer, St Michael   Per pint: £1.25
(B) Beery aromas with peppery-hopped flavour. £5.50 per 10x25cl bottles or £11.99 for 24x25cl bottles. [*5%, Alsace, France*]

Traditional Premium Ale, Caledonian, St Michael
Per pint: £1.47

Ⓢ Beautiful hoppy aroma, good bitterness and depth. In a way, it's just a good straightforward bitter – but that can be difficult to find in a bottle. £1.29 per 50cl bottle. [*4.4%, England*]

Atlanta Ice, St Michael
Per pint: £1.66

Fresh and easy-drinking, with more flavour than most other American beers and, indeed, most other Ice Beers. £4.15 per 4x35.5cl bottles. [*5%, USA*]

MORRISONS

Number of stores *81*
Opening hours *Mondays–Saturdays 8a.m.–8p.m., Sundays 10a.m.–4p.m.*
Maximum range *450 wines, 350 beers, 250 spirits*
Alternative methods of payment *Cash, cheque with card, Access, Switch*
Local delivery *None*
Discounts *None*
Refund policy? *Refund or replace*
Other services *Free loan of glasses*

Comment Morrisons are moving south to Banbury and Kent. This pleases me because I enjoy their stores, which have wide aisles and different departments dressed up to look like shop fronts, and I hope they will not lose this nice little touch. Stuart Purdie is a one-man buying department, just as Finnerty is at Budgen, and like him is pretty damn good at it. Morrisons have dramatically improved their performance in *SuperBooze* this year. It shows what can be done when enough wines of the right calibre are submitted, because the total range is essentially not that much different from last year's.

Red Wines

The Bulgarian Vintners' NV Cabernet Sauvignon & Merlot £2.69

> If you want a Bulgarian Cabernet-Merlot for less than £3, I could recommend only two this year, and although this does not merit the bronze medal awarded to the one from Suhindol (Kwik Save, £5.19 in

For details of 'Stock Me and Buy One' see pages xi–xii.

magnums), if you prefer a more mature, mellow style, this would be the one for you. [*Svischtov, Bulgaria*]

Côtes-du-Lubéron 1995 Rhône Valley Red Wine, Pol Romain £2.99

Peppery-jammy red with enough acidity to accompany a bowl of underripe tomatoes! [*Côtes-du-Lubéron, Rhône, France*]

Côtes-du-Rhône NV Gabriel Meffre, Morrisons £3.19

ℬ Fresh and authentically peppery medium-bodied red, with plenty of easy-drinking fruit. [*Côtes-du-Rhône, France*]

South African Red NV Wonderfully Fruity, Morrisons £3.25

The light body of this wine belies its richness and fruitiness, but it is the label that intrigues me most, as it has a charming ethnic-style painting that has been crammed into too little space, and far too much text. Not only is there far too much text for a front label, but each line has its own typeface. Quite peculiar. [*Paarl, South Africa*]

Valdezaro 1996 Chilean Cabernet Sauvignon £3.29

Lightweight wine with sweet wine-gum fruit. [*Maule, Chile*]

La Source 1994 Cabernet Sauvignon, Vin de Pays d'Oc £3.35

ℬ Best-structured Cabernet in its price category. Nice with a steak. [*Southern France, France*]

Amazon NV Brazilian Cabernet Sauvignon £3.75

A tasty red with a touch of sweetness on the finish. [*Rio Grande do Sul, Brazil*]

Big Frank's Red 1995 Minervois £3.99
Thick and tasty fruit. [*Minervois, Southern France, France*]

Bovlei Winery 1995 Merlot £3.99
Ⓢ The pure blackcurrant aroma and flavour of this wine might be too opulent for some hardened red-wine drinkers, but many people will find it a joy to drink. [*Wellington, South Africa*]

Uggiano 1994 Chianti dei Colli Fiorentini £4.69
Ⓑ This Chianti has a smoothness on the finish that suggests some cask-ageing in used, not new, oak. The flavours in this wine are extended when drinking with food. Will improve a year or two in bottle. [*Tuscany, Italy*]

Hanwood 1995 Cabernet Sauvignon, McWilliams
£4.79
Ⓑ This is not your typical Oz Cabernet, from the bouquet – which displays a floral finesse – to the hint of peaches on the palate – which could indicate a touch of noble botrytis – the understated use of oak and firm tannins on the finish. [*South Eastern Australia, Australia*]

Château Saint Galier 1995 Graves £4.99
Ⓢ A sweet, perfumed, ripe-fruit aroma, with a good depth of flavour, lovely menthol after-aromas and enough silky tannins for food. [*Graves, Bordeaux, France*]

Cranswick Estate 1995 Shiraz £4.99
Rich, thick and tasty, with slight coffee oak for added interest and a certain smoothness. [*Riverina, NSW, Australia*]

Uggiano 1995 Chianti Classico £4.99

(G) The soft, smooth vanilla-oak might not be everybody's idea of Chianti, but this wine has good typicity of fruit and the correct structure. It also happens to be of such extraordinary quality, tasting more like a £6.99 or even a £7.99 wine, that I would have queried the price, had it not been for the fact that the 1992 vintage got a gold last year at £4.39! [*Tuscany, Italy*]

Bin 444 Cabernet Sauvignon 1994 Wyndham Estate
£5.25

(S) A definite step up in structure and complexity, the flavours unfolding with time, which makes it a fine food wine that is capable of further ageing. [*South Eastern Australia, Australia*]

Crozes-Hermitage 1994 Cave de Tain l'Hermitage
£5.85

(S) Stylish and well-focused. [*Crozes-Hermitage, Rhône, France*]

Parducci 1994 Petite Sirah £6.99

(B) Although all lovers of four-by-two will quickly latch on to the creamy-coconutty oak in this wine, which does deserve recommendation, at almost £7 I had not intended to make it a medal winner, but for the fact that the oak builds into smooth, coffee tones on the palate. [*California, USA*]

Châteauneuf-du-Pape 1994 Domaine du Vieux Lazaret
£8.49

(S) A lovely, soft, stylish expression of Châteauneuf-du-Pape. Under blind conditions I thought there must be more Mourvèdre there than usual, but when I later discovered the wine was from Vieux Lazaret, I doubted that this would be so, as the *domaine* generally uses just 5 per cent of that variety. Vieux Lazaret is the source and producer of Tesco's Les Arnevals and Marks & Spencer's Les Couversets. [*Châteauneuf-du-Pape, Rhône, France*]

White Wines

Vin de Pays de l'Aude White NV Foncalieu, Morrisons £2.89

This blended dry white wine is dominated by Sauvignon Blanc, the fruit of which, although modest in quality, is cleaner and more intense than in most Sancerre costing more than twice as much. [*Southern France, France*]

Côtes-du-Roussillon NV Foncalieu, Morrisons £2.95

ℬ This extremely fresh, crisp and zippy dry white wine makes a very good aperitif. [*Côtes-du-Roussillon, Southern France, France*]

TR2 Medium Dry White Wine 1995 Reserve, Wyndham Estate £3.99

S Definitely on the sweet side of medium-dry, this very fresh wine has succulent, peachy fruit. [*South Eastern Australia, Australia*]

Zimmermann NV Rivaner £3.99

ℬ Drier than most German wines in this category, which makes it better with food. [*Pfalz, Germany*]

Solana 1994 Torrontés & Treixadura £4.19

B Toasty-lemon bottle-aromas carry through from the nose to the fruit on the palate. Made in collaboration with Aussie winemaker Don Lewis. [*Val do Mino, Spain*]

Saint-Denis Fine White Burgundy NV Chardonnay
£4.99

B Some people might not notice it, but this has been bottled with a touch too much sulphur. But for that, the gently rich and elegant fruit in this wine might have earned it a silver medal. If you find the sulphur objectionable, lay the wine down for 18–24 months and it will become absorbed and turn into toasty bottle-aromas. What I cannot understand, however, is how the Burgundian authorities permit the use of a brand name that could be mistaken for Morey-St.-Denis, one of its prestigious *grands crus*? This white Saint-Denis is much better than the red. [*Burgundy, France*]

Preiss-Zimmer Gewurztraminer 1995 Vin d'Alsace Tradition £5.29

B I was tempted to give this a silver medal, but am glad now that I did not, since my appreciation was due more to this being the cheapest, and thus first, Alsace in the Gewürztraminer tasting. The step up in class, quality and character was significant, but not really deserving anything more than a bronze (good as that may be). This wine does, however, have a very elegant, spice-laden structure that promises further development. [*Alsace, France*]

Wyndham Estate 1995 Oak Cask Chardonnay £5.65

B Everything you would expect from an oaky Oz

Chardonnay, with a fine balance between acidity and ripe-sweetness of fruit. [*Hunter Valley, NSW, Australia*]

Sparkling Wines

Sacred Hill 1995 Whitecliff Sauvignon Blanc £6.99
Because of its nose, nearly did not get even a recommendation; but it's not so much off-putting as different, when tasted blind with other Sauvignon Blanc wines, as is the flavour – very rich, intense and for sipping rather than gulping. [*Hawkes Bay, New Zealand*]

Champagne Paul Hérard NV Blanc de Noirs Brut
£11.39
This soft, creamy Champagne comes from an underrated producer in the Aube. [*Champagne, France*]

Fortified Wines

Amontillado Sherry NV Morrisons £3.59
Creamy-rich with a long medium-sweet, toffee-treacle intensity on the finish. More like a genuinely old Amontillado. Very impressive for the price. [*Jerez, Spain*]

Rozès 1991 Late Bottled Vintage Port £6.99
Invigorating, fiery fruit with a smooth, mellow finish. [*Douro, Portugal*]

Cockburn's Anno 1989 Late Bottled Vintage Port
£9.99

Ⓢ Exquisitely elegant to drink now, but will, however, be a far more complex Port if aged for another five years. [*Douro, Portugal*]

Beers

Keoghan's Ale, Draught, Federation Brewery
Per pint: £0.96

Very creamy-malty nose. I originally kicked this out at the tasting stage, but after failing to recommend a single widgetized bitter under about £1.30 per pint, I picked this as the best available in its category. £2.99 per 4x44cl widgetized cans. [*4.7%, Tyne & Wear, England*]

Budweiser Budvar   Per pint: £1.35

Ⓖ Elegant, refreshing and perfectly hopped, this classic really is the business. £1.19 per 50cl bottle. [*5%, Czech Republic*]

Beamish Draught Irish Stout   Per pint: £1.38

Ⓑ It's amazing how the smoky-bitterness permeates this brew despite the creamy widgetized effect. £4.29 per 4x44cl widgetized cans. [*4.2%, County Cork, Ireland*]

Murphy's Draught Irish Stout   Per pint: £1.42

Ⓑ Very soft, mild and sweet, but there is a cardboardy aftertaste to Murphy's this year (detected in samples from all outlets) which demotes it from silver to bronze. £4.39 per 4x44cl widgetized cans. [*4%, Ireland & UK*]

Nastro Azzurro, Premium Beer, Peroni Per pint: £1.46
Ⓑ Rich and easy drinking, with a touch of sweetness on the palate. £0.85 per 33cl bottle. [*5.2%, Italy*]

Pendle Witches Brew, Strong Lancashire Ale, Moorhouse's Per pint: £1.47
Ⓑ Not for bitter drinkers, but good for those who prefer a softer, more mellow brew. £1.29 per 50cl bottle. [*5.1%, Lancashire, England*]

Daniels Hammer Strong Ale, Thwaites Per pint: £1.47
Ⓖ Lovely satisfying richness, with really mellow flavour, yet clean and crisp with a sharp finish. £1.29 per 50cl bottle. [*5.2%, England*]

Draught Guinness Per pint: £1.48
Ⓖ Draught Guinness stands out from other draught stout sold in cans because of the intensity of its smoky-toasty-malty aroma. It is every bit as smoky as Beamish, but has such a greater depth of other top-quality ingredients that this smokiness is not immediately apparent. What is more easily perceived is the lovely roasted-barley tones that give Guinness the satisfying edge other stouts lack. £4.59 per 4x44cl widgetized cans. [*4.1%, Dublin, Ireland, and London, England*]

Marston's Pedigree Bitter Per pint: £1.49
Ⓑ Very fresh and clean, almost sweet. £1.49 per 56.8cl bottle. [*4.5%, Burton-on-Trent, England*]

Gillespie's Draught Malt Stout, Scottish & Newcastle Breweries Per pint: £1.51
Ⓢ One of the most distinctive widgetized stouts on the market, Gillespie's is more malty-mellow than its

Irish counterparts. £4.69 per 4x44cl widgetized cans.
[*4%, Edinburgh, Scotland*]

Old Fart, Premium Strength Beer, Merrimans Brewery Per pint: £1.53
ℬ Richer and sweeter than last year. £1.35 per 50cl bottle. [*5%, Leeds, England*]

Brewers Droop, Marston Moor Brewery Per pint: £1.53
Easy-drinking, light-flavoured ale with the taste of pears and an interesting label. £1.35 per 50cl bottle. [*5%, York, England*]

Black Sheep Ale, Paul Theakston's Black Sheep Brewery Per pint: £1.53
𝒢 Mellow, full and stylish, with a good bitter flavour and some nutty-smoky complexity on the finish. A delight to drink. £1.35 per 50cl bottle. [*4.4%, North Yorkshire, England*]

Waggle Dance Traditional Honey Beer, Vaux
Per pint: £1.54
𝒮 This soft, full, luscious ale with perfumed-hop aromas, clean, off-dry malty taste and a crisp finish is apparently named after the dance honey bees execute when they have located nectar. £1.49 per 55cl bottle. [*5%, Sunderland, England*]

Boddingtons Manchester Gold Per pint: £1.55
𝒮 A superior silver medal in widgetized bitter terms, this brew is in a similar style to the basic Boddingtons Draught, but has more depth of bitter flavour. £4.79 per 4x44cl widgetized cans. [*4.8%, Manchester, England*]

Cumberland Ale, Jennings Brothers Per pint: £1.58
A sweetish, clean, fresh, easy-supping brew for non-beer-drinkers! £1.39 per 50cl bottle. [*4.2%, Cumbria, England*]

Kilkenny Irish Beer Draught, St Francis Abbey Brewery, Guinness Per pint: £1.61
ⓑ Sweet and creamy. £4.99 per 4x44cl widgetized cans. [*5%, Kilkenny & Dublin, Ireland*]

Murphy's Draught Irish Stout Per pint: £1.69
ⓖ Widgetized Murphy's in a bottle is vastly superior to the canned version because it has an edge and wisp of smoke. There is also no cardboard taint. £1.49 per 50cl widgetized bottle. [*4%, Ireland & UK*]
☞ THE BEST VALUE DARK BEER OF THE YEAR

Marston's Oyster Stout, Bottle Conditioned
Per pint: £1.69
ⓢ Although very smooth and easy drinking, this brew lacks the intensity, bitterness and complexity of a great stout when it hits the shelf, but having kept a few bottles over the last year, I have noticed how the flavour deepens and mellows after 6 months' cellaring. £1.49 per 50cl bottle. [*4.5%, Burton-on-Trent, England*]

Hobgoblin Extra Strong Ale, Wychwood Brewery
Per pint: £1.69
ⓢ Fresh and fragrant with a smoky-pear flavour. £1.49 per 50cl bottle. [*5.5%, Oxfordshire, England*]

Sneck Lifter, Jennings Brothers Per pint: £1.69
ⓑ Less sweet, more smoky-peppery than last year. £1.49 per 50cl bottle. [*5.1%, Cumbria, England*]

Tangle Foot Strong Ale, Badger Brewery
Per pint: £1.69

A perfumed, light, easy-drinking ale with a clean finish. £1.49 per 50cl bottle. [*5%, Dorset, England*]

Pilsner Urquell
Per pint: £1.70

G Smooth, flowery and fragrant, with the classic Urquell taste, crisp-fragrant finish and a nice slightly bitter touch. £0.99 per 33cl bottle. [*4.4%, Pilsen, Czech Republic*]

Pete's Wicked Ale
Per pint: £1.74

B A strong liquorice taste with a citric finish. £1.09 per 35cl bottle. [*5.1%, USA*]

Riggwelter Strong Yorkshire Ale, Black Sheep Brewery
Per pint: £1.76

G A great but most unusual beer; its aromatics are closer to fortified wine than ale, and the intensely flavoured, smooth palate, with distinctive wood-smoke complexity, is more for sipping than supping. £1.55 per 50cl bottle. [*5.7%, Yorkshire, England*]

☞ THE BEST QUALITY BITTER OF THE YEAR

Marston's India Export Pale Ale, Head Brewers Choice
Per pint: £1.76

S Citric notes heighten the palate while spicy-smoky aromas add complexity to the finish. £1.55 per 50cl bottle. [*5.5%, Burton-on-Trent, England*]

Spitfire Bottle Conditioned Bitter, Shepherd Neame
Per pint: £1.76

S Distinctive pear-hoppy aroma and flavour, nicely dry, well-hopped finish. Not quite up to last year's standard, but an excellent beer nevertheless.

£1.55 per 50cl bottle. [*4.7%, Kent, England*]

Marston's Burton S.P.A.   Per pint: £1.81

(G) Totally different from Marston's Export Pale Ales, this brew is creamy-smooth with delicately floral hoppy aromas and a distinctive bitter finish. A lovely head too. £1.59 per 50cl bottle. [*6.2%, Burton-on-Trent, England*]

☞ THE BEST QUALITY LIGHT BEER OF THE YEAR

Grolsch Premium Lager   Per pint: £1.88

(G) Very fruity, crisp and deep flavoured. A classic. £1.49 per 45cl bottle. [*5%, Groenlo, Holland*]

Staropramen, Prague Breweries   Per pint: £1.98

(B) Light, perfumed and elegant. £1.15 per 33cl bottle. [*5%, Prague, Czech Republic*]

Carlsberg Elephant, Strong Imported Beer

                                        Per pint: £2.38

(S) This strong, heady lager with an intense finish is a classic. £1.15 per 27cl bottle. [*7.2%, Copenhagen, Denmark*]

PLYMCO

A group of 40 superstores, supermarkets and late-night shops in the Torbay–Cornwall area that belong to the Plymouth & South Devon Co-operative Society. Plymco stores stock most of the Co-op wines and beers tasted, plus a significant range of independently purchased products. Please see the main **Co-op** entry for recommendations.

PRESTO

Part of the Argyll group, Presto has 170 stores, all of which sell exactly the same wines as its big sister chain Safeway – although the range of what you can actually buy in each outlet is narrower owing to the smaller size of these typically local, supermarket-type stores. Please see the **Safeway** entry for recommendations.

QUINSWORTH

This supermarket group in Northern Ireland was purchased by Tesco in early 1997.

SAFEWAY

Number of stores *410*
Opening hours *Monday–Saturday 8.30a.m.–8p.m. (some stores open until 10p.m.), Sunday 10a.m.–4p.m.*
Maximum range *400 wines, 149 beers, 150 spirits*
Alternative methods of payment *Cheque with card, Switch and Delta debit cards, Access, Visa*
Local delivery *Not provided, but will help carry goods to car if requested*
Discounts *5 per cent discount on six bottles or more of wine over £2.99*
Refund policy? *No comment*
Other services *A free glass service in most stores, with four sizes to choose from*

Comment After the blind tasting results have been manipulated by the database and transmitted to my word-processing software, it is always fascinating to see how well each supermarket has done – but I had to do a double-take on this one because Safeway notched up two more golds than last year and an extra silver, yet its performance relative to other supermarkets dropped significantly. How come? The overall number of recommended wines and beers dipped from an incredible 93 (a feat that will probably never be equalled by any retailer in the future) to 'just' 70, yet this was still an excellent result – this year's top-performing supermarket had just 66 products recommended but the reduction had a dramatic effect on Safeway's performance this year, when the top three supermarkets alone shared no fewer than 42 gold medal winners, compared with 27 last year. If anything it demonstrates how close the best supermarkets are in this country, and I'm sure it will encourage Liz Robertson MW and her team to bounce back next year – which, from an analysis of Safeway's performance, they could easily do just by submitting more fortified wines. In the meantime, there is a wealth of wine and beer goodies to choose from.

Red Wines

Vin de Pays de Vaucluse 1996 Du Peloux, Safeway
£2.99
This fresh, light and peppery red has the refreshing acidity of a white wine with just a touch of tannin. [*Rhône, France*]

Bulgarian Cabernet Sauvignon 1992 Barrel Matured, Vinprom, Safeway £3.29
Light but not lacking, this wine has easy-drinking, blackcurrant fruit. [*Svischtov, Bulgaria*]

Romanian Pinot Noir 1993 Special Reserve, Rovit SA, Safeway £3.69
Tastes freshened-up for a 1993 Romanian Pinot Noir, and with a distinctly blackcurrant fruit flavour, it could be pepped-up as well. [*Podgoria Dealul Mare, Romania*]

Rosenview 1996 Cinsaut £3.79
Fresh, easy-drinking, fruity red. Better on its own than with food. [*Coastal Region, South Africa*]

Balbi Vineyard 1996 Malbec £3.99
Dark and deep coloured, but lighter-bodied and more fruit-driven than Balbi Vineyard's cheaper Malbec-Syrah blend. Peppery fruit. [*Mendoza, Argentina*]

134 SAFEWAY

Bulgarian Cabernet Sauvignon 1991 Reserve, Vini, Safeway £3.99
B Most unusually for a red wine, the fruit is definitely peachy. Firm oak. [*Sliven, Bulgaria*]

Casa di Giovanni 1994 Oak Aged, Safeway £3.99
S The grapes in this wine have retained some typicity of their Sicilian origins, even though they are dominated by oak. The fruit element of the flavour builds up very substantially in the mouth. [*Sicily, Italy*]

Landskroon 1996 Cinsaut Shiraz £3.99
B Rich and tangy. [*Paarl, South Africa*]

Minervois 1995 Domaine Roche Vue £3.99
B A firm, tannic, yet tasty red that makes an ideal accompaniment to warming winter stews, casseroles and *cassoulets*. [*Minervois, Southern France, France*]

Tocornal NV Cabernet-Malbec £3.99
Soft, easy blackcurrant fruit. [*Central Valley, Chile*]

Zagara 1995 Nero d'Avola £3.99
S Vibrantly fresh fruit with refreshing acidity, ideal with tomato-based pasta dishes. [*Sicily, Italy*]

Chilean Cabernet Sauvignon 1996 Viña San Pedro, Safeway £4.39
Beaujolais-style red made from Cabernet Sauvignon. [*Lontue, Chile*]

Breakaway 1995 Grenache Shiraz £4.49
S Loads of gluggy fruit. [*South Australia, Australia*]

Shiraz 1996 McWilliam's, Safeway £4.69
B Minty-cedary oak dominates, but the fruit is

fresh and sappy, suggesting it will come through given a few months. [*South Eastern Australia, Australia*]

La Chasse du Pape Réserve 1995 Côtes-du-Rhône £4.99

Soft and fruity with a nice mix of Rhône spice on the finish. [*Côtes-du-Rhône, France*]

Rosenview 1996 Cabernet Sauvignon £4.99

Ⓑ Soft, plummy fruit. [*Stellenbosch, South Africa*]

Villa Montes 1994 Merlot Oak Aged Reserve £4.99

Ⓢ The perfumed blackcurranty aromas are still knitting together, but the creamy-coffee oak builds on the finish. A ten-minute aeration does wonders now, but this really needs another year in bottle. [*Curico, Chile*]

Oaked Cabernet Sauvignon 1996 Thomas Hardy, Safeway £5.29

Ⓢ A nicely structured wine with oodles of fruit and grippy tannins to follow. [*South Eastern Australia, Australia*]

Oaked Shiraz NV Thomas Hardy, Safeway £5.29

Ⓑ Quite jammy, more Grenache in style than Syrah, but very easy and enjoyable to drink. [*South Eastern Australia, Australia*]

La Cuvée Mythique 1994 Vin de Pays d'Oc £5.99

Ⓑ Still quite tight, this wine needs another 12 months to open up and mellow out. [*Southern France, France*]

Peter Lehmann 1995 Cabernet Sauvignon £7.49

Ⓑ Sweet, creamy-cedary fruit. [*Barossa, South Australia, Australia*]

Jacana 1995 Pinotage Reserve £8.99
G Top-quality Pinotage made in the style of top-
quality Zinfandel, with opaque purple-black colour,
huge, thick, intense berry flavours, and an
unashamedly massive splattering of American oak.
Made by Australian-trained British winemaker Hugh
Ryman, this could not be a greater contrast to his other
Pinotage under the Impala label (*see* Kwik Save).
[*Stellenbosch, South Africa*]

Hardys 1994 Cabernet Sauvignon £9.99
S Very tasty, rich, sappy fruit. Lovely now, but will
improve after another year or two in bottle.
[*Coonawarra, South Australia, Australia*]

White Wines

Pinot Blanc 1996 Nagyréde Estate £3.29
Invitingly fresh aroma with crisp, lemony fruit on the
palate. [*Nagyréde, Hungary*]

Chardonnay Oaked 1996 Mátra Mountain £3.49
B Better-focused fruit makes this superior to
Waitrose's oaked Hungarian Chardonnay, also from
Kym Milne. [*Nagyréde, Hungary*]

**La Coume de Peyre 1996 Vin de Pays des Côtes-de-
Gascogne** £3.49
B A fresh, crisp, yet gluggy off-dry white with
plenty of fruit. [*South Western France, France*]

Bordeaux Blanc Sec 1995 Aged in Oak, Safeway £3.99
B Light, dry and delicately fruity with a perfumed

aroma and, despite the label, very little indication of oak. [*Bordeaux, France*]

Chilean Sauvignon Blanc 1996 Viña San Pedro, Safeway £3.99

ⓑ Very fresh, clean and dry with a delicately fruity finish. [*Lontue, Chile*]

Château du Plantier 1995 Entre-Deux-Mers £3.99
Fresh, dry and lightly fruity. [*Entre-Deux-Mers, Bordeaux, France*]

Riverview 1995 Chardonnay-Pinot Gris £3.99

ⓑ Intensely flavoured dry white dominated by Pinot Gris (despite its minority shareholding) and with a touch of liquorice-spice on the finish. [*Csopak, Hungary*]

Touraine 1995 Sauvignon Blanc, BRL Hardy £3.99

ⓑ The apricot fruit in this wine made it one of the best Touraine Sauvignon I have tasted, narrowly missing silver medal status. [*Touraine, Loire, France*]

Chardonnay Colombard 1996 Wingara, Safeway £4.29

ⓑ Very succulent, fruity white for summertime drinking. [*Victoria, Australia*]

La Baume Sauvignon Blanc 1996 Vin de Pays d'Oc, Philippe de Baudin £4.99

ⓢ The Aussies do it again: this solid silver winner from the sunny south of France was immeasurably better than Loire Sauvignon costing half as much again. Hey guys, ever thought of trying your hand at Sancerre or Pouilly-Fumé? [*Southern France, France*]

Oaked Chardonnay 1996 Thomas Hardy, Safeway
£4.99

Ⓢ A beautifully rich and fresh dry white wine with nicely understated oak. [*South Eastern Australia, Australia*]

Peter Lehmann 1996 Semillon £4.99

Ⓑ Knocked the spots off the normally excellent Lindemans Hunters Valley Semillon; this has a real limey richness. [*Barossa, South Australia, Australia*]

Australian Marsanne 1996 Murchison Vineyard, Safeway £6.49

Ⓑ Very fresh, floral, lavender-scented fruit dipped in refreshing, crisp acidity with a touch of spritz. [*Goulburn Valley, Australia*]

Vergelegen 1995 Chardonnay £6.49

Ⓢ Fresh, lemony intensity. [*Stellenbosch, South Africa*]

The Million Vineyard 1995 Chardonnay, Barrel Fermented £7.99

Ⓢ Tasty, rich and so ripe it's almost sweet. No kiwi herbaceousness whatsoever. [*Gisborne, New Zealand*]

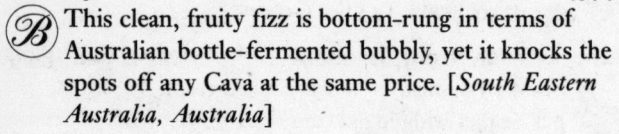

Sparkling Wines

Australian Sparkling Wine NV Brut Reserve, Seppelt, Safeway £4.99

Ⓑ This clean, fruity fizz is bottom-rung in terms of Australian bottle-fermented bubbly, yet it knocks the spots off any Cava at the same price. [*South Eastern Australia, Australia*]

Asti Dolce NV Perlino, Safeway £5.49
Soft and very easy to drink, this was significantly better than Tesco's Asti, which did not survive the tasting, even though it was from the same supplier. This also had the edge over the recommended Asti from Sainsbury's and Marks & Spencer, but was not quite worthy of a bronze. [*Asti, Piedmont, Italy*]

Champagne Chartogne-Taillet NV Brut, Cuvée Sainte-Anne £15.99
(G) Pure gold for lovers of toasty-rich, creamy Champagne. [*Champagne, France*]

Fortified Wines

Moscatel de Valencia 1995 Vicente Gandia, Safeway £3.59
(G) Softer than either the Castillo de Liria (*see* Kwik Save *and* Co-operative) or Gandia's non-vintage Moscatel de Valencia (*see* Somerfield), yet even more concentrated in flavour, just as zesty and equally intense in sweetness. Very fresh. [*Valencia, Spain*]

Beers

Safeway Strong Bitter Per pint: £0.93
(B) Good full-flavoured bitterness at this price. £3.29 per 4x50cl cans. [*4.5%, England*]

Safeway Irish Stout, Draught Per pint: £0.96
(B) Smoky Beamish-style widgetized stout. £2.99 per 4x44cl widgetized cans. [*4.1%, Ireland*]

Safeway Bière d'Alsace, French Lager Per pint: £1.13

Ⓑ Although the brewer of this is probably the same firm that brewed various beers that did not survive the tasting process, this particular bottling is one of the best 25cl beers on the market today. £4.99 per 10x25cl bottles. [*5%, Alsace, France*]

Guinness Original Stout Per pint: £1.42

Ⓑ Dense, dark, bitter chocolate, coffee and liquorice. Quite stern, but great with a Stilton ploughmans. £1.25 per 50cl bottle. [*4.3%, London, England*]

Coopers Sparkling Ale Per pint: £1.50

Ⓢ Almost a hop-pillow aroma (not so common this year), with a rich, mellow-tangy, sweet-and-sour flavour. £0.99 per 37cl bottle. [*5.8%, South Australia, Australia*]

Gillespie's Draught Malt Stout, Scottish & Newcastle Breweries Per pint: £1.51

Ⓢ One of the most distinctive widgetized stouts on the market, Gillespie's is more malty-mellow than its Irish counterparts. £4.69 per 4x44cl widgetized cans, available in Scotland only. [*4%, Edinburgh, Scotland*]

Budweiser Budvar Per pint: £1.53

Ⓖ Elegant, refreshing and perfectly hopped, this classic really is the business. £1.35 per 50cl bottle. [*5%, Czech Republic*]

Waggle Dance Traditional Honey Beer, Vaux
Per pint: £1.54

Ⓢ This soft, full, luscious ale with perfumed-hop aromas, clean, off-dry malty taste and a crisp finish is

apparently named after the dance honey bees execute
when they have located nectar. £1.49 per 55cl bottle.
[5%, Sunderland, England]

Boston Beer, Whitbread   Per pint: £1.55
This sweet and creamy 'American' beer is brewed
under licence in the UK. £4.79 per 4x44cl widgetized
cans. [4.6%, England]

**Black Sheep Ale, Paul Theakston's Black Sheep
Brewery**   Per pint: £1.58
(G) Mellow, full and stylish, with a good bitter flavour
and some nutty-smoky complexity on the finish. A
delight to drink. £1.39 per 50cl bottle. [4.4%, North
Yorkshire, England]

Tennent's Robert Burns Scottish Ale   Per pint: £1.60
(B) Panders to those who prefer sweet, malty brews.
£1.55 per 55cl bottle, available in Scotland only.
[4.2%, Glasgow, Scotland]

Caffrey's Draught Irish Ale   Per pint: £1.61
(B) Sweet and creamy. £4.99 per 4x44cl widgetized
cans. [4.8%, Co. Antrim, UK]

**Kilkenny Irish Beer Draught, St Francis Abbey
Brewery, Guinness**   Per pint: £1.61
(B) Sweet and creamy too. £4.99 per 4x44cl
widgetized cans. [5%, Kilkenny & Dublin, Ireland]

Fuller's Refreshing Summer Ale   Per pint: £1.65
Refreshing yes, but also surprisingly full and
mellow, lifted by a zesty finish. £1.45 per 50cl bottle.
[3.9%, London, England]

CH'TI Bière de Garde en Nord, Amber Beer
Per pint: £1.66

(S) This classic *bière de garde* has a lovely golden-hued copper colour, a rich, smooth, sweet malty taste, and peppery hops on the finish. £2.19 per 75cl bottle. [*5.9%, Bénifontaine, France*]

6X Export, Wadworth
Per pint: £1.69

(S) Tasty and smooth with refined, malty bitter notes and none of the sour sultana-malty character that blighted this brew last year. £1.49 per 50cl bottle. [*5%, Devizes, England*]

Pilsner Urquell
Per pint: £1.70

(G) Smooth, flowery and fragrant, with the classic Urquell taste, crisp-fragrant finish and a nice slightly bitter touch. £0.99 per 33cl bottle. [*4.4%, Pilsen, Czech Republic*]

Hoegaarden White Beer, Bottle Conditioned
Per pint: £1.70

(B) This has a classic, soapy-spicy aroma and stewed, spiced-apple flavour. £0.99 per 33cl bottle. [*5%, Brussels, Belgium*]

Carlsberg Ice Beer
Per pint: £1.70

(S) One of the better ice beers. £0.99 per 33cl bottle. [*5.6%, England*]

Stella Artois Dry, Export Strength Premium Beer, Whitbread
Per pint: £1.72

This light, flowery Pilsner-style beer is a decent lunchtime lager – especially considering the brand's naff reputation among serious beer drinkers and the fact that it is brewed in the UK by Whitbread, rather

than in Belgium by Stella Artois itself. £4.99 per
6x27.5cl bottles. [5.5%, England]

Hobgoblin Extra Strong Ale, Wychwood Brewery
Per pint: £1.76
Fresh and fragrant with a smoky-pear flavour.
£1.55 per 50cl bottle. [5.5%, Oxfordshire, England]

Fuller's London Pride, Premium Ale   Per pint: £1.76
This fresh, intense, hoppy-malty brew is
particularly well suited to the bottling process and
always hits home for those who prefer genuinely dry,
authentically bitter beers. £1.55 per 50cl bottle. [4.7%,
London, England]

Tangle Foot Strong Ale, Badger Brewery
Per pint: £1.76
A perfumed, light, easy-drinking ale with a clean
finish. £1.55 per 50cl bottle. [5%, Dorset, England]

Fuggles Imperial Strong Ale, Castle Eden Brewery
Per pint: £1.76
A widgetized bitter for hardened bitter drinkers!
The wonderful aroma of Fuggles hops comes
streaming through the creamy head, with an assertive,
hoppy bitterness dominating the finish. £1.55 per 50cl
widgetized bottle. [5.5%, Co. Durham, England]

☞ SPECIAL BEER AWARD OF THE YEAR

Murphy's Draught Irish Stout   Per pint: £1.76
Widgetized Murphy's in a bottle is vastly
superior to the canned version because it has an edge
and wisp of smoke. There is also no cardboard taint.
£1.55 per 50cl widgetized bottle. [4%, Ireland & UK]

☞ THE BEST VALUE DARK BEER OF THE YEAR

Old Speckled Hen, Strong Fine Ale, Morland

Per pint: £1.81

ⓢ A refreshing and tasty beer with a characterful maltiness in both the aroma and on the palate, and the barest hint of smoke. £1.59 per 50cl bottle. [5.2%, Oxfordshire, England]

Staropramen, Prague Breweries

Per pint: £2.05

ⓑ Light, perfumed and elegant. £1.19 per 33cl bottle. [5%, Prague, Czech Republic]

Grolsch Premium Lager

Per pint: £2.08

ⓖ Very fruity, crisp and deep flavoured. A classic. £1.65 per 45cl bottle. [5%, Groenlo, Holland]

SAINSBURY'S

Number of stores *380*
Opening hours *Varies widely from store to store*
Maximum range *500 wines, 300 beers, 200 spirits*
Alternative methods of payment *Cheque with card, Switch and Delta debit cards, Access, American Express, Visa, Eurocard*
Delivery *Not provided from any of the stores, but will help carry goods to car if requested*
Discounts *Various multi-buy offers*
Refund policy? *Refund or replace on complaint*
Other services *Sale or return, ice*

Comment One analyst was recently quoted as saying that Sainsbury's 'management credibility is at an all-time low', and certainly the return of Allan Cheesman, which I hailed in the first edition, has done nothing to help. Much of the trouble was not originally of his making, as the profits of the entire group, not just the wine department, have dived over the last couple of years. Although Sainsbury's now appears to be clawing back some of its sales from other supermarkets, an independent analysis of store-switching quotes the group as having lost £9 million of business to its arch-rival Tesco, as former Sainsbury's customers expressed their feelings with both their feet and pockets. Tesco cannot seem to do anything wrong, while Sainsbury's cannot do anything right. Where Cheesman has gone wrong is in dragging Sainsbury's wine PR back to the days when there were few wine journalists and the supermarkets took no notice of them anyway.

It's not just *SuperBooze* (and its readers) that Cheesman couldn't care less about. I have it in writing from the man himself that he is 'supporting just one guide' and that turns out to be written by Malcolm Gluck, who just so happens to be the wine editor of Sainsbury's magazine, which does the integrity of both of them no good. And it does nothing for the Sainsbury family name either.

Red Wines

Australian Shiraz Cabernet NV Sainsbury's
£14.49 (3-litre wine box)
Light, cedary fruit with a fresh, creamy finish. [*South Eastern Australia, Australia*]

Sainsbury's El Conde NV Vino de Mesa Tinto £2.99
A light but long-flavoured wine with lots of fruit and creamy-coconutty oak that turns coffeeish in the mouth. Lovely combination of yumminess and elegance for the price. [*Mesa, Spain*]

Sainsbury's Sangiovese NV Bodegas Peñaflor £3.49
Quite fat for Sangiovese, but with good, grippy tannins for food. Made by flying Aussie winemaker Peter Bright. [*Mendoza, Argentina*]

Costières de Nîmes 1995 Les Garrigues, Sainsbury's
£3.75
Rich, rustic and characterful red with chunky fruit and a smooth finish. [*Costières de Nîmes, Southern France, France*]

Sainsbury's Cabernet Sauvignon 1995 Fiuza & Bright
£3.79
Flying Aussie winemaker Peter Bright made this amazingly soft and fruity wine. [*Ribatejo, Portugal*]

Red Wines

Banrock Station 1996 Mataro Grenache Shiraz, Hardys
£3.99

Ⓑ Smoky-creamy aromas, jammy fruit. [*South Eastern Australia, Australia*]

Bush Vine Grenache 1995 Limited Edition £3.99

Ⓑ This is one that can all too easily be ignored when in tasting mode, but try it with food and the flavours come tumbling out. I also suspect it could repay ageing for 12–18 months. [*Coteaux du Languedoc, Southern France, France*]

Sainsbury's Tempranillo NV Bodegas Peñaflor £3.99

Ⓑ Although there are some excellent Spanish Tempranillo in the under-£4 bracket, the wines from that country at around £4 are very disappointing this year, despite some promising names among the submissions, and this Argentinian effort makes far more interesting drinking. The wine has an attractive, tangy-raspberry fruit with a good dash of oak on the finish. [*Mendoza, Argentina*]

Sainsbury's Australian Shiraz 1995 Austral Wines
£4.85

Richest–cheapest Shiraz, but not the most elegant. Creamy. [*Barossa, South Australia, Australia*]

Claret NV Cuvee Prestige, Sainsbury's £4.99

Ⓑ Soft and easy, with nice, grippy grape tannins, this wine has been made with respect for local style and tradition by Australian winemaker Mandy Jones. [*Bordeaux, France*]

South Bay Vineyards NV American Pinot Noir, Sainsbury's £4.99

B Not the succulently fruity style that first made me sit up and take notice of South Bay Vineyards Pinot Noir. This wine is rather more obvious and down-to-earth, with upfront coconutty American oak that is too dominant for the likes of Pinot Noir enthusiasts; but for those who like coconutty wines, this certainly merits a bronze. [*USA*]

Sainsbury's Burgundy NV Guichard Potheret £5.45

Dark for Pinot Noir, particularly a relatively inexpensive one, but there is firm fruit that will accompany lasagne or moussaka well, and promises to develop favourably over the next 12 months. [*Burgundy, France*]

Orobio Rioja Reserva 1990 Artadi, Sainsbury's Selected Vintage £6.95

B Rich, mellow and mature fruit with spicy-complexity and soft, drying tannins on the finish. [*Rioja, Spain*]

Lindemans Padthaway 1995 Pinot Noir £8.45

B Thick, tasty Pinot Noir fruit with enough succulence on the finish to warrant a bronze. [*Padthaway, South Australia, Australia*]

Château La Vieille Cure 1990 Sainsbury's Selected Vintage £10.95

G Gold at £11 just has to be good, and this very rich wine with its long, cedary-chocolaty fruit is just that. [*Fronsac, Bordeaux, France*]

White Wines

Muscadet 1996 Les Celliers de la Sanguèze £2.95
Fresh, clean, light-bodied fruit with a correctly lean structure. [*Muscadet, Loire, France*]

Sainsbury's Mosel NV Ehemalig Kurfürstliche Weinkellerei £2.99
⑬ Sweet-tangy fruit with a spritzy finish. [*MSR, Germany*]

Hungarian Pinot Gris NV Szölöskert Cooperative, Sainsbury's £3.19
⑤ Not exactly Pinot Gris, but stands out in the medium-dry category for its gushy fruit and real depth of flavour. If you want grapy-German gulpability, buy the Muscat Ottonel from Co-operative, but if you want a more vinous wine that is better with food, this is the best-cheapest choice. [*Nagyréde, Hungary*]

Sainsbury's Bordeaux Sauvignon NV Jean-Paul Jauffret £3.49
⑬ Very fresh, gentle fruit, nicely dry with a crisp finish. [*Bordeaux, France*]

Gentil 'Hugel' 1995 Alsace £4.65
Although an interesting mélange of Alsace varieties, this does not compare with Hugel's famous 'Gentil' of the past. This wine is produced by blending together made wines of no particular origin, whereas Hugel's historic Sporen Gentil was made exclusively from grapes grown on the great Sporen slope (now a *Grand Cru*), where the varieties were already mixed and thus pressed and fermented together. Such wine aged

gracefully for thirty years or more, whereas this Gentil will be at its best between three and four years of age. [*Alsace, France*]

Galet Vineyards 1996 Roussanne Barrel Reserve, Sainsbury's £4.99
Quite fat, but very fresh. Should partner winter salads with hot ingredients like potato, bacon etc very well, but best drunk by Christmas 1997. [*Gard, Southern France, France*]

Sainsbury's White Burgundy NV Guichard Potheret
£4.99
(B) Quite a substantial flavour for such a soft and easy wine. [*Burgundy, France*]

Muscadet de Sèvre-et-Maine Sur Lie 1995 Sainsbury's Classic Selection £5.95
The cool, crisp, gentle fruit in this wine has a nice lean structure, but a rather fatter aftertaste than most Muscadet. [*Muscadet de Sèvre et Maine, Loire, France*]

Chablis, Sainsbury's Classic Selection 1995 Domaine Sainte Celine £7.45
(B) This clean, fruit-dominated Chablis gets marks for freshness. [*Chablis, Burgundy, France*]

Rosé Wines

Chilean Cabernet Sauvignon Rosé NV Sainsbury's
£3.49
(B) Full, rich and tasty, with quite a deep colour. This is like a red wine without any tannin. [*Curico, Chile*]

Domaine de Sours 1996 Bordeaux Rosé £4.99

Ⓢ This delicious, stylish wine is absolutely clean, very fresh, with plenty of delicate fruit and a nice spritz on the finish. [*Bordeaux, France*]

Sparkling Wines

Sainsbury's Asti NV Casa Vinicola IVASS £5.49

Very soft in texture, with a gentle sweetness. [*Asti, Piedmont, Italy*]

Seaview Pinot Noir Chardonnay 1993 Brut £8.49

Ⓖ The big, rich, toasty fruit in this wine is indicative of how the 1994 will go (*see* Somerfield). [*South Australia, Australia*]

Yalumba Cuvée One Prestige NV Pinot Noir/ Chardonnay £8.49

A very fruity fizz. Not in the same class as Seaview's Pinot Noir Chardonnay (*see* Sainsbury's *and* Somerfield). [*South Australia, Australia*]

Sainsbury's Champagne NV Blanc de Noirs Brut
£11.99

The sort of soft and easy style that offends no one at a reception or party, but is good enough for regular Champagne imbibers. [*Champagne, France*]

Sainsbury's Champagne NV Extra Dry, Duval-Leroy
£12.95

Ⓑ Fresh, elegant, aperitif-style. [*Champagne, France*]

Sainsbury's Champagne NV Brut Rosé, Beaumet
£13.95
B A soft, fruity, summer-drinking Champagne.
[*Champagne, France*]

Sainsbury's Vintage Champagne 1991 Blanc de Blancs Brut, UVCB
£14.95
S This smooth concoction of perfumed fruit is a blatant flatterer. [*Champagne, France*]

Fortified Wines

Sainsbury's Oloroso NV Old Dry Sherry, Morgan Bros
£3.29 (half-bottle)
S Very oaky, with a crisp, distinctly dry finish.
[*Jerez, Spain*]

Sainsbury's Vintage Character Port NV Taylor Fladgate & Yeatman
£6.99
B The sweet, chocolaty fruit is very appealing, but the separation of alcohol on the finish must demote this from a silver to bronze. [*Douro, Portugal*]

Pedro Ximénez Cream of Cream NV Alvear, Sainsbury's
£3.95 (half-bottle)
B Very thick, oil-like viscosity; very very sweet indeed, but lacks the acidity or intensity required for balance. [*Montilla, Spain*]

Sainsbury's LBV Port 1990 Temilobos
£7.99
S Spicy-tangy-cedary aromas, with rich and sweet fruit on the palate. Lovely now, but will still develop, so don't worry about leaving this unopened for a few years. [*Douro, Portugal*]

Sainsbury's Madeira NV Cossart Gordon

£4.49 (half-bottle)

Tangy-sweet, Bual-like baked fruit. [*Madeira, Portugal*]

Sainsbury's Madeira NV Dry Sercial 5 Year Old £8.99

(G) Fine, crisp and deeply flavoured with a long, intense, off-sweet, slightly spicy finish. You might not like Madeira, but it is hard to imagine a better quality Madeira at this price, so it's a good choice to cut your teeth on. [*Madeira, Portugal*]

Mick Morris Liqueur Muscat NV Rutherglen

£4.99 (half-bottle)

(G) Huge, thick, rich, oil-like and incredibly, tooth-tinglingly, sweet, with toffee-toasty-coffee complexity. Serious stuff from chuckling Mick Morris. [*Rutherglen, Victoria, Australia*]

Sainsbury's Vintage Port 1985 Quinta Dona Matilde

£14.95

(G) Although delicious in a grippy, fiery, youthful way now, this really deserves another 10 years' ageing. [*Douro, Portugal*]

Beers

Sainsbury's Bière des Flandres, French Lager

Per pint: £0.68

Recommended because, with the exception of Blonderaü Pils (*see* Budgens), there's nothing else worth recommending at this price point! Inoffensive telly beer. £2.99 per 10x25cl bottles. [*3%, Flandres, France*]

Parkin's Special Bitter, Sainsbury's   Per pint: £0.79
Clean and smooth with a touch of bitter hops. £2.79
per 4x50cl cans. [4%, *England*]

Sainsbury's Bière d'Alsace, French Lager
Per pint: £0.91
(B) The cheapest lager or lager-style to get a medal!
£3.99 per 10x25cl bottles. [4.9%, *Alsace, France*]

Sainsbury's Stolz Pilsner, Authentic German Beer
Per pint: £1.02
(S) Delicate hoppy aromas belie the deep, mellow
flavour of this own-label brew, which is fresh and crisp
on the finish. £4.49 per 10x25cl bottles. [5%,
Dortmund, Germany]

Sainsbury's Cerveza de España, Premium Spanish Lager   Per pint: £1.13
(B) Easy-drinking, sweet and mellow lager-style beer.
£4.99 per 10x25cl bottles. [5%, *Zaragoza, Spain*]

Sainsbury's German Pilsener, Premium Lager
Per pint: £1.16
(S) Deep flavoured, yet very crisp and correct, with
nice hoppy aromas. £2.69 per 4x33cl bottles. [4.9%,
Brunswick, Germany]

Adnams Suffolk Strong Ale   Per pint: £1.44
(B) A good, tasty brew with a nicely hopped bitter
finish. £4.45 per 4x44cl cans. [4.5%, *Suffolk, England*]

Sainsbury's Blackfriars Porter   Per pint: £1.76
(B) More sherry notes than last year, less coffee.
£1.55 per 50cl bottle. [5.5%, *England*]

Riggwelter Strong Yorkshire Ale, Black Sheep Brewery
Per pint: £1.81

(G) A great but most unusual beer; its aromatics are closer to fortified wine than ale, and the intensely flavoured, smooth palate with distinctive wood-smoke complexity is more for sipping than supping. £1.59 per 50cl bottle. [*5.7%, Yorkshire, England*]

☞ THE BEST QUALITY BITTER OF THE YEAR

Staropramen Dark Lager, Prague Breweries
Per pint: £2.05

Disappointing after last year's brew; where's the creamy-coffee and chicory? £1.19 per 33cl bottle. [*4.6%, Prague, Czech Republic*]

SAVACENTRE

A group of 12 hypermarkets, Savacentre was originally a collaboration between Sainsbury's and British Home Stores, but has been totally owned by Sainsbury's for several years now. Each Savacentre hypermarket is supposed to carry the complete range of Sainsbury's wines, beers and spirits, but a test conducted by *SuperBooze* on the Reading store in May 1997 found that the range on display fell far short of this claim. Please see the **Sainsbury's** entry.

SOLO

Having shrunk to just 17 stores from 26 last year, the SoLo trading name is gradually being phased out, as some outlets are converted to Somerfield or Food Giant and others sold off. For the range of wines and beers recommended, see the **Somerfield** entry.

SOMERFIELD

STOCK ME AND BUY ONE

Number of stores *440*
Opening hours *Vary widely, but can be summarized as Monday–Saturday 8.30a.m.–6.30p.m., Sunday 10a.m.–4p.m.*
Maximum range *410 wines, 163 beers, 122 spirits*
Alternative methods of payment *Cheque with card, Switch and Delta debit cards, Access, American Express, Visa*
Local delivery *Not provided, but will help carry goods to car if requested*
Discounts *None*
Refund policy? *With Tesco and Waitrose, Somerfield offers the most comprehensive guarantee in the entire off-licence sector, refunding your money even if the wine is perfectly OK and you just happen not to like it!*
Other services *In-store tastings*
Parent company *Somerfield is the parent and owns Food Giant, Gateway and SoLo*

Comment Somerfield truly excelled when judged on its wine only, but was let down by a very poor beer showing – which must be particularly galling to Angela Mount, whom I described last year as Britain's most underrated wine buyer. I look forward to next year, when one hopes the wine and beer departments can work in unison.

Red Wines

Cabernet Sauvignon Vin de Pays d'Oc NV Les Vignerons du Val d'Orbieu, Somerfield £3.35
Another easy-drinking, blackcurranty Cabernet, but this has a food wine structure and is more vinous in character than most others in its price category.
[*Southern France, France*]

For details of 'Stock Me and Buy One' see pages xi–xii.

Santara Tempranillo 1996 Conca de Barberà £3.35

This deep purple coloured wine from Englishman Hugh Ryman is far better than the Merlot, the 1993 of which was the first Santara wine I tasted. This Tempranillo is far more expressive of its Spanish origins, not just because it is of course made from an indigenous variety, but also because of the vinification style, which reminds me of a traditional Rioja *vino nuevo*. Very much fruit-driven and macerated, but not at all Beaujolais-like, this has deep, fat fruit and a hint of tobacco plant blossom on the finish. Drink on its own or with simple food. Should be fine up to spring 1998, but do not keep too long. [*Conca de Barberà, Spain*]

Rawson's NV Ruby Cabernet Merlot £3.49

Soft and easy, with a hint of blackcurrant jam in the fruit. [*Breede River Valley, South Africa*]

Chilean Cabernet Sauvignon 1995 Viña Cornellana, Somerfield £3.99

Toasty bottle-aromas on nose and finish, but the fruit on the palate is pure blackcurrants. [*Rapel, Chile*]

Montepulciano d'Abruzzo 1995 Bianchi £3.99

Fresh and elegant, with richer, riper, better-focused fruit than most Italian reds at this price. [*Abruzzi, Italy*]

Rioja NV Almaraz, Somerfield £3.99

Wonderfully succulent and fruity, mellowed by background oak. [*Rioja, Spain*]

Vignetti Casterna 1994 Valpolicella, Pasqua £4.45

A real full-bodied Valpolicella with a deep colour

and excellent brooding, black-fruit flavour is rare
enough, but at less than £4.50 it's a miracle. [*Italy*]

**Château Valoussière 1995 Coteaux-du-Languedoc,
Brut de Cuve** £4.49

⓷ A deep, dark wine, thick with nicely tannic fruit.
Good with stews and casseroles. [*Coteaux-du-Languedoc, Southern France, France*]

Soltero 1994 Rosso di Sicilia, Settesoli £4.49

⓷ Rich and oaky, with vibrantly fresh fruit and
grippy tannins. [*Sicily, Italy*]

Domaine La Tuque Bel-Air 1994 Côtes-de-Castillon
£4.95

Ⓢ This firm, fruity and characterful claret would be
ideal with pink lamb. [*Côtes-de-Castillon, Bordeaux, France*]

James Herrick 1995 Cuvée Simone, Vin de Pays d'Oc
£4.99

⓷ This has thickened up since last year, dropping
from silver to bronze for current drinking, but there
is some violet finesse, suggesting that it is only going
through a phase in development and will improve
over the next year or two to reach even greater
heights than promised last year. [*Southern France, France*]

Crozes-Hermitage 1995 Groupe Jean-Paul Selles £5.49

⓷ The sort of smoky-raspberry Syrah that develops
a more blackcurrant richness with a little bottle-age.
[*Crozes-Hermitage, Rhône, France*]

Quinta de Pancas 1995 Cabernet Sauvignon £5.49

⓷ Firm, tannic fruit and a big depth of flavour.

Excellent with roast lamb, but will be even better in
two or three years. [*Estremadura, Portugal*]

Chianti Classico 1995 Montecchio £5.99
S Lovely balance of ripe fruit and fine tannins.
Brilliant drinking now, but will be even better in 2–3
years. [*Tuscany, Italy*]

**Chianti Classico, Villa Primavera 1995 Conti
Serristori, Somerfield** £5.99
S This is not your average supermarket wine. In
fact, I think Somerfield's buyer Angela Mount must
have been off her supermarket trolley when she bought
this big, thick, dense, dark, tannic, backward wine, but
you should buy this and lay it down for five years
because it is going to be sensational. [*Tuscany, Italy*]

Viña Caña Reserva 1987 Rioja, Somerfield £5.99
G Very fresh, zesty oak for a 10-year-old red; this
wine has been kept vital by its relatively high acidity,
which is very attractive and useful with food. [*Rioja, Spain*]

Château Saint Robert 1993 Graves £6.45
B Does this coconutty claret herald an onslaught of
Bordeaux wines dominated by American oak? [*Graves, Bordeaux, France*]

Wolf Blass Cabernet Sauvignon 1995 Yellow Label
£6.99
B Closed on the nose, but nicely fresh, with elegant,
creamy-coconutty fruit on the palate. [*South Australia, Australia*]

Penfolds Bin 128 1994 Shiraz £7.99

B Fresh, easy drinking, oaky-fruit. [*Coonawarra, South Australia, Australia*]

Châteauneuf-du-Pape 1995 Domaine de la Solitude

£9.49

S Rich smoky-creamy fruit. This elegant, sumptuous wine is definitely superior to Morrison's Domaine du Vieux Lazaret, but it's £1 more expensive and thus receives equal silver-medal status. [*Châteauneuf-du-Pape, Rhône, France*]

White Wines

South African Dry White NV W1226, Somerfield £2.99

B Fresh, easy, off-dry and clean: everything that most Loire Chenin is not! [*Cape, South Africa*]

Vin de Pays des Côtes-de-Gascogne 1995 DG 32800, Somerfield £2.99

B Côtes-de-Gascogne is always noticeable in a blind tasting of assorted dry white wines as it invariably has more intensity of clean, crisp, fruity flavour. This one was the cheapest I tasted, and quite delicious too, with a hint of sweetness to balance the spritz on the finish. [*South Western France, France*]

Domaine Bordeneuve 1996 Vin de Pays des Côtes-de-Gascogne £3.65

B An attractively crisp, dry white wine fattened up on the finish with sweetness of ripe fruit. [*South Western France, France*]

Chilean Sauvignon Blanc NV Sagrada Familia, Somerfield £3.99

ⓑ Grassy-lemony aroma, with fresh lively fruit on the palate. There was a considerable spritz to this wine, which might have been due to the fact that it was a tank sample of the then forthcoming 1997-based blend – but it was not at all unpleasant for all that. [*Chile*]

Rioja Barrel Fermented 1995 Almenar, Somerfield
£3.99

ⓑ Lightly oaked, dry white of some elegance, with creamy-apricot fruit and a touch of coconut. Excellent with a starter of smoked haddock in a light cheese sauce served on a bed of fresh tagliatelle. [*Rioja, Spain*]

Le Trulle 1996 Chardonnay £4.39

ⓑ Extraordinarily fresh for such a southerly Italian white, this wine has real Chardonnay flavour and plenty of fruit, illustrating just how much flying winemakers (Kym Milne in this instance) and modern technology have raised standards in that part of the world. [*Apulia, Italy*]

Australian Chardonnay NV Somerfield £4.65

ⓑ Elegantly oaky Chardonnay with a bright, ripe, fruity finish. [*South Eastern Australia, Australia*]

Scharzhofberger Riesling Kabinett 1995 Müller-Burggraef £4.85

ⓑ Crisp, spritzy Riesling fruit with a fine, tangy, medium-sweet balance. [*MSR, Germany*]

James Herrick 1996 Chardonnay, Vin de Pays d'Oc
£4.99

ⓢ A perfect demonstration of the supermarket

wine-buyer's art, this wine developed from nothing
special in April of this year to silver medal quality by
June, and promises to be at its peak between autumn
and Christmas, but will remain enjoyable for another
year. A fresh and lively wine in a Mâcon-like style with
lovely ripe acidity. [*Southern France, France*]

Gewurztraminer Vin d'Alsace 1996 Cave des Vignerons Turckheim, Somerfield £5.95

S This wine has a certain finesse, as if it contained
some classy components in addition to the bulk of
basic, village-quality Gewurztraminer. It has very rich
fruit, and will get progressively more spicy over the
next 2–3 years. Very well selected this end. [*Alsace, France*]

Penfolds The Valleys 1995 Chardonnay £6.95

S A lovely lemony richness charged with acidity for
a fresh, zippy finish. [*Clare and Eden Valleys, South Australia, Australia*]

Jacana 1996 Chardonnay £6.99

Very skilfully produced by Australian-trained British
flying winemaker Hugh Ryman, this wine has an
attractive succulence of fruit that is lifted by an
invigorating spritz on the finish. [*Stellenbosch, South Africa*]

Coopers Creek 1996 Sauvignon Blanc £7.49

G Deliciously ripe gooseberry fruit with a long,
intense, zippy finish. [*Marlborough, New Zealand*]

Jamiesons Run 1996 Chardonnay £7.99

B A light, gentle wine with tropical fruit flavour.
[*Coonawarra, South Australia, Australia*]

Lindemans 1994 Coonawarra Botrytis Riesling
£5.99 (half-bottle)

ⓖ Sumptuous richness, beautifully focused Riesling fruit and impeccable acidity balance. [*Coonawarra, South Australia, Australia*]

Sparkling Wines

Seaview Pinot Noir Chardonnay 1994 Brut £8.49

ⓖ Smooth and creamy, the richness of fruit builds gently in the mouth to a wonderfully satisfying flavour that is all fruit now, but will become increasingly toasty over the next 12 months. [*South Australia, Australia*]

Champagne Prince William NV Brut Reserve £11.99
Fresh and young, but will develop, so if you like biscuity or toasty mellowness in your Champagne, save this for Christmas. [*Champagne, France*]

Champagne Prince William NV Blanc de Blancs Brut
£15.29

ⓑ Attractively creamy fruit to drink now or keep for 12 months. [*Champagne, France*]

Champagne Prince William NV Rosé Brut £15.29

ⓖ Very soft, succulent fruit, made by Henri Mandois in such an easy-drinking style that I cannot imagine anyone not enjoying this Champagne. [*Champagne, France*]

Fortified Wines

Moscatel de Valencia NV Vicente Gandia, Somerfield
£3.39

(G) Very fresh and zesty, with intensely sweet, gorgeously zesty Muscat fruit. Difficult to tell the difference between this and Castillo de Liria (*see* Kwik Save *and* Co-operative) under blind conditions, although the different shape of the bottle is a dead give-away. My notes, however, indicate this is more lemon-zesty, while the Castillo is orange-zesty. [*Valencia, Spain*]

Frontignan NV Vin de Liqueur £5.49

(B) Very sweet, peachy-Muscat fruit, very soft, without the acidity or zest of the Spanish or South African Moscatels, but charming none the less. [*Frontignan, Southern France, France*]

The Navigators 1989 LBV Port, Somerfield £7.15

(B) Concentrated, powerful flavour. [*Douro, Portugal*]

Beers

None of the Somerfield beers survived the rigorous *SuperBooze* blind-tasting test. The number of submissions was much fewer than in previous years; let's hope that a larger number of better-selected beers will be submitted for future editions.

STEWARTS

This supermarket group in Northern Ireland was purchased by Tesco in early 1997.

TESCO

Number of stores *580*
Opening hours *Most open Monday–Thursday 8.30a.m.–8p.m., Friday 8.30a.m.–9p.m., Saturday 8a.m.–8p.m., Sunday 10a.m.–4p.m.*
Maximum range *800 wines, 100 beers, 300 spirits*
Alternative methods of payment *Cheque with card, Switch, Access, Visa*
Local delivery *Through Tesco Direct (Freephone 0800 403403)*
Discounts *Last year it was an unspecified quantity discount 'in some stores', but this year you are advised to 'contact head office for details'. What have you got to lose?*
Refund policy? *With Somerfield and Waitrose, Tesco offers the most comprehensive guarantee in the entire off-licence sector, refunding your money even if the wine is perfectly OK and you just happen not to like it!*
Other services *Loan of glasses in larger stores; permanent tasting area in larger stores*

Comment The market leader in the UK, with 23.3 per cent of all supermarket sales, Tesco took over three Irish groups in spring 1997 – Quinsworth, Crazy Prices and Stewarts – making it the number one grocery chain in Northern Ireland and the Republic as well. Although the company is publicly committed to sourcing as much produce as possible locally in Northern Ireland, this is obviously not possible with wine, so some Tesco products are bound to creep on to the shelves sooner or later. Tesco is one of the three best-performing supermarket groups in *SuperBooze* this year.

Red Wines

Claret NV Yvon Mau, Tesco £2.98
B The cheapest red Bordeaux I can recommend, this bronze medal winner makes an ideal luncheon claret. [*Bordeaux, France*]

Bonarda NV Picajuan Peak £3.29
B Soft, fat, chocolaty fruit with mellow bottle aromas. [*Mendoza, Argentina*]

Cape Cinsaut NV Tesco £3.49
B Sweet, jammy fruit with sherbetty finish. [*Coastal Region, South Africa*]

Chimango NV Tempranillo Malbec, Tesco £3.49
Soft and fruity, with a smoky-wine gum flavour. [*Mendoza, Argentina*]

Great with Steak 1995 Merlot, Vin de Pays d'Oc, Tesco
£3.49
The least exciting of Tesco's three 'Great With' wines, but easy and enjoyable drinking all the same. The fruit is quite elegant, yet has the structure to take a steak, if that's what you want. Its length and smooth tannins could equally well go with pasta or vegetarian dishes. [*Southern France, France*]

Sangiovese NV Picajuan Peak £3.49
Half-way between Chianti and Beaujolais. [*Mendoza, Argentina*]

Cabernet Sauvignon 1995 Campo dos Frades £3.99
S The quality and concentration of fruit and the smooth oak finish make this a classy wine for the price.

Made by Australian winemaker Peter Bright. [*Ribatejo, Portugal*]

Claret Réserve NV Yvon Mau, Tesco £3.99
ⓑ Soft and tasty in a frank Bordeaux style, with a good, drying finish. [*Bordeaux, France*]

Côtes-du-Rhône 1993 Domaine de Pauline £3.99
Tastier than most sub-£4 Côtes-du-Rhône. [*Côtes-du-Rhône, France*]

Domaine de Jouclary 1993 Cabardès £3.99
ⓑ Packed with chocolaty-toasty fruit. Firm tannic finish. [*Cabardès, Southern France, France*]

Chianti Rufina 1995 Fratelli Grati, Tesco £4.29
ⓑ Real fruit in a cheap Chianti! [*Tuscany, Italy*]

Le Trulle 1994 Primitivo del Salento £4.49
ⓑ Raspberry–liquorice fruit. Much more expressive than the vintage. [*Apulia, Italy*]

Beyers Truter NV Pinotage, Tesco £4.99
ⓑ Upfront, tangy fruit, but with a good dry finish underpinned by accessible tannins. As good with food as without. [*Stellenbosch, South Africa*]

Chianti Classico 1994 Ampelos, Tesco £4.99
ⓑ Plenty of fruit, good typicity, nice tannins; a very well-selected own-label Chianti. [*Tuscany, Italy*]

Château du Bluizard 1995 Beaujolais-Villages £4.99
Not a medal winner, but certainly worthy of recommendation. There were several cheaper Beaujolais, but this was the best-cheapest, and I had to taste up to £5.99 before I found better, or even

comparable, flavour and structure. [*Beaujolais, Burgundy, France*]

Domaine Georges Bertrand 1994 Corbières, Cuvée Spéciale £4.99
⑤ Fresh, thick and tasty blackcurrant fruit mellowed by oak aromas and with enough tannin structure to accompany food. [*Corbières, Southern France, France*]

Fitou Oak Aged 1995 Baron de la Tour £4.99
⑤ Firm-flavoured, chocolate-box fruit with smooth tannins on the finish. [*Fitou, Southern France, France*]

James Herrick 1995 Cuvée Simone, Vin de Pays d'Oc
£4.99
Ⓑ This has thickened up since last year, dropping from silver to bronze for current drinking, but there is some violety finesse, suggesting that it is only going through a phase in development, and will improve over the next year or two to reach even greater heights than promised last year. [*Southern France, France*]

Jennsberg 1995 Cabernet Sauvignon Merlot £4.99
Ⓑ Intense, inky fruit. [*Paarl, South Africa*]

La Vieille Ferme 1994 Côtes-du-Rhône Réserve £4.99
Ⓑ This wine is made from organically cultivated grapes and has a much greater depth of fruit and finesse compared with the basic *cuvée*. [*Côtes-du-Rhône, France*]

Schoone Gevel 1995 Merlot £4.99
Ⓖ If you can keep your hands off this deep, silky-rich wine for 3–4 years, it will gain even more complexity and finesse. [*Franschhoek-Vallei, South Africa*]

Vintage Claret Aged in New Oak 1995 Yvon Mau, Tesco
£4.99

B Fresh and tasty claret, with the oak mentioned on the label manifesting itself more as a smooth texture than imparting any significant aroma or flavour. [*Bordeaux, France*]

Western Cape Shiraz/Cabernet Sauvignon 1995 Tesco
£4.99

S British-based and Australian-trained John Worontschak returns to the southern hemisphere to make this deliciously fresh, creamy-cedary red. [*Western Cape, South Africa*]

Beaumes de Venise 1994 Côtes-du-Rhône-Villages, Carte Noire
£5.49

Sweet punchy fruit, nice tannins. [*Côtes-du-Rhône, France*]

Viña Mara 1990 Rioja Reserva, Tesco £5.49
B Very smooth, with tasty fruit and vanilla oak. [*Rioja, Spain*]

Diemersdal 1996 Syrah £5.99
S This fruit-driven wine is soft, stylish and elegant. [*Coastal Region, South Africa*]

Diemersdal 1996 Merlot £5.99
S Succulent, juicy fruit. [*Coastal Region, South Africa*]

Domaine de Conroy 1994 Brouilly £5.99
B Not typical Beaujolais, but it has plenty of good, tasty, fat and soft fruit. [*Brouilly, Beaujolais, Burgundy, France*]

Châteauneuf-du-Pape 1996 S.A. V.J.Q., Tesco £6.99

Ⓢ Unless I received a wrongly labelled wine, this must be the ultimate demonstration of the supermarket wine-buyer's art of finding wines that are ready to drink, as its orange-hued colour and sweet, mellow-peppery fruit is almost a parody of a fully matured Châteauneuf-du-Pape. God only knows how long it will last, but it should still be drinking well this Christmas, and despite its instant-age, it is a strangely satisfying Châteauneuf-du-Pape. [*Châteauneuf-du-Pape, Rhône, France*]

McLaren Vale Shiraz 1994 Maglieri, Tesco £6.99

Ⓢ A rich and powerful wine with heaps of smoky-creamy fruit. [*McLaren Vale, South Australia, Australia*]

South African Premium Shiraz 1995 Tesco £6.99

Elegant and fruity. [*Western Cape, South Africa*]

Barolo 1992 Giacosa Fratelli £7.99

Ⓢ Hint of classic tar complexity on the nose, with fine, rich, mellow berry-cherry fruits on palate and a long, dry, flavoursome finish. A wine that builds in the glass. [*Barolo, Piedmont, Italy*]

Barolo 1992 Cantine Gemma £7.99

Ⓖ Classic orange-hued Barolo with toasty bottle-aromas mingling with beautifully ripe, rich, mellow fruit. [*Barolo, Piedmont, Italy*]

Clos Malverne 1995 Auret £7.99

Ⓖ An extraordinary aroma of strawberries, translating into gorgeously succulent fruit on the

palate. A seductive wine to drink on its own, but not with food. [*Stellenbosch, South Africa*]

Châteauneuf-du-Pape 1995 Le Chemin des Mulets
£8.99

Ⓑ Quite a powerful Châteauneuf-du-Pape, yet very accessible, making it very flexible with or without food. [*Châteauneuf-du-Pape, Rhône, France*]

St.-Julien 1993 Raoul Johnston, Tesco £8.99

Ⓑ This is a bronze going on silver, and if all generic Bordeaux was as good as this, it would be an amazing world. Certainly I want to see supermarkets raise their generic Bordeaux standards to this sort of quality – but can they sell generic wines for £9? [*St.-Julien, Bordeaux, France*]

White Wines

Hock NV Maas Nathan, Tesco £2.19

Ⓑ Fresh, grapy and medium sweet. [*Rhein, Germany*]

French Dry White Wine NV Bouey, Tesco £2.79

Extremely fresh, early-picked (but not green), dry white style. [*France*]

Chenin Blanc NV Vin de Pays du Jardin de la France, Tesco £2.99

Ⓑ As it says on the back label, appley-lemony fruit. [*Loire, France*]

White Wines

Great with Fish 1996 Vin de Pays de l'Aude, Tesco
£3.49

Ⓑ The 'Great With' concept was generally well received when launched in April 1997, but the actual wines got a bit of a hammering. I was in the minority who thought that the 'Great With Fish' wine was really quite good, with its crispness nicely balanced by a touch of fatness in the fruit – so I am pleased to see it also succeeded under blind tasting conditions. [*Southern France, France*]

Chenin Blanc 1996 Barrel Fermented, Ryland's Grove
£3.99

Ⓢ Soft, creamy, tropical fruits, with some *sur lie* fullness and a touch of creamy-oak. [*Stellenbosch, South Africa*]

Domaine de Saubagnère 1995 Sauvignon Colombard, Vin de Pays des Côtes-de-Gascogne £3.99

Ⓑ Not much Sauvignon contribution to this wine, but it does have lovely perfumed, tangy fruit with a refreshingly crisp finish. [*South Western France, France*]

Domaine Saubagnère 1995 Vin de Pays des Côtes-de-Gascogne, Les Domaines, Tesco £3.99

An elegant dry white with fairly rich fruit. Try it with asparagus. [*South Western France, France*]

Muscadet NV Les Celliers du Prieuré, Tesco £3.99

Fresh, crisp and clean, with gentle fruit, a long, flavoursome finish and a nicely lean style. Although significantly better than the cheaper Muscadets recommended this year, this wine is at least a third more expensive, hence not quite a bronze. [*Muscadet, Loire, France*]

Schoone Gevel 1996 Chardonnay Reserve £5.99
  Very fresh fruit with a nice touch of oak. [*Franschhoek-Vallei, South Africa*]

Réserve Chardonnay 1995 Vin de Pays d'Oc, Vignobles James Herrick £6.99
  Ⓢ Very fresh, succulent and juicy Chardonnay fruit, with an underlying hint of oak for a touch of complexity. [*Southern France, France*]

Jackson Estate 1996 Sauvignon Blanc £7.99
  Ⓖ Classic ripe gooseberry fruit wrapped in fine, crisp acidity. Wonderful stuff! [*Marlborough, New Zealand*]

Niederhäuser Hermannsberg Riesling Spätlese 1992 Staatliche Weinbaudomäne £5.89
  Ⓢ Incredibly rich, with a sweetness that borders on Auslese level. [*Nahe, Germany*]

Rosé Wines

Cabernet de Saumur Rosé NV Cave des Vignerons de Saumur, Tesco £3.29
  Ⓑ Delicate pale peach in colour, with a very fresh aroma, elegantly dry fruit and a nice intensity of flavour. [*Saumur, Loire, France*]

Van Loveren 1996 Blanc de Noir Red Muscadel £3.49
  Ⓑ Fresh, flowery, medium-sweet aromatic Muscat fruit. [*Robertson, South Africa*]

Sparkling Wines

Yalumba Cuvée Two Prestige NV Cabernet Sauvignon
£8.49

B Deep, dark and (according to its back label) 'mischievous', this fizzy red wine has big, oaky notes on nose and palate, with a minty Cabernet flavour. [*South Australia, Australia*]

Seppelt 1992 Sparkling Shiraz Bottle Fermented £8.99

S Big oaky Shiraz aroma, although less oak dominance than Yalumba's sparkling Cabernet Sauvignon (see above). This heady wine has bags of fruit and a rich, raisiny complexity, making it the ideal accompaniment to almost any dish containing blue cheese. [*South Australia, Australia*]

Tesco Champagne Blanc de Blancs NV Brut Cuvée Speciale £13.99

S Luxuriantly rich and creamy, with a fine biscuity complexity. [*Champagne, France*]

Fortified Wines

Finest Special Reserve Port NV Real Companhia, Tesco £5.49

S Very smooth. [*Douro, Portugal*]

Manzanilla Superior Sherry NV Sanchez Romate, Tesco £3.35 (half-bottle)

Intense *flor* nose, crisp, delicate palate. [*Sanlúcar de Barrameda, Jerez, Spain*]

LBV Port 1990 Smith Woodhouse, Tesco £7.29
Ⓖ In the company of other Ports, this smells very much like a creamy–fruity unfortified wine. I would certainly age it another 3–5 years. [*Douro, Portugal*]

Finest Madeira NV Madeira Wine Company, Tesco
£7.99
Ⓑ Tangy-sweet baked prunes give this a Bual-like style. [*Madeira, Portugal*]

10 Year Old Tawny Port NV Smith Woodhouse, Tesco
£9.99
Ⓢ There was a big gap in the price of Tawny Ports from £6.99 to this (and Marks & Spencer's Tawny) at £9.99, and there was an equally big step up in texture, richness and sweetness. [*Douro, Portugal*]

W. & J. Graham's Six Grapes Port NV £11.99
Ⓑ Rich, smooth, sweet, chocolaty fruit, with lots of after-aromas and fiery-tingly spice on the finish. [*Douro, Portugal*]

Beers

Tesco Strong Yorkshire Bitter Per pint: £0.98
Full-flavoured for the price, with a touch of peppery hops and bitterness on the finish. £3.45 per 4x50cl cans. [*5%, Yorkshire, England*]

German Pilsener Bier, Tesco Per pint: £1.14
Ⓢ Refreshing to the bottom of the glass. £3.99 per 6x33cl bottles. [*4.9%, Dortmund, Germany*]

Guinness Original Stout Per pint: £1.18
Dense, dark, bitter chocolate, coffee and liquorice. Quite stern, but great with a Stilton ploughmans. £3.65 per 4x44cl cans. [*4.3%, Dublin & London, Ireland & England*]

Castle Lager, SA Breweries Per pint: £1.31
This fresh, easy-drinking brew will be enjoyed by those who prefer a sweetish lager, but South Africa is not going to set the beer world alight in the same way as it has the wine world. £4.69 per 6x34cl bottles. [*5%, South Africa*]

Vratislav Lager, Tesco Per pint: £1.31
Soft, smooth and flowery, with a lightly toasted malt flavour. £1.15 per 50cl bottle. [*5%, Czech Republic*]

Kronenbourg 1664, Courage Ltd Per pint: £1.38
Its deep gold colour belies the fresh, hoppy aroma and crisp flavour beneath. Considering this is canned, not bottled, and brewed in the UK by Courage rather than in Strasbourg by Kronenbourg, it is surprisingly good, with a very authentic character. £4.29 per 4x44cl cans. [*5%, Middlesex, England*]

Murphy's Draught Irish Stout Per pint: £1.42
Very soft, mild and sweet, but there is a cardboardy aftertaste to Murphy's this year (detected in samples from all outlets) which demotes it from silver to bronze. £4.39 per 4x44cl widgetized can. [*4%, Ireland & UK*]

Festive Ale, Bottle Conditioned, King & Barnes
Per pint: £1.50

🅢 Deep, mellow and satisfying; what more do you want from a festive ale? Would go well with the turkey and chipolatas. In fact, forget the turkey – this would go well with bangers and mash. £1.45 per 55cl bottle. [*5.3%, Horsham, Sussex, England*]

Black Sheep Ale, Paul Theakston's Black Sheep Brewery
Per pint: £1.53

🅖 Mellow, full and stylish, with a good bitter flavour and some nutty-smoky complexity on the finish. A delight to drink. £1.35 per 50cl bottle. [*4.4%, North Yorkshire, England*]

Tesco Porter Select Ales, Marston Thompson & Evershed
Per pint: £1.58

An off-dry Porter with some sherry notes, but a shade too fizzy. £1.39 per 50cl bottle. [*5%, England*]

Budweiser Budvar
Per pint: £1.58

🅖 Elegant, refreshing and perfectly hopped, this classic really is the business. £1.39 per 50cl bottle. [*5%, Czech Republic*]

Tesco Select Ales India Pale Ale, Bottle Conditioned, Marston Thompson & Evershed
Per pint: £1.58

🅢 A deep-flavoured pale ale with a fine, assertive, malty taste. £1.39 per 50cl bottle. [*5%, Burton-on-Trent, England*]

Kilkenny Irish Beer Draught, St Francis Abbey Brewery, Guinness
Per pint: £1.61

🅑 Sweet and creamy. £4.99 per 4x44cl widgetized cans. [*5%, Kilkenny and Dublin, Ireland*]

Caffrey's Draught Irish Ale Per pint: £1.61

B Sweet and creamy. £4.99 per 4x44cl widgetized cans. [*4.8%, Co. Antrim, UK*]

Waggle Dance Traditional Honey Beer, Vaux
Per pint: £1.64

S This soft, full, luscious ale with perfumed-hop aromas, clean, off-dry malty taste and a crisp finish is apparently named after the dance honey bees execute when they have located nectar. £1.59 per 55cl bottle. [*5%, Sunderland, England*]

Exmoor Gold, Gold Hill Brewery Per pint: £1.69

S Light golden colour, perfumed hoppiness, very soft, delicate flavour. A very individual beer. £1.49 per 50cl bottle. [*5%, Somerset, England*]

Moretti, Birra Friulana Per pint: £1.70

B Crisp, apple-sharp, light but not lacking Italian lager-style beer with a clean finish. £0.99 per 33cl bottle. [*4.5%, Italy*]

Fischer Tradition, Bière Blonde Spéciale d'Alsace
Per pint: £1.74

B Lovely, refreshing, peppery-hop aromas. This is completely different from, and vastly superior to, last year's brew, which was recommendable but failed to pick up a medal. £1.99 per 65cl bottle. [*6.5%, Alsace, France*]

The Famous Taddy Porter, Samuel Smith
Per pint: £1.75

G Extremely rich and intense, with coffee notes and a very dry, creamy finish. £1.69 per 55cl bottle. [*5%, Yorkshire, England*]

Young's Ram Rod, Strong Ale   Per pint: £1.76
Tasted against bitters, Ram Rod is like a strong, rich
lager. £1.55 per 50cl bottle. [5%, *London, England*]

Bud Ice, Anheuser-Busch Inc.   Per pint: £1.80
Not recommended as such, just included so that I can
put in print that I honestly wonder if Anheuser-Busch
could be sued for the following claim about this watery
beer: 'Our exclusive ice brewing process produces a
rich, smooth taste that's remarkably easy to drink.'
£4.19 per 4x33cl bottles. [5.2%, *St. Louis, USA*]

Hobgoblin Extra Strong Ale, Wychwood Brewery
       Per pint: £1.81
(S) Fresh and fragrant with a smoky-pear flavour.
£1.59 per 50cl bottle. [5.5%, *Oxfordshire, England*]

Sneck Lifter, Jennings Brothers   Per pint: £1.81
Less sweet, more smoky-peppery than last year. £1.59
per 50cl bottle. [5.1%, *Cumbria, England*]

Batemans XXXB Classic Bitter   Per pint: £1.81
(G) Batemans could not be sued under the Trade
Descriptions Act, for this is indeed classic bitter. A
lovely, well-hopped, Goldings aroma is followed by a
fresh, smooth flavour of pears and malt, underpinned
by fine, hoppy bitterness, with an intense finish. £1.59
per 50cl bottle. [4.8%, *Lincolnshire, England*]

Spitfire Bottle Conditioned Ale, Shepherd Neame
       Per pint: £1.81
(S) Distinctive pear-hoppy aroma and flavour, nicely
dry, well-hopped finish. Not quite up to last year's
standard, but an excellent beer nevertheless. £1.59 per
50cl bottle. [4.7%, *Kent, England*]

Marston's Burton S.P.A.   Per pint: £1.81

(G) Totally different from Marston's Export Pale Ales, this brew is creamy-smooth with delicately floral hoppy aromas and a distinctive bitter finish. A lovely head too. £1.59 per 50cl bottle. [6.2%, *Burton-on-Trent, England*]

☞ THE BEST QUALITY LIGHT BEER OF THE YEAR

Monkey Wrench Strong Ale, Daleside Brewery
                                                                             Per pint: £1.92

(S) Rich and mellow, with a sweet, malty taste. According to the label, the Witty family have been brewing since the thirteenth century! £1.69 per 50cl bottle. [5.3%, *Yorkshire, England*]

Old Growler, Nethergate Brewery   Per pint: £1.92

(B) Nicely bitter and with a good length of flavour, but lacks the complexity required for a medal. £1.69 per 50cl bottle. [5.5%, *Suffolk, England*]

St Peter's Golden Ale, St Peter's Brewery Per pint: £1.92

(S) This delightfully fresh brew is a cross between the lightest pale ale and an elegant Pilsner. The green flask-type bottle might look more like a receptacle for gin than beer, but is apparently a replica of an eighteenth-century beer bottle. The packaging certainly stands out on the shelf. £1.69 per 50cl bottle. [4.7%, *Suffolk, England*]

Fuller's 1845, Bottle Conditioned Celebration Strong Ale   Per pint: £1.99

(S) Deep, full, bitter-toffee, malty flavour, with an intense liquorice finish and smoky-peppery hops on the aftertaste. £1.75 per 50cl bottle. [6.3%, *London, England*]

Staropramen, Prague Breweries Per pint: £2.05

ℬ Light, perfumed and elegant. £1.19 per 33cl bottle. [*5%, Prague, Czech Republic*]

Staropramen Dark Lager, Prague Breweries

Per pint: £2.05

Disappointing after last year's brew: where's the creamy-coffee and chicory? £1.19 per 33cl bottle. [*4.6%, Prague, Czech Republic*]

Carlsberg Elephant, Strong Imported Beer

Per pint: £2.38

𝒮 This strong, heady lager with an intense finish is a classic. £1.15 per 27cl bottle. [*7.2%, Copenhagen, Denmark*]

WAITROSE

Number of stores *117*
Opening hours *Vary from store to store, but majority are open Monday and Tuesday 8.30a.m.–6p.m., Wednesday and Thursday 8.30a.m.–8p.m., Friday 8.30a.m.–9p.m., Saturday 8.30a.m.–6p.m., Sunday 10a.m.–4p.m. or 11a.m.–5p.m. (90 branches)*
Maximum range *550 wines, 280 beers, 150 spirits*
Alternative methods of payment *Cheque with card, Switch and Delta debit cards, Access, Visa*
Local delivery *Not provided except through Waitrose Direct, a mail order service provided under the auspices of sister company Findlater Mackie Todd (phone 0181 543 0966 for details) – you can pay for this service with a Lewis Partnership Account Card, as well as Visa, Mastercard or cheque; Waitrose supermarket staff will help carry goods to car if requested*
Discounts *5 per cent off a whole case of any wine not subject to another offer, and 12 bottles for the price of 11 on any 'Wines of the Month'*
Refund policy? *With Somerfield and Tesco, Waitrose offers the most comprehensive guarantee in the entire off-licence sector, refunding your money even if the wine is perfectly OK and you just happen not to like it!*
Other services *Sale or return on party purchases. Free loan of glasses. Gift vouchers for use in either Waitrose or John Lewis stores.*

Comment If Morrisons can move south, why can't Waitrose move north to redress the balance? I know there are a lot of potential Waitrose shoppers up there. At least with Waitrose Direct, this group's famously eclectic wine range is available to everyone in the country, whether they are north of Watford or not. But now that you can buy Waitrose wine at supermarket prices delivered free to your doorstep, what about beers? Waitrose has a wealth of regional brews, but they are available at local branches only, and it's nothing short of southern prejudice that beer-drinkers are not privy to the same facility as wine-drinkers. I'll offer Waitrose a deal: if they include beers in their Waitrose Direct service, I'll consider regional brews as being available nationally, which will enable me to include them in my tastings, and this should do wonders for the performance of Waitrose beers in *SuperBooze*. At the moment the beers reviewed lag behind the wines, but potentially they should be almost as exciting. It's ironic that Waitrose should be one of the two top-performing supermarkets in *SuperBooze*, even with a lacklustre beer performance. If Waitrose submitted its entire range of regional wines, I think Chris Dee of Booths would have a real fight on his hands. I'm not sure who would win – especially if Booths redoubled its efforts – but it would make for a fun tasting finding out!

Red Wines

Ridgewood 1996 Mataro-Grenache £3.69
Ⓑ A light-bodied, fresh and easy-drinking red that definitely merits a bronze for lovers of coconutty oak. [*South Eastern Australia, Australia*]

Montepulciano d'Abruzzo 1995 Umani Ronchi £3.95
Ⓑ A spicy, high-toned, medium-bodied red of good typicity, and some elegance and style for the price. [*Abruzzi, Italy*]

Cabernet Sauvignon/Shiraz 1996 Du Toitskloof Wine Cellar £3.99
Ⓢ The blackcurranty fruit in this wine is so soft and easy-drinking that it is much better on its own than with food. [*Worcester, South Africa*]

Concha y Toro 1996 Merlot £3.99
ⓑ Fresh, medium-bodied fruit with a good hint of *macération carbonique* and soft oak. An elegant, tasty red for the price. [*Rapel, Chile*]

Ermitage du Pic St.-Loup 1996 Coteaux du Languedoc, Maurel Vedeau, Waitrose £3.99
ⓑ An example of careful use of *macération carbonique* to lift the richness of fruit, making the wine softer and more elegant than it would otherwise be. [*Coteaux-du-Languedoc, Southern France, France*]

Long Mountain 1995 Shiraz £4.35
Fresh and vital blackberry–blackcurrant fruit on nose and palate, with a lively finish. [*Western Cape, South Africa*]

Château Saint-Maurice 1995 Côtes-du-Rhône £4.49
ⓑ Soft and stylish red with elegant fruit. [*Côtes-du-Rhône, France*]

Château Saint Auriol 1994 Corbières £4.99
ⓑ Elegant yet really quite powerfully flavoured wine, with enough fruit to match its serious food wine structure. [*Corbières, Southern France, France*]

Enate Tinto 1995 Cabernet Sauvignon Merlot £4.99
ⓢ A rich and tasty red that is already mellow, suggesting it would be best consumed before Christmas 1997; otherwise, look out for the next vintage. [*Somontano, Spain*]

James Herrick 1995 Cuvée Simone, Vin de Pays d'Oc
£4.99
ⓑ This has thickened up since last year, dropping from silver to bronze for current drinking, but there is

some violety finesse, suggesting that it is only going
through a phase in development, and will improve over
the next year or two to reach even greater heights than
promised last year. [*Southern France, France*]

Diemersdal 1996 Pinotage £5.49

(S) Succulent fruit with fine tannins and a dry finish.
[*Coastal Region, South Africa*]

Falcoaria 1994 Almeirim £5.49

(G) Heaps of very rich fruit, with a hint of plummy-
spice, and lifted by a touch of sweetness. [*Almeirim,
Portugal*]

Cosme Palacio y Hermanos 1995 Rioja £5.75

(G) Stunning richness of fruit supported by delicious,
coconutty oak. Really quite classy, with good grippy
tannins for food. [*Rioja, Spain*]

Prunotto Fiulot 1995 Barbera d'Alba £5.75

(G) An elegant and characterful Barbera with
deliciously soft and silky fruit. [*Piedmont, Italy*]

Clos Malverne 1996 Pinotage £6.49

(S) Elegant fruit aroma, quite assertive fruit on the
palate, with firm oak tannins on the finish.
[*Stellenbosch, South Africa*]

Fetzer Valley Oaks 1994 Cabernet Sauvignon £6.49

(B) Very fresh and tasty with cedary-oak aromas.
[*California, USA*]

**Bourgogne Hautes-Côtes-de-Beaune 1995 Tête de
Cuvée, Les Caves des Hautes-Côtes** £6.99

(S) Elegantly rich and pure Pinot fruit on nose and
palate, with fine tannins on the finish. [*Burgundy,
France*]

Red Wines

Tatachilla 1995 Merlot, Clarendon Vineyard £7.45
Ⓢ Big and black, with rich, oaky aromas and dense blackcurrant fruit underpinned by grippy tannins. So complete that food only detracts. [*McLaren Vale, South Australia, Australia*]

Warwick Estate 1993 Cabernet Franc £7.95
Ⓢ Although an up-and-coming style, pure Cabernet Franc is still quite rare outside the Loire Valley. Oak seems to dominate the nose of this medium to full-bodied wine, but the fruit is persistent on the palate and really exerts itself on the finish. [*Stellenbosch, South Africa*]

Browns of Padthaway 1995 Shiraz T-Trellis £7.99
Ⓑ A medal-winner not really to my taste, owing to its strange salty-iodine acidity balance, but it is very much like the 1994 vintage I included in the last edition, and I know that some readers really enjoyed the peculiarities of that wine. [*Padthaway, South Australia, Australia*]

Poggio A'Frati 1991 Rocca di Castagnoli, Chianti Classico Riserva £7.99
Ⓑ For lovers of mature Chianti only, this orange-hued wine has cedary-mellow fruit of great typicity and plenty of firm tannins to support it. [*Tuscany, Italy*]

Château Sénéjac 1993 Haut-Médoc £8.45
Ⓑ Cold toast aroma with firm chocolaty fruit on the palate and a perfumed aftertaste. This distinctive wine will not appeal to everyone. [*Haut-Médoc, Bordeaux, France*]

Avignonesi 1993 Vino Nobile di Montepulciano £8.75
Ⓖ A classy food wine with elegant, creamy fruit and

fine tannins. Lovely length. Will age gracefully.
[*Tuscany, Italy*]

Esk Valley 1995 Merlot Cabernet Sauvignon £8.99
ⓑ Rich, soft, cedary-oaky fruit. [*Hawkes Bay, New Zealand*]

L de La Louvière 1994 Pessac-Léognan £9.45
ⓢ Toasty nose, lovely thick, tannic fruit with the positive stamp of oak. [*Pessac-Léognan, Graves, Bordeaux, France*]

Clos Saint Michel 1995 Châteauneuf-du-Pape £9.95
ⓑ Much thicker-tasting fruit than last year's 1994 gold medal winner, but with time it will lose this and become quite elegant and perfumed. [*Châteauneuf-du-Pape, Rhône, France*]

Corbans 1994 Marlborough Pinot Noir Private Bin
£9.99
ⓑ If you can get past the cedary-oak, there's real Pinot Noir fruit here. A wine of serious depth, capable of ageing 2–3 years. [*Marlborough, New Zealand*]

Marqués de Murrieta Ygay 1989 Rioja Reserva Especial £10.95
ⓢ Rich, cedary fruit, superb acidity and fine, dry tannin finish. This Rioja might seem expensive, but it has the potential to age gracefully over 10 years or more, by which time aficionados of this style will think the price paid today was a snip. [*Rioja, Spain*]

Avignonesi 1993 Pinot Nero di Valdicapraia £11.45
ⓖ A classy food wine with elegant, creamy fruit and fine tannins. Lovely length. Will age gracefully.
[*Tuscany, Italy*]

Church Road Reserve 1994 Cabernet Sauvignon Merlot
£11.99

G This might seem expensive, but it is one of New Zealand's three or four greatest reds. It has the quality of a fine *cru classé* claret, but at less than half the price. A fabulous example of how to balance power, complexity and finesse. [*Hawkes Bay, New Zealand*]

Cornas 1994 M. Chapoutier
£12.95

S This wonderful wine would be a gold medal winner if it happened to be a few pounds cheaper, but even so, for a £13 wine to earn a silver it has to be a bit special. With such soft, stylish, perfumed, blackberry fruit and a very satisfying finish, you would be forgiven for thinking that food would only detract from its enjoyment, yet it makes an extraordinarily good accompaniment to roast pork or turkey. [*Cornas, Rhône, France*]

Château La Lagune 1993 Haut-Médoc
£23.50

S Significantly superior to Château La Vieille Cure (*see* Sainsbury's), but in view of its £23.50 price – more than twice as much as Vieille Cure – it only gets a silver. Only! [*Haut-Médoc, Bordeaux, France*]

White Wines

Domaine de Planterieu 1996 Vin de Pays des Côtes-de-Gascogne, Maïté Dubuc-Grassa
£3.65

S Deliciously ripe, clean, crisp fruit, for drinking with or without food. [*South Western France, France*]

Bodega Jacques y Francois Lurton 1996 Pinot Gris

£3.99

Ⓢ Not exactly Pinot Gris, but lovely richness of fruit for the price – and it might even develop some spicy bottle-aromas by Christmas. [*Mendoza, Argentina*]

Currawong Creek 1996 Chardonnay £3.99

This typical Oz Chardonnay has one of those excellent yellow cork substitutes, which are vastly superior to the first generation of plastic corks and can easily be re-inserted after extraction. [*South Eastern Australia, Australia*]

Fairview 1996 Chenin Blanc £3.99

Ⓢ Fresh, clean, crisp and deliciously fruity. [*Paarl, South Africa*]

Southern Creek 1996 Semillon-Chardonnay, Hardys

£3.99

Ⓑ Good fruit, simply easy to enjoy. [*South Eastern Australia, Australia*]

Muscadet de Sèvre-et-Maine Sur Lie 1996 Pierre Guéry, Waitrose £4.35

Correctly dry, with very fresh, spritz-enhanced fruit. [*Muscadet de Sèvre-et-Maine, Loire, France*]

Agramont 1995 Viura Chardonnay £4.75

Ⓑ Another year in bottle and the oak is even more obvious. [*Navarra, Spain*]

Colombara 1996 Soave Classico, Zenato £4.95

Ⓑ Fresh, light-bodied, elegant Soave with real depth of flavour and good typicity, but drink now because the 1995 (which some branches of Asda still

White Wines

stock) is nowhere near as attractive, although it was a bronze medal winner last year. [*Veneto, Italy*]

Penfolds Koonunga Hill 1996 Chardonnay £4.99
Ⓢ Rich, lemony-oaky fruit. [*South Australia, Australia*]

Valdivieso 1996 Chardonnay £4.99
Ⓑ This wine has enough sweet, ripe, upfront fruit to warrant a silver medal, but for a lack of acidity which makes it a tad too fat. [*Andes Foothills, Chile*]

Château Terres Douces 1995 Cuvée Prestige £5.49
Ⓢ Coconut-dominated, but stylish rather than gauche coconut, with fine, dry, elegant fruit. [*Bordeaux, France*]

Top 40 Chardonnay NV Vin de Pays d'Oc, Foncalieu
£5.49
Ⓑ Very fresh and fruity; the flavour of this wine will increase in intensity if kept for another 12 months. [*Southern France, France*]

Schloss Schönborn 1989 Geisenheimer Mäuerchen Riesling Spätlese £5.95
Ⓑ Rich, medium-sweet apricot fruit. [*Rheingau, Germany*]

Penfolds 1994 Barrel Fermented Semillon £5.99
Ⓢ Intense, like Rose's pure lime juice. [*South Australia, Australia*]

Weingut Toni Jost 1994 Bacharacher Schloss Stahleck Riesling Kabinett £6.95
Ⓢ Gorgeous Riesling fruit with a lively medium-sweet balance heightened by spritzy finish. [*Mittelrhein, Germany*]

Mamre Brook 1995 Chardonnay £6.99

G Lovely creamy-citrus aroma, with beautifully fresh, tasty oaky-fruit that is succulent and juicy to the very finish. [*South Eastern Australia, Australia*]

Pouilly-Fumé 1996 Domaine J.M. Masson-Blondelet
£7.49

G The crisp, ripe, yet slightly herbaceous fruit in this wine stands up to the best New Zealand Sauvignon Blancs. [*Pouilly-Fumé, Loire, France*]

Lawson's Dry Hills 1996 Sauvignon Blanc £7.99

G Intensely dry yet absolutely ripe fruit, with a very crisp, zippy finish. [*Marlborough, New Zealand*]

Thelema 1996 Sauvignon Blanc £8.75

B The spritzy finish elevates the perception of acidity, which in turn highlights the fruit. This is the best South African Sauvignon Blanc I've tasted all year, and although £8.75 is the going price for this fast-rising star on the Cape wine firmament, it can only rank as a bronze considering the superior quality of so many other Sauvignon Blanc wines much cheaper than this. Even the French can get a gold with Pouilly-Fumé at £1.26 less than this (see above). [*Stellenbosch, South Africa*]

Rosemount Estate 1995 Chardonnay Show Reserve
£9.99

G If you think this toasty Chardonnay is very rich, with its intense, penetrating fruit flavour, you should try Rosemount Roxburgh, since this is essentially the Estate Chardonnay with a splash of Roxburgh. [*Hunter Valley, NSW, Australia*]

Belondrade y Lurton 1994 Rueda £10.95
Ⓖ Although the back label suggests ageing until
1999–2000, I find the balance between fruit and elegant
oak perfect now. A wonderful dry white wine that is
well worth its seemingly steep price. [*Rueda, Spain*]
☞ THE BEST QUALITY WHITE WINE OF THE YEAR

Brown Brothers 1995 Late Harvested Riesling £6.99
(half-bottle)
Ⓢ Sweeter than Lindemans and quite brilliant in
style and quality, but not in the same class. Very fresh
and clean, with toothsome richness. [*King Valley,
Victoria, Australia*]

Rosé Wines

Winter Hill Rosé 1996 Vin de Pays de l'Aude £3.29
Ⓑ Fresh, tasty, clean and dry. Good with pasta.
[*Southern France, France*]

Sparkling Wines

**Comtesse de Die Tradition 1995 Clairette de Die,
Première Cuvée** £6.45
Ⓑ Very flowery aroma, really quite perfumed, but
the fruit comes through on the palate, with hints of
peach. Definitely sweet in style, but not as sweet as
Asti. [*Clairette de Die, Rhône, France*]

Krone Borealis 1993 Brut £6.99
Ⓢ This South African fizz has established its ability
to age well, requiring four years to develop its creamy-

biscuity complexity. [*Coastal Region, South Africa*]

Waitrose Champagne Blanc de Blancs NV Brut, NM-123 £13.95

G A classic Champagne that is full of rich, ripe, creamy-biscuity fruit. Absolutely delicious. [*Champagne, France*]

Quartet NV Brut £14.95

G I do not blame anyone for wondering why this deserves a gold medal, but this is one of the two or three greatest sparkling wines outside Champagne, and if you keep it for at least two years you will discover why. [*Anderson Valley, USA*]

Fortified Wines

Waitrose Oloroso Sherry NV Medium Sweet, Emilio Lustau £4.65

B Quite stylish for a relatively cheap, sweet sherry. Sweeter than its 'medium' designation implies. [*Jerez, Spain*]

Dry Amontillado Sherry NV Solera Jerezana, Waitrose £5.25

B Leans more towards fino than most Amontillado, particularly on the finish. Very fresh and elegant, with an off-dry finish. [*Jerez, Spain*]

Dry Oloroso Sherry NV Solera Jerezana, Waitrose £5.25

Sweetened up for a so-called 'Dry' Oloroso, but has a good, firm flavour and a tingling intensity on the finish. [*Jerez, Spain*]

Rich Cream Sherry NV Solera Jerezana, Waitrose
£5.25

(B) Very sweet, powerful and long, with a rich, raisiny finish. [*Jerez, Spain*]

Dry Fly Medium Sherry NV Amontillado, Findlater's
£5.75

(B) Light, medium-dry and fresh. [*Jerez, Spain*]

Waitrose Late Bottled Vintage Port 1990 Bottled in 1996 by Smith Woodhouse
£7.85

(S) Powerful, tangy and satisfying. Very rich and very sweet. [*Douro, Portugal*]

Noval NV 10 Year Old Tawny Port
£13.45

(S) Tasty, elegant and spicy, with good Tawny wood showing on the finish. [*Douro, Portugal*]

Warre's 1982 Traditional Late Bottled Vintage Port
£13.95

(B) This gets a bronze for current drinking because although it has a lovely liquorice intensity at the moment, it is not as smooth as it should be and will benefit from at least another five years – which is remarkable for a 1982 (not one of the best vintages). [*Douro, Portugal*]

Apostoles Palo Cortado Muy Viejo NV Gonzalez Byass
£9.95 (half-bottle)

(G) Huge, rich and mind-blowingly complex, with a vast, long, burnt-honeyed richness on the finish. [*Jerez, Spain*]

Matusalem Oloroso Dulce Muy Viejo NV Gonzalez Byass
£9.95 (half-bottle)

(G) The equivalent of almost £20 a bottle, but its

Beers

Waitrose Strong Lager   Per pint: £0.90
Tastes more like a cheap Californian jug wine than a beer of any description, but at least it tastes of *something*, which is a positive point at this price level. £2.79 per 4x44cl cans. [*4.6%, England*]

Waitrose French Lager   Per pint: £1.13
Deeper and more tangy-mellow than the others in the tasting up to and at this price-point. £4.99 per 10x25cl bottles. [*5%, France*]

Waitrose Czech Lager   Per pint: £1.24
Soft, delicate perfumed Pils style. Very consistent. £1.09 per 50cl bottle. [*5%, Vratislavice, Czech Republic*]

Waitrose Westphalian Lager   Per pint: £1.29
A tasty, easy-drinking brew. £2.99 per 4x33cl bottles. [*5%, Germany*]

Waitrose Scottish Ale, Caledonian Brewery
           Per pint: £1.65
Elegantly perfumed hoppy aroma, with a clean, delicate hoppy-malt flavour and a wisp of smoke on the finish. £1.45 per 50cl bottle. [*4.8%, Edinburgh, Scotland*]

WELLWORTHS

Joint owners with Safeway of the new Safeways Stores Ireland, which operates 15 stores in Northern Ireland.

THE WINE & BEER RANKINGS

Virtually all the wines described under each supermarket can be found here, listed in ascending price order by type, style, region and country. If you are looking for a specific wine or beer that does not come under any of the following categories, consult the index to see if it is reviewed in this year's *SuperBooze*. I cannot emphasize too much that you should not ignore non-medal wines or beers. It is only common sense to buy up gold medal winners in preference to silver, silver before bronze, and bronze before non-medal winners, but this inevitably means that the highest-scoring beers and wines are the first to walk off the shelf. Readers should realize that even the lowest-scoring products have survived the rigorous tasting, and are therefore highly recommended. Have faith: buy the non-medal-winners and judge the value of this book by what you think of them.

Note: Where a price seems to be out of order, this will be due to a non-standard bottle-size (most are either half-bottles or 2-litre and 3-litre wine boxes).

RED WINES

Argentina

This country still has a lot to prove in the medium price range and above, but being the fifth largest wine-producing country in the world should enable it to satisfy our more basic needs. Prices ranged from £2.99 to £4.99.

	Argentine Dry Red NV Bright Brothers	£2.99	Co-operative
Bronze	Bonarda NV Picajuan Peak	£3.29	Tesco
	Balbi Vineyard 1995 Malbec Syrah	£3.29	Kwik Save
	Chimango NV Tempranillo Malbec, Tesco	£3.49	Tesco
	Sangiovese NV Picajuan Peak	£3.49	Tesco
	Sainsbury's Sangiovese NV Bodegas Peñaflor	£3.49	Sainsbury's
Bronze	Valle de Vistalba 1995 Barbera, Casa Nieto & Senetiner	£3.99	Booths
	Balbi Vineyard 1996 Malbec	£3.99	Safeway
Bronze	Sainsbury's Tempranillo NV Bodegas Peñaflor	£3.99	Sainsbury's
	Valle de Vistalba 1995 Malbec, Casa Nieto & Senetiner	£4.49	Co-operative
Bronze	La Rural 1996 Malbec	£4.49	Asda

Bordeaux

These wines are not made from a single grape but blended from various varieties, most importantly Cabernet Sauvignon for flavour and structure and Merlot for softness. Contrary to popular belief, however, the Cabernet Sauvignon is not the staple of all fine Bordeaux, as it accounts for only 18 per cent of the vines cultivated in the region. The choice and quality was much better this year, although it would have been nice to find a gold medal winner under a fiver from the most

RED WINES

famous red wine region in the world. Prices of wines tasted ranged from £2.95 to £23.50.

Bronze	Claret NV Yvon Mau, Tesco	£2.98	Tesco
Bronze	Claret NV Paul Barbe, Asda	£2.99	Asda
	Claret Bordeaux NV Co-op	£3.49	Co-op
Bronze	Claret Réserve NV Yvon Mau, Tesco	£3.99	Tesco
Silver	Château la Brunette 1995 Bordeaux	£4.15	Booths
Gold	Château Pierrousselle 1995 Bordeaux, Co-op	£4.59	Co-op
	Prestige Oak-Aged Claret 1994 Saint Vincent Baron	£4.69	Co-operative
Silver	Domaine La Tuque Bel-Air 1994 Côtes-de-Castillon	£4.95	Somerfield
Bronze	Booths Oak Aged Vintage Claret 1994 Bordeaux Supérieur	£4.99	Booths
	Cadet Claret 1995 Baron Philippe de Rothschild	£4.99	Budgens
Silver	Château Saint Galier 1995 Graves	£4.99	Morrisons
Bronze	Claret NV Cuvée Prestige, Sainsbury's	£4.99	Sainsbury's
Bronze	Vintage Claret Aged in new oak 1995 Yvon Mau, Tesco	£4.99	Tesco
Silver	Château de Parenchère 1995 Bordeaux Supérieur	£5.25	Asda
Bronze	Château Saint Robert 1993 Graves	£6.45	Somerfield
Bronze	Château Sénéjac 1993 Haut-Médoc	£8.45	Waitrose
Silver	Château Monlot Capet 1993 St.-Emilion Grand Cru	£8.49	Co-op
	Mouton Cadet Réserve 1994 Baron Philippe de Rothschild	£8.99	Budgens
Bronze	St.-Julien 1993 Raoul Johnston, Tesco	£8.99	Tesco
Silver	L de La Louvière 1994 Pessac-Léognan	£9.45	Waitrose
Gold	Château La Vieille Cure 1990 Sainsbury's Selected Vintage	£10.95	Sainsbury's
Silver	Château La Lagune 1993 Haut-Médoc	£23.50	Waitrose

Bulgaria

The consistency of these wines is not what it used to be, but a few individual wines can be found. Prices ranged from the equivalent of £2.60 to £3.99.

Bronze	Bulgarian Country Wine NV Cabernet Sauvignon & Merlot, Domaine Boyar	£5.19	Kwik Save
	The Bulgarian Vintners' NV Cabernet Sauvignon & Merlot	£2.69	Morrisons
Bronze	Bulgarian Merlot & Cabernet Sauvignon 1995 Domaine Boyar	£2.89	Kwik Save
Bronze	Elhovo 1992 Cabernet Sauvignon Reserve, Domaine Boyar	£3.19	Kwik Save
Bronze	Bulgarian Merlot Reserve 1992 Domaine Boyar	£3.19	Kwik Save
	Bulgarian Cabernet Sauvignon 1992 Barrel Matured, Vinprom, Safeway	£3.29	Safeway
Bronze	Bulgarian Cabernet Sauvignon 1991 Reserve, Vini, Safeway	£3.99	Safeway

Cabernet Sauvignon

Although it is the noblest grape variety of Bordeaux, you will rarely find a Bordeaux wine made entirely from Cabernet Sauvignon. It has a greater ability than any other variety to transplant its essential characteristics into the wines it produces, hence its proliferation throughout the world. Great quality Cabernet Sauvignon can be made in every New World country, not to mention the great value wines, which stretch much further to encompass the mass-producing vineyards of Spain, Eastern Europe and elsewhere. Last year Romania overtook Bulgaria as the cheapest source of Cabernet Sauvignon, but the cheapest recommended this year is Bulgarian – and the cheapest Cabernet submitted was in fact French. Prices ranged from £2.79 to £11.99

Bronze	Elhovo 1992 Cabernet Sauvignon Reserve, Domaine Boyar	£3.19	Kwik Save

204 RED WINES

	Bulgarian Cabernet Sauvignon 1992 Barrel Matured, Vinprom, Safeway	£3.29	Safeway
	Valdezaro 1996 Chilean Cabernet Sauvignon	£3.29	Morrisons
	Cabernet Sauvignon Vin de Pays d'Oc NV Les Vignerons du Val d'Orbieu, Somerfield	£3.35	Somerfield
Bronze	La Source 1994 Cabernet Sauvignon, Vin de Pays d'Oc	£3.35	Morrisons
	Chapel Hill NV Cabernet Sauvignon	£3.49	Londis
	Chapel Hill NV Cabernet Sauvignon	£3.49	Co-op
Bronze	Marble Mountain 1995 St.-George Cabernet Sauvignon, Asda	£3.49	Asda
Silver	Young Vatted Cabernet Sauvignon 1995 Pietroasa Vineyards	£3.49	Budgens
	Amazon NV Brazilian Cabernet Sauvignon	£3.75	Morrisons
	Sainsbury's Cabernet Sauvignon 1995 Fiuza & Bright	£3.79	Sainsbury's
Bronze	Bulgarian Cabernet Sauvignon 1991 Reserve, Vini, Safeway	£3.99	Safeway
Silver	Cabernet Sauvignon 1995 Campo dos Frades	£3.99	Tesco
Bronze	Chilean Cabernet Sauvignon 1995 Viña Cornellana, Somerfield	£3.99	Somerfield
Bronze	Four Rivers 1995 Cabernet Sauvignon	£3.99	Co-op
	Chilean Cabernet Sauvignon 1996 Viña San Pedro, Safeway	£4.39	Safeway
	Cabernet Sauvignon 1995 Angove's, Co-op	£4.49	Co-op
Silver	Palmeras Estate 1995 Oak Aged Cabernet Sauvignon	£4.49	Booths
	Virginie 1994 Cabernet Sauvignon, Vin de Pays d'Oc	£4.49	Booths
	Penfolds Rawson's Retreat Bin 35 1995 Cabernet Sauvignon-Shiraz-Ruby Cabernet	£4.69	Londis
Bronze	Hanwood 1995 Cabernet Sauvignon, McWilliams	£4.79	Morrisons
Silver	Casa Leona 1995 Reserve Cabernet Sauvignon, St Michael	£4.99	M&S

Bronze	Casa Porta 1995 Cabernet Sauvignon	£4.99	**Londis**
Bronze	Rosenview 1996 Cabernet Sauvignon	£4.99	**Safeway**
Gold	Rowan Brook Cabernet Sauvignon 1994 Winemaker's Reserve Oak Aged, Asda	£4.99	**Asda**
Silver	Bin 444 Cabernet Sauvignon 1994 Wyndham Estate	£5.25	**Morrisons**
Silver	Oaked Cabernet Sauvignon 1996 Thomas Hardy, Safeway	£5.29	**Safeway**
Bronze	Mont-Marçal 1991 Cabernet Sauvignon Reserva	£5.49	**Booths**
Bronze	Quinta de Pancas 1995 Cabernet Sauvignon	£5.49	**Somerfield**
Silver	Cono Sur 1995 Cabernet Sauvignon, Selection Reserve	£5.59	**Co-operative**
	Canyon Road 1994 Cabernet Sauvignon, St Michael	£5.99	**M&S**
Bronze	Fetzer Valley Oaks 1994 Cabernet Sauvignon	£6.49	**Waitrose**
Bronze	Wolf Blass Cabernet Sauvignon 1995 Yellow Label	£6.99	**Londis**
Bronze	Wolf Blass Cabernet Sauvignon 1995 Yellow Label	£6.99	**Somerfield**
Bronze	Peter Lehmann 1995 Cabernet Sauvignon	£7.49	**Safeway**
Gold	Rosemount Estate 1995 Cabernet Sauvignon	£7.49	**Europa**
Bronze	Nexus 1994 San Simone	£7.99	**Budgens**
Bronze	The Ridge Wines 1995 Coonawarra Cabernet, St Michael	£8.99	**M&S**
Silver	Hardys 1994 Cabernet Sauvignon	£9.99	**Safeway**
Gold	Rosemount 1993 Orange Vineyard Cabernet Sauvignon, St Michael	£11.99	**M&S**

Cabernet-based Blends

Apart than Bordeaux (dealt with separately above), Bordeaux-type blends from Eastern Europe and the New World still dominate this category, with Chile and South Africa on the rise this year. The juicy Merlot is the classic blending partner, but Shiraz and Malbec are the New World favourites. Prices ranged from £2.49 to £11.99.

RED WINES

Bronze	Bulgarian Country Wine NV Cabernet Sauvignon & Merlot, Domaine Boyar	£5.19	Kwik Save
	The Bulgarian Vintners' NV Cabernet Sauvignon & Merlot	£2.69	Morrisons
Bronze	Chilean Long Slim Red 1994 Cabernet Merlot, Co-op	£3.49	Co-op
Bronze	Chilean Cabernet Merlot 1995 Vinicola Las Taguas, Asda	£3.79	Asda
Silver	Cabernet Sauvignon/Shiraz 1996 Du Toitskloof Wine Cellar	£3.99	Waitrose
	Parras Valley 1994 Cabernet Sauvignon-Merlot, St Michael	£3.99	M&S
	Tocornal NV Cabernet-Malbec	£3.99	Safeway
Silver	Enate Tinto 1995 Cabernet Sauvignon Merlot	£4.99	Waitrose
Bronze	Jennsberg 1995 Cabernet Sauvignon Merlot	£4.99	Tesco
Bronze	Palacio de la Vega 1993 Navarra	£4.99	Budgens
Bronze	Carmen 1995 Grande Vidure Cabernet Reserve	£6.99	Booths
Bronze	Leasingham Domain 1994 Cabernet Sauvignon Malbec	£6.99	Co-op
	Saints 1994 Cabernet Merlot, St Michael	£6.99	M&S
Silver	Château Reynella 1994 Basket Pressed Cabernet Merlot	£7.99	Asda
Gold	Clos Malverne 1995 Auret	£7.99	Tesco
Gold	Church Road Reserve 1994 Cabernet Sauvignon Merlot	£11.99	Waitrose

Cabernet Franc

As last year, the majority of these wines were from the Loire Valley. Although there have been a couple of good vintages, most were not so much lean as mean, and grossly overpriced. Prices ranged from £3.99 to £7.95.

	Pepperwood Grove 1995 Cabernet Franc	£3.99	Budgens
Silver	Warwick Estate 1993 Cabernet Franc	£7.95	Waitrose

Chianti

Including other Sangiovese or Sangiovese-dominated blends

The chief Chianti grape variety is Sangiovese, which is also used for other Italian wines, including Brunello di Montalcino and Vino Nobile di Montepulciano. As with most of Italy's most famous wines, the quality can range from dire to stunning. Some of the most exciting Sangiovese wines are the so-called 'super-Tuscan' Cabernet/Sangiovese blends and New World Sangiovese, an up-and-coming, if relatively rare, category of wine owing to the premium charged. Prices ranged from £2.99 to £11.99.

	Sainsbury's Sangiovese NV Bodegas Peñaflor	£3.49	Sainsbury's
	Sangiovese NV Picajuan Peak	£3.49	Tesco
	Chianti 1995 Piccini, Co-op	£3.99	Co-op
Bronze	Chianti Rufina 1995 Fratelli Grati, Tesco	£4.29	Tesco
Bronze	Uggiano 1994 Chianti dei Colli Fiorentini	£4.69	Morrisons
Bronze	Chianti Classico 1994 Ampelos, Tesco	£4.99	Tesco
Gold	Uggiano 1995 Chianti Classico	£4.99	Morrisons
Silver	Castelgreve 1995 Chianti Classico	£5.49	Co-operative
Silver	Chianti Classico 1995 Montecchio	£5.99	Somerfield
Silver	Chianti Classico, Villa Primavera 1995 Conti Serristori, Somerfield	£5.99	Somerfield
	Chianti Classico 1995 Basilica Cafaggio, St Michael	£6.99	M&S
Bronze	Poggio A'Frati 1991 Rocca di Castagnoli, Chianti Classico Riserva	£7.99	Waitrose
Gold	Avignonesi 1993 Vino Nobile di Montepulciano	£8.75	Waitrose
Gold	Canfera 1994 Single Vineyard, St Michael	£8.99	M&S
Gold	Avignonesi 1993 Vino Nobile di Montepulciano	£9.99	Budgens

French Vins de Pays

Hugely varied range of styles and quality, including some of the most exciting new developments in French winemaking. Great for bargain hunters. Prices ranged from £2.39 to £5.99.

	Baron d'Arignac 1996 Vin de Pays de l'Aude	£2.55	Budgens
Bronze	Montagne Noire Red NV Vin de Pays de l'Aude, Asda	£2.99	Asda
	Skylark Hill Syrah 1995 Vin de Pays d'Oc	£2.99	Kwik Save
	Vin de Pays de Vaucluse 1996 Du Peloux, Safeway	£2.99	Safeway
	Cabernet Sauvignon Vin de Pays d'Oc NV Les Vignerons du Val d'Orbieu, Somerfield	£3.35	Somerfield
Bronze	La Source 1994 Cabernet Sauvignon, Vin de Pays d'Oc	£3.35	Morrisons
	Great with Steak 1995 Merlot, Vin de Pays d'Oc, Tesco	£3.49	Tesco
	Tramontane 1996 Syrah, Vin de Pays d'Oc, Asda	£3.49	Asda
Bronze	La Baume Syrah Grenache 1995 Vin de Pays d'Oc,	£3.99	Co-operative
	Syrah 1996 Vin de Pays d'Oc, Paul Sapin, St Michael	£3.99	M&S
Silver	Domaine Jeune 1996 Cepage Counoise, Vin de Pays du Gard, St Michael	£4.49	M&S
	Virginie 1994 Cabernet Sauvignon, Vin de Pays d'Oc	£4.49	Booths
Bronze	James Herrick 1995 Cuvée Simone, Vin de Pays d'Oc	£4.99	Somerfield
Bronze	James Herrick 1995 Cuvée Simone, Vin de Pays d'Oc	£4.99	Tesco
Bronze	James Herrick 1995 Cuvée Simone, Vin de Pays d'Oc	£4.99	Waitrose
Bronze	La Domeque, Tête de Cuvée 1995 Vieilles Vignes Syrah, Vin de Pays d'Oc	£4.99	Asda
	Merlot Vin de Pays d'Oc 1996 Baron Philippe de Rothschild	£4.99	Europa
Bronze	La Cuvée Mythique 1994 Vin de Pays d'Oc	£5.99	Safeway

Gamay

Mostly Beaujolais. Sometimes a Mâcon Rouge is submitted – though God only knows why – and occasionally a Passetoutgrains, an *appellation* that has improved over the years and sometimes makes more sense in a Pinot Noir tasting. Beaujolais generally lacks fruit and will be grossly overpriced, but good Beaujolais is worth trying, even if it seldom represents good value in comparison to almost every other red wine in the world. If it is the peardrop fermentation character rather than the varietal style you enjoy, go for a cheap New World red made by *macération carbonique*. Prices ranged from £3.49 to £7.99.

	Château du Bluizard 1995 Beaujolais-Villages	£4.99	Tesco
Bronze	Domaine de Conroy 1994 Brouilly	£5.99	Tesco
	Fleurie 1995 Clos de la Chapelle des Bois	£6.85	Asda
	Morgon, Les Charmes 1994 Domaine Brisson	£6.99	Co-op
	Brouilly 1995 Georges Duboeuf	£7.99	Co-operative
Silver	Fleurie 1995 Paul Boutinot	£7.99	Booths

Italy

Other than Chianti (see earlier). The range, quality and value of Italian red wines are rapidly improving. Prices ranged from £2.49 to £9.99.

Bronze	Gabbia d'Oro NV Vino Rosso	£2.39	Kwik Save
Bronze	Montepulciano d'Abruzzo 1995 Umani Ronchi	£3.95	Waitrose
	Trentino Pinot Nero 1995 La Vis, Asda	£3.99	Asda
Silver	Montepulciano d'Abruzzo 1995 Bianchi	£3.99	Somerfield
Silver	Zagara 1995 Nero d'Avola	£3.99	Safeway
Silver	Casa di Giovanni 1994 Oak Aged, Safeway	£3.99	Safeway
Silver	Vignetti Casterna 1994 Valpollicella, Pasqua	£4.45	Somerfield
Bronze	Soltero 1994 Rosso di Sicilia, Settesoli	£4.49	Somerfield
Bronze	Le Trulle 1994 Primitivo del Salento	£4.49	Tesco

RED WINES

Bronze	Le Canne 1995 Boscaini Bardolino Classico Riserva	£4.99	Co-op
Silver	Rozzano 1995 Villa Pigna	£4.99	Asda
Gold	Prunotto Fiulot 1995 Barbera d'Alba	£5.75	Waitrose
Bronze	Barolo 1992 Cantina Terre del Barolo	£7.99	Co-op
Silver	Barolo 1992 Giacosa Fratelli	£7.99	Tesco
Gold	Barolo 1992 Cantine Gemma	£7.99	Tesco
Bronze	Nexus 1994 San Simone	£7.99	Budgens
Gold	Avignonesi 1993 Pinot Nero di Valdicapraia	£11.45	Waitrose

Malbec

Pure and blended

Responsible for the famed 'black wines' of Cahors, the Malbec is usually used in a secondary blending role these days, although it is occasionally allowed to dominate a blend, and a few pure varietals can be found. Prices ranged from £3.29 to £4.99.

	Balbi Vineyard 1995 Malbec Syrah	£3.29	Kwik Save
	Balbi Vineyard 1996 Malbec	£3.99	Safeway
Bronze	La Rural 1996 Malbec	£4.49	Asda
	Valle de Vistalba 1995 Malbec, Casa Nieto & Senetiner	£4.49	Co-operative
Silver	Valdivieso 1996 Malbec	£4.99	Asda

Merlot

Pure and blended

The Merlot is a great Bordeaux grape and capable of producing luscious, velvety red wine. It is also very fashionable. Although perceived as a relatively light, supple grape that will soften a Cabernet-dominated blend, it can also be one of the biggest, richest and most majestically structured of all grape varieties, as Château Pétrus proves. Prices ranged from £2.79 to £8.99.

Bronze	Romanian Merlot 1996 Kwik Save	£2.79	Kwik Save
Bronze	Bulgarian Merlot & Cabernet Sauvignon 1995 Domaine Boyar	£2.89	Kwik Save

Bronze	Deep Pacific 1996 Merlot–Cabernet Sauvignon	£2.99	Kwik Save
Bronze	Bulgarian Merlot Reserve 1992 Domaine Boyar	£3.19	Kwik Save
	Great with Steak 1995 Merlot, Vin de Pays d'Oc, Tesco	£3.49	Tesco
	Frontier Island Merlot 1994 Hungarian Country Wine	£3.59	Europa
Silver	Bovlei Winery 1995 Merlot	£3.99	Morrisons
Bronze	Concha y Toro 1996 Merlot	£3.99	Waitrose
Bronze	Libertas 1994 Merlot	£3.99	Europa
	Marques de Monistrol 1993 Merlot	£3.99	Co-op
	Robertson 1996 Merlot	£4.29	Co-op
Silver	Bisquertt 1995 Merlot	£4.79	Co-operative
Silver	Casa Leona 1996 Reserve Merlot, St Michael	£4.99	M&S
Bronze	La Fortuna 1996 Merlot	£4.99	Londis
	Merlot Vin de Pays d'Oc 1996 Baron Philippe de Rothschild	£4.99	Europa
Gold	Schoone Gevel 1995 Merlot	£4.99	Tesco
Silver	Villa Montes 1994 Merlot Oak Aged Reserve	£4.99	Safeway
Silver	Diemersdal 1996 Merlot	£5.99	Tesco
Silver	Château Fourtanet 1993 Côtes-de-Castillon	£6.49	Co-op
Silver	Tatachilla 1995 Merlot, Clarendon Vineyard	£7.45	Waitrose
Silver	Viñas del Vero 1994 Merlot	£7.99	Europa
Bronze	Esk Valley 1995 Merlot Cabernet Sauvignon	£8.99	Waitrose

New Zealand

It is the leafy character or herbaceousness of these wines that generally stands out in a blind tasting, but this is gradually being eradicated through better canopy management. No wine better demonstrates this than Church Road Reserve, this year's Best Quality Red Wine of the Year. Prices ranged from £4.49 to £11.99

Bronze	Waimanu NV Premium Dry Red Wine	£4.49	Budgens
	Saints 1994 Cabernet Merlot, St Michael	£6.99	M&S

212 RED WINES

Bronze	Esk Valley 1995 Merlot Cabernet Sauvignon	£8.99	Waitrose
Bronze	Corbans 1994 Marlborough Pinot Noir Private Bin	£9.99	Waitrose
Gold	Church Road Reserve 1994 Cabernet Sauvignon Merlot	£11.99	Waitrose

Pinotage

This grape is to South Africa what Zinfandel is to California and Shiraz to Australia. The range was as erratic as ever, but with more wines of real style and quality than last year. Prices ranged from £3.99 to £8.99.

Bronze	Impala 1996 Pinotage	£3.99	Kwik Save
Silver	Pinotage 1995 Bovlei Winery	£3.99	Co-operative
	South African Pinotage NV Clear Mountain	£3.99	Budgens
Bronze	Beyers Truter NV Pinotage, Tesco	£4.99	Tesco
Bronze	Cape Afrika 1992 Pinotage	£4.99	Co-op
Silver	Diemersdal 1996 Pinotage	£5.49	Waitrose
Silver	Clos Malverne 1996 Pinotage	£6.49	Waitrose
Gold	Jacana 1995 Pinotage Reserve	£8.99	Safeway

Pinot Noir

The world's most elusive classic red wine grape. More Pinot Noirs disappoint than excite, even in Burgundy, but it is capable of producing a red wine of incomparable finesse and grace. Prices ranged from £2.99 to £16.95.

Bronze	Pinot Noir 1995 River Route Selection	£3.19	Asda
Bronze	Classic Pinot Noir 1993 Posta Romana	£3.39	Londis
	Romanian Pinot Noir 1993 Special Reserve, Rovit SA, Safeway	£3.69	Safeway
	Trentino Pinot Nero 1995 La Vis, Asda	£3.99	Asda
Gold	Jennsberg 1996 Pinot Noir, Asda	£4.49	Asda
Bronze	South Bay Vineyards NV American Pinot Noir, Sainsbury's	£4.99	Sainsbury's

	Sainsbury's Burgundy NV Guichard Potheret	£5.45	Sainsbury's
Silver	Redwood Trail Pinot Noir 1995 Coastal Vintners	£5.49	Londis
	Bourgogne Pinot Noir 1995 Charles Viénot	£5.99	Budgens
Silver	Côte-de-Beaune-Villages 1995 Jules Vignon, Co-op	£6.49	Co-op
Silver	Bourgogne Hautes-Côtes-de-Beaune 1995 Tête de Cuvée, Les Caves des Hautes-Côtes	£6.99	Waitrose
Bronze	Fixin 1994 Les Vins Pierre Leduc	£6.99	Co-op
Bronze	Lindemans Padthaway 1995 Pinot Noir	£8.45	Sainsbury's
Bronze	Corbans 1994 Marlborough Pinot Noir Private Bin	£9.99	Waitrose
Gold	Avignonesi 1993 Pinot Nero di Valdicapraia	£11.45	Waitrose

Portugal

Things continue to buzz in Portugal, with real fruit being found in what used to be astringently dry and unappealing wines. Prices ranged from £2.49 to £6.29.

Gold	José Neiva 1994 Oak Aged	£2.49	Booths
Bronze	Vinha Nova NV Vinho de Mesa Tinto	£2.99	Booths
Bronze	Floral Vinho Tinto Reserva 1994 Caves Aliança	£3.49	Booths
	Dão 1994 Co-op	£3.59	Co-op
Bronze	Bright Brothers 1994 Old Vines	£3.70	Asda
	Sainsbury's Cabernet Sauvignon 1995 Fiuza & Bright	£3.79	Sainsbury's
	Espiga 1995 Vinho Tinto	£3.89	Booths
Silver	Cabernet Sauvignon 1995 Campo dos Frades	£3.99	Tesco
Silver	Duque de Viseu 1992 Dão	£5.49	Co-op
Bronze	Quinta de Pancas 1995 Cabernet Sauvignon	£5.49	Somerfield
Gold	Falcoaria 1994 Almeirim	£5.49	Waitrose

Rhône

Including everything from the Rhône apart from Syrah or Syrah-dominated wines, this category is dominated by Côtes-du-Rhône at the bottom end and Châteauneuf-du-Pape at the top. Prices ranged from £2.69 to £13.95

	Côtes-du-Lubéron 1995 Rhône Valley Red Wine, Pol Romain	£2.99	Morrisons
	Côtes-du-Rhône NV F. Dubessy	£2.99	Kwik Save
Bronze	Côtes-du-Rhône NV Gabriel Meffre, Morrisons	£3.19	Morrisons
	Côtes-du-Rhône NV Co-op	£3.49	Co-op
	Côtes-du-Ventoux 1995 La Falaise	£3.49	Booths
Bronze	Bush Vine Grenache 1995 Limited Edition	£3.99	Sainsbury's
	Côtes-du-Rhône 1993 Domaine de Pauline	£3.99	Tesco
Gold	Côtes-du-Rhône 1996 Aged in Oak, Roger Bernoin	£3.99	Asda
Bronze	Château Saint-Maurice 1995 Côtes-du-Rhône	£4.49	Waitrose
	Domaine de Grangeneuve 1995 Coteaux-du-Tricastin, Cuvée Tradition	£4.49	Asda
	Château Malijay 1995 Fontanilles, Côtes-du-Rhône	£4.59	Budgens
	La Chasse du Pape Réserve 1995 Côtes-du-Rhône	£4.99	Safeway
Bronze	La Vieille Ferme 1994 Côtes-du-Rhône Réserve	£4.99	Tesco
	Beaumes de Venise 1994 Côtes-du-Rhône-Villages, Carte Noire	£5.49	Tesco
	Vacqueyras 1995 Cuvée du Marquis de Fonseguille	£5.49	Co-op
	Gigondas 1995 Fleuron des Vignes	£6.29	Co-op
Bronze	Gigondas 1995 Domaine de la Mourielle	£6.89	Co-operative
Silver	Châteauneuf-du-Pape 1996 S.A. V.J.Q., Tesco	£6.99	Tesco
Silver	Châteauneuf-du-Pape 1994 Domaine du Vieux Lazaret	£8.49	Morrisons

Bronze	Châteauneuf-du-Pape 1994 Cellier des Princes	£8.99	Co-op
Bronze	Châteauneuf-du-Pape 1995 Le Chemin des Mulets	£8.99	Tesco
Silver	Châteauneuf-du-Pape 1995 Domaine de la Solitude	£9.49	Somerfield
Bronze	Clos Saint Michel 1995 Châteauneuf-du-Pape	£9.95	Waitrose

Rhône-Rangers

Essentially Southern Rhône in style, as above, but made outside the Rhône itself, mostly in the New World, this category consists mainly of Grenache, pure or blended, and Mourvèdre (also known as Mataro) based blends. Prices ranged from £2.99 to £8.99.

Bronze	Cape Cinsaut NV Tesco	£3.49	Tesco
Bronze	Ridgewood 1996 Mataro-Grenache	£3.69	Waitrose
Silver	Kingston 1995 Grenache	£3.79	Co-operative
	Rosenview 1996 Cinsaut	£3.79	Safeway
Bronze	Banrock Station 1996 Mataro Grenache Shiraz, Hardys	£3.99	Sainsbury's
Bronze	La Baume Syrah Grenache 1995 Vin de Pays d'Oc	£3.99	Co-operative
Bronze	Landskroon 1996 Cinsaut Shiraz	£3.99	Safeway
Silver	Breakaway 1995 Grenache Shiraz	£4.49	Safeway
Silver	Mount Hurtle 1995 Grenache Shiraz	£4.49	Asda

Rioja

Including other Tempranillo and Tempranillo-dominated blends

Rioja had its own way for a long time, then Tempranillo from Navarra got some attention, and now it's even coming from Valdepeñas in La Mancha and from as far afield as Argentina – although other New World countries have been slow to pick up on its popularity. Prices ranged from £3.13 to £10.95.

RED WINES

Silver	Tempranillo NV Stowells of Chelsea	£12.49	Co-operative
Silver	Tempranillo Oak Aged NV Co-op	£3.29	Co-op
Silver	Santara Tempranillo 1996 Conca de Barberà	£3.35	Somerfield
	Chimango NV Tempranillo Malbec, Tesco	£3.49	Tesco
Bronze	Hoya de Cadenas 1989 Reserva	£3.99	Co-operative
Silver	Rioja NV Almaraz, Somerfield	£3.99	Somerfield
Bronze	Sainsbury's Tempranillo NV Bodegas Peñaflor	£3.99	Sainsbury's
Bronze	Rioja Tempranillo 1994 Bodegas Age, St Michael	£4.99	M&S
	Roseral 1994 Rioja, St Michael	£4.99	M&S
Silver	Marqués de Cacérès 1992 Rioja	£5.19	Co-operative
	Ochoa 1995 Tempranillo-Garnacha	£5.19	Europa
Bronze	Viña Mara 1990 Rioja Reserva, Tesco	£5.49	Tesco
Gold	Cosme Palacio y Hermanos 1995 Rioja	£5.75	Waitrose
Gold	Viña Caña Reserva 1987 Rioja, Somerfield	£5.99	Somerfield
	Cune 1994 Rioja	£6.19	Europa
Silver	Gran Condal 1990 Rioja Reserva	£6.49	Co-op
Gold	Artadi 1994 Viñas de Gain, Rioja	£6.49	Booths
Silver	Baron de Ley 1991 Rioja Reserva	£6.79	Asda
Bronze	Orobio Rioja Reserva 1990 Artadi, Sainsbury's Selected Vintage	£6.95	Sainsbury's
Bronze	Faustino V 1991 Rioja Reserva	£7.49	Londis
	Siglo Reserva 1988 Rioja	£7.99	Co-operative
Silver	Marqués de Murrieta Ygay 1989 Rioja Reserva Especial	£10.95	Waitrose

Spain

Other than Rioja

Supermarkets have always been keen on inexpensive Spanish wines, and the choice of better-quality Spanish wines has increased significantly over the last 12 months. Prices ranged from £2.59 to £9.75.

	Flamenco NV Spanish Full Red	£2.59	Kwik Save
Silver	Viña Alarba 1995 Calatayud	£2.99	Booths

Bronze	La Falleras 1996 St Michael	£2.99	M&S
Silver	Sainsbury's El Conde NV Vino de Mesa Tinto	£2.99	Sainsbury's
	Diego de Almagro 1993 Felix Solis	£3.19	Budgens
	Marques de Monistrol 1993 Merlot	£3.99	Co-op
Gold	Guelbenzu 1995 Jardin	£4.99	Booths
Silver	Enate Tinto 1995 Cabernet Sauvignon Merlot	£4.99	Waitrose
Bronze	Palacio de la Vega 1993 Navarra	£4.99	Budgens
Bronze	Mont-Marçal 1991 Cabernet Sauvignon Reserva	£5.49	Booths
Silver	Viñas del Vero 1994 Merlot	£7.99	Europa
Silver	Pago de Carraovejas 1994 Ribera del Duero	£9.75	Booths

Syrah/Shiraz

As last year, this primarily involves Australian Shiraz and Northern Rhônes (such as Crozes-Hermitage), with Syrah/Shiraz-dominated blends treated separately (*see* next category). In France, youthful Syrah has a raspberry character, but can develop plummy-blackcurrant fruit and silky-spicy finesse, particularly in the best vintages after a couple of years in bottle. Prices ranged from £3.29 to £12.95.

	Skylark Hill Syrah 1995 Vin de Pays d'Oc	£2.99	Kwik Save
	Tramontane 1996 Syrah, Vin de Pays d'Oc, Asda	£3.49	Asda
	Syrah 1996 Vin de Pays d'Oc, Paul Sapin, St Michael	£3.99	M&S
	Long Mountain 1995 Shiraz	£4.35	Waitrose
Bronze	Shiraz 1996 McWilliam's, Safeway	£4.69	Safeway
Bronze	Crozes-Hermitage 1994 Quinson	£4.75	Budgens
	Sainsbury's Australian Shiraz 1995 Austral Wines	£4.85	Sainsbury's
	Cranswick Estate 1995 Shiraz	£4.99	Morrisons
Bronze	La Domeque, Tête de Cuvée 1995 Vieilles Vignes Syrah, Vin de Pays d'Oc	£4.99	Asda
	Shiraz 1995 Oak Matured, St Michael	£4.99	M&S
	Vine Vale Shiraz 1995 Peter Lehmann	£4.99	Co-operative

RED WINES

Bronze	Oaked Shiraz NV Thomas Hardy, Safeway	£5.29	Safeway
Bronze	Crozes-Hermitage 1995 Groupe Jean-Paul Selles	£5.49	Somerfield
Silver	Crozes-Hermitage 1994 Cave de Tain l'Hermitage	£5.85	Morrisons
	Bankside Shiraz 1994 Hardys	£5.99	Asda
Silver	Diemersdal 1996 Syrah	£5.99	Tesco
Silver	Lindemans Bin 50 1995 Shiraz	£5.99	Co-operative
Silver	Shiraz 1994 Baileys	£6.49	Co-op
Silver	Wolf Blass Shiraz Cabernet Sauvignon 1995 Red Label	£6.49	Londis
Bronze	Parducci 1994 Petite Sirah	£6.99	Morrisons
Silver	McLaren Vale Shiraz 1994 Maglieri, Tesco	£6.99	Tesco
	South African Premium Shiraz 1995 Tesco	£6.99	Tesco
Bronze	Browns' of Padthaway 1995 Shiraz T-Trellis	£7.99	Waitrose
Bronze	Penfolds Bin 128 1994 Shiraz	£7.99	Somerfield
Silver	Penfolds Kalimna Bin 28 1994 Shiraz	£8.99	Co-operative
Gold	Penfolds Kalimna Bin 28 1993 Shiraz	£8.99	Asda
Bronze	Shiraz 1995 Coonawarra Winegrowers, St Michael	£8.99	M&S
Silver	Plantagenet 1994 Shiraz	£10.75	Booths
Silver	Cornas 1994 M. Chapoutier	£12.95	Waitrose

Syrah/Shiraz-dominated Blends

With one exception, an entirely Australian category as far as the wines that survived the tasting go. With this blender's workhorse, Aussie winemakers do seem to produce better quality, better balanced wines at significantly cheaper prices. Prices ranged from £3.33 to £6.59.

Bronze	Pelican Bay NV Australian Shiraz-Cabernet	£3.59	Kwik Save
	Australian Shiraz Cabernet NV Sainsbury's	£14.49	Sainsbury

Silver	Kingston 1996 Shiraz Mataro	£3.99	**Co-op**
Bronze	James Herrick 1995 Cuvée Simone, Vin de Pays d'Oc	£4.99	**Somerfield**
Bronze	James Herrick 1995 Cuvée Simone, Vin de Pays d'Oc	£4.99	**Tesco**
Bronze	James Herrick 1995 Cuvée Simone, Vin de Pays d'Oc	£4.99	**Waitrose**
Silver	Western Cape Shiraz/Cabernet Sauvignon 1995 Tesco	£4.99	**Tesco**
Silver	Honey Tree Shiraz Cabernet 1996 Rosemount Estate, St Michael	£5.50	**M&S**
Silver	Rosemount Estate 1996 Shiraz Cabernet	£5.99	**Co-operative**

Zinfandel

Primarily a Californian category, because this grape is as American as cherry pie (even if it is the same variety as the Italian Primitivo). What makes the Zinfandel so full of stars and stripes is the use of all-American oak, whereas your average California winemaker uses French oak for Cabernet Sauvignon and other classic varieties. As a style, Zinfandel is hard to pin down. Each bunch ripens unevenly, and depending on where and how it's grown, the yield can vary by as much as tenfold. Thus, Zinfandel is used for everything from sparkling and blush to red and fortified, and there is a tremendous variation in the styles of red wine produced, with berry fruits and some spiciness being the only common denominators. Unfortunately, this year's Zinfandel submissions were generally a miserable bunch. Prices ranged £4.29 to £5.99

| | Sutter Home 1994 Zinfandel | £4.29 | **Budgens** |
| Bronze | Le Trulle 1994 Primitivo del Salento | £4.49 | **Tesco** |

WHITE WINES

Argentina

Most of the white wines from this country are even more basic than the reds, but Argentina has something of a reputation for its flowery, muscat-like Torrontes grape, and *bordelais* Jacques Lurton has dabbled successfully with the Alsace variety Pinot Gris. Prices ranged from £2.99 to £4.99.

Bronze	Etchart 1996 Cafayate Torrontes	£3.99	**Co-operative**
Silver	Bodega Jacques y Francois Lurton 1996 Pinot Gris	£3.99	**Waitrose**

Bordeaux

Dry Style

The world's most famous red wine region is a minefield when it comes to dry white wines. This category is specifically for blended wines. Dry white Bordeaux made entirely from Sauvignon Blanc are found under that section further on. Prices ranged from £3.39 to £5.49.

Bronze	Bordeaux Blanc Sec 1995 Aged in Oak, Safeway	£3.99	**Safeway**
	Château du Plantier 1995 Entre-Deux-Mers	£3.99	**Safeway**
	Château Pierrousselle 1995 Entre-Deux-Mers, Co-op	£3.99	**Co-op**
Silver	Château Terres Douces 1995 Cuvée Prestige	£5.49	**Waitrose**

Chardonnay

Pure and blended

Almost as many Chardonnays as last year, but I did not receive one as cheap as Asda's Hungarian Chardonnay 1995 Private Reserve, which was only £2.49 last time round. Asda is selling the 1996 for £3.29, and it still deserves a bronze, which illustrates just what a bargain the previous vintage was. Although I found some nice white Burgundies, far too many were poorly made; it does not look as if even supermarket muscle can force the Burgundians to accept the humiliation of having a flying winemaker foisted on them – more's the pity. Prices range from £2.99 to £21.75.

	Badger Hill 1994 Chardonnay Oak Barrel Fermented	£2.99	Co-operative
Silver	Bulgarian Vintage Blend 1995 Chardonnay & Sauvignon Blanc, Domaine Boyar	£2.99	Budgens
Bronze	Hungarian Chardonnay 1996 Private Reserve, Neszmély Winery	£3.29	Asda
	Chilean Long Slim White 1996 Chardonnay Semillon, Co-op	£3.49	Co-op
Bronze	Chardonnay Oaked 1996 Mátra Mountain	£3.49	Safeway
	Pelican Bay NV Australian Chardonnay, Kwik Save	£3.59	Kwik Save
	Casa Leona 1996 Chardonnay, St Michael	£3.99	M&S
	Currawong Creek 1996 Chardonnay	£3.99	Waitrose
Bronze	Montagne Noire Chardonnay 1996 Vin de Pays d'Oc, Asda	£3.99	Asda
Silver	Santara 1995 Chardonnay	£3.99	Co-op
Silver	Santara 1995 Chardonnay	£3.99	Booths
	South Australia Chardonnay 1995 W1226, Asda	£3.99	Asda
Bronze	Trentino Chardonnay 1996 La Vis, Asda	£3.99	Asda
Bronze	Riverview 1995 Chardonnay-Pinot Gris	£3.99	Safeway
Bronze	Chardonnay Colombard 1996 Wingara, Safeway	£4.29	Safeway
Bronze	Le Trulle 1996 Chardonnay	£4.39	Somerfield

WHITE WINES

Bronze	Chardonnay 1995 Jidvei Winery	£4.49	Budgens
	Domaine Mandeville Chardonnay 1996 Vin de Pays d'Oc, St Michael	£4.49	M&S
Gold	Rowan Brook Chardonnay 1996 Winemaker's Reserve Oak Aged, Asda	£4.49	Asda
Bronze	Australian Chardonnay NV Somerfield	£4.65	Somerfield
	Bourgogne Chardonnay 1996 Charles Viénot	£4.99	Budgens
Silver	Chardonnay Bin 65 1996 Lindemans, St Michael	£4.99	M&S
Gold	Chardonnay par Yves Grassa 1996 Barrel Fermented, Vin de Pays des Côtes-de-Gascogne	£4.99	Asda
Bronze	Cuckoo Hill Oak Barrel Chardonnay 1995 Vin de Pays d'Oc	£4.99	Co-operative
Silver	Fiuza 1995 Chardonnay	£4.99	Co-op
Gold	Grande Cuvée Chardonnay 1995 Laroche, Vin de Pays d'Oc	£4.99	Budgens
Silver	James Herrick 1996 Chardonnay, Vin de Pays d'Oc	£4.99	Somerfield
Silver	James Herrick 1995 Chardonnay, Vin de Pays d'Oc	£4.99	Europa
	Mâcon-Igé 1996 Les Vignerons d'Igé	£4.99	Budgens
Silver	Oaked Chardonnay 1996 Thomas Hardy, Safeway	£4.99	Safeway
Silver	Penfolds Koonunga Hill 1996 Chardonnay	£4.99	Waitrose
Bronze	Sainsbury's White Burgundy NV Guichard Potheret	£4.99	Sainsbury's
Bronze	Saint-Denis Fine White Burgundy NV Chardonnay	£4.99	Morrisons
Bronze	Valdivieso 1996 Chardonnay	£4.99	Asda
Bronze	Valdivieso 1996 Chardonnay	£4.99	Waitrose
	Redwood Trail Chardonnay 1994 By Sterling Vineyards	£5.49	Londis
Bronze	Top 40 Chardonnay NV Vin de Pays d'Oc, Foncalieu	£5.49	Waitrose
Silver	Kaituna Hills 1996 Chardonnay, St Michael	£5.50	M&S
Bronze	Wyndham Estate 1995 Oak Cask Chardonnay	£5.65	Morrisons

Chardonnay

	Schoone Gevel 1996 Chardonnay Reserve	£5.99	Tesco
Bronze	Chardonnay Viognier 1996 Juanico, St Michael	£5.99	M&S
Bronze	Wolf Blass Chardonnay Semillon 1996	£5.99	Londis
Silver	Saint-Véran 1996 Domaine des Deux Roches	£6.49	Asda
Silver	Vergelegen 1995 Chardonnay	£6.49	Safeway
Silver	Penfolds The Valleys 1995 Chardonnay	£6.95	Somerfield
Bronze	Chablis NV Guy Mothe, Asda	£6.99	Asda
	Jacana 1996 Chardonnay	£6.99	Somerfield
Gold	Mamre Brook 1995 Chardonnay	£6.99	Waitrose
	Montagny Premier Cru 1995 Les Vignes de la Croix, St Michael	£6.99	M&S
Bronze	Petit Chablis 1996 C.V.C., St Michael	£6.99	M&S
Silver	Riddoch 1994 Chardonnay	£6.99	Booths
Silver	Rosemount Estate 1996 Chardonnay	£6.99	Budgens
Silver	Réserve Chardonnay 1995 Vin de Pays d'Oc, Vignobles James Herrick	£6.99	Tesco
Silver	Saints 1995 Chardonnay, St Michael	£6.99	M&S
Bronze	Wolf Blass Chardonnay Barrel Fermented 1996	£6.99	Londis
Bronze	Chablis, Sainsbury's Classic Selection 1995 Domaine Sainte Céline	£7.45	Sainsbury's
Silver	Rosemount Estate 1995 Chardonnay, St Michael	£7.50	M&S
	Chablis 1994 Les Maitres Goustiers, SA L.R.	£7.99	Londis
Bronze	Chablis 1995 C.V.C., St Michael	£7.99	M&S
Silver	Château Reynella 1995 Chardonnay	£7.99	Asda
Bronze	Haan 1996 Barossa Valley Chardonnay, St Michael	£7.99	M&S
Bronze	Jamiesons Run 1996 Chardonnay	£7.99	Somerfield
	Ninth Island 1996 Chardonnay	£7.99	Booths
Silver	The Millton Vineyard 1995 Chardonnay, Barrel Fermented	£7.99	Safeway
Bronze	Vine Vale Vineyard 1996 Chardonnay, St Michael	£8.99	M&S
Gold	Rosemount Estate 1995 Chardonnay Show Reserve	£9.99	Waitrose

224 WHITE WINES

Silver	Chablis Premier Cru Fourchaume 1995 Domaine du Colombier	£10.99	**Asda**
	Chablis Premier Cru Fourchaume 1994 Domaine du Colombier	£11.99	**Asda**
Gold	Rosemount 1995 Orange Vineyard Chardonnay, St Michael	£11.99	**M&S**
Silver	Mas de Daumas Gassac 1995 Vin de Pays de l'Hérault	£15.49	**Booths**

Chenin Blanc

Dry style

Two Loire wines qualified, which was two more than the year before, but there were far more Vouvrays submitted than all the rest of the New World Chenin put together, and the solitary survivor is a terrible indictment of the Loire's ability to handle its most famous grape variety. South Africa has always made pleasant, easy-drinking wines from this grape, and is now beginning to turn out slightly more serious renditions – but if Burgundy is likely to benefit from flying winemakers, then the Loire desperately needs a flying doctor. Prices ranged from £2.79 to £5.99.

Silver	Jade Peaks 1996 Chenin Blanc	£2.79	**Kwik Save**
Bronze	Chenin Blanc NV Vin de Pays du Jardin de la France, Tesco	£2.99	**Tesco**
Bronze	Impala 1996 Cape White	£2.99	**Kwik Save**
Bronze	South African Dry White NV W1226, Somerfield	£2.99	**Somerfield**
Silver	Chenin Blanc 1996 Barrel Fermented, Ryland's Grove	£3.99	**Tesco**
Silver	Fairview 1996 Chenin Blanc	£3.99	**Waitrose**
Bronze	Long Mountain 1995 Chenin Blanc	£3.99	**Londis**
Silver	Vouvray 1996 Hand Picked, Denis Marchais	£4.99	**Asda**

French Vins de Pays

Chardonnay dominates, but it is not the only grape available. Prices ranged from £2.99 to the equivalent of £5.98.

	Valblanc 1995 Colombard, Vin de Pays du Gers	£2.79	**Budgens**
	Vin de Pays de l'Aude White NV Foncalieu, Morrisons	£2.89	**Morrisons**
Bronze	Chenin Blanc NV Vin de Pays du Jardin de la France, Tesco	£2.99	**Tesco**
	Skylark Hill Very Special White NV Vin de Pays d'Oc, Kwik Save	£2.99	**Kwik Save**
Bronze	Vin de Pays des Côtes-de-Gascogne 1995 DG 32800, Somerfield	£2.99	**Somerfield**
Bronze	Vin de Pays des Côtes-de-Gascogne 1996 Asda	£2.99	**Asda**
	Vin de Pays du Gers 1996 St Michael	£2.99	**M&S**
Bronze	Domaine L'Argentier 1995 Terret, Vin de Pays des Côtes-de-Thau	£3.49	**Budgens**
Bronze	Great with Fish 1996 Vin de Pays de l'Aude, Tesco	£3.49	**Tesco**
Bronze	La Coume de Peyre 1996 Vin de Pays des Côtes-de-Gascogne	£3.49	**Safeway**
Silver	Montagne Noire 1996 Sauvignon Blanc, Vin de Pays d'Oc, Asda	£3.49	**Asda**
	Vin de Pays des Côtes-de-Gascogne 1996 Patrick Azcué, St Michael	£3.49	**M&S**
Bronze	Domaine Bordeneuve 1996 Vin de Pays des Côtes-de-Gascogne	£3.65	**Somerfield**
Silver	Domaine de Planterieu 1996 Vin de Pays des Côtes-de-Gascogne, Maïté Dubuc-Grassa	£3.65	**Waitrose**
Bronze	Domaine de Saubagnère 1995 Sauvignon Colombard, Vin de Pays des Côtes-de-Gascogne	£3.99	**Tesco**
	Domaine Saubagnère 1995 Vin de Pays des Côtes-de-Gascogne, Les Domaines, Tesco	£3.99	**Tesco**

WHITE WINES

	Domaine Villeroy-Castellas 1996 Sauvignon Blanc, Vin de Pays des Sables du Golfe du Lion	£3.99	**Budgens**
Bronze	Montagne Noire Chardonnay 1996 Vin de Pays d'Oc, Asda	£3.99	**Asda**
	Sauvignon Blanc Vin de Pays d'Oc NV Foncalieu, Co-op	£3.99	**Co-op**
	Domaine Mandeville Chardonnay 1996 Vin de Pays d'Oc, St Michael	£4.49	**M&S**
Bronze	Virginie 1995 Vermentino, Vin de Pays d'Oc	£4.69	**Booths**
Gold	Chardonnay par Yves Grassa 1996 Barrel Fermented, Vin de Pays des Côtes-de-Gascogne	£4.99	**Asda**
Bronze	Cuckoo Hill Oak Barrel Chardonnay 1995 Vin de Pays d'Oc	£4.99	**Co-operative**
Silver	Cuckoo Hill Viognier NV Vin de Pays d'Oc	£4.99	**Asda**
Bronze	Cuckoo Hill Viognier 1995 Vin de Pays d'Oc	£4.99	**Co-operative**
Gold	Grande Cuvée Chardonnay 1995 Laroche, Vin de Pays d'Oc	£4.99	**Budgens**
Silver	James Herrick 1996 Chardonnay, Vin de Pays d'Oc	£4.99	**Somerfield**
Silver	James Herrick 1995 Chardonnay, Vin de Pays d'Oc	£4.99	**Europa**
Silver	La Baume Sauvignon Blanc 1996 Vin de Pays d'Oc, Philippe de Baudin	£4.99	**Safeway**
	La Domeque, Tête de Cuvée 1996 Vieilles Vignes Blanc, Vin de Pays d'Oc	£4.99	**Asda**
Bronze	Top 40 Chardonnay NV Vin de Pays d'Oc, Foncalieu	£5.49	**Waitrose**
Silver	Réserve Chardonnay 1995 Vin de Pays d'Oc, Vignobles James Herrick	£6.99	**Tesco**
Silver	Mas de Daumas Gassac 1995 Vin de Pays de l'Hérault	£15.49	**Booths**

German-style

This medium-sweet category encompasses the likes of Liebfraumilch, Hock, Niersteiner, Piesporter *et al*, and I am as surprised as anyone to have awarded two gold medals in this section. Prices ranged from just £2.17 to £3.99.

Bronze	Hock NV Peter Bott	£2.17	Kwik Save
Bronze	Hock 1996 K. Linden, Kwik Save	£4.35	Kwik Save
Bronze	Hock NV Maas Nathan, Tesco	£2.19	Tesco
Bronze	Hock Deutscher Tafelwein NV Zeller Barl Kellerei, Londis	£2.69	Londis
Bronze	Piesporter Michelsberg 1996 K. Linden	£2.97	Kwik Save
Bronze	Langenbach Kabinett 1995 Binger St.-Rochuskapelle	£2.99	Co-operative
Gold	Liebfraumilch 1996 Rheinhessen, St Michael	£2.99	M&S
Silver	Mosel Deutscher Tafelwein NV St.-Urbanus Weinkellerei, Co-op	£2.99	Co-op
Silver	Niersteiner Gutes Domtal NV Zeller Barl Kellerei, Londis	£2.99	Londis
Bronze	Sainsbury's Mosel NV Ehemalig Kurfürstliche Weinkellerei	£2.99	Sainsbury's
Gold	St.-Laurens 1996 QbA Pfalz	£2.99	Kwik Save
Silver	Hock 1996 Deutscher Tafelwein Rhein, St Michael	£3.99	M&S
Bronze	Cape Afrika 1996 Rhine Riesling	£3.99	Co-op
Bronze	Zimmermann NV Rivaner	£3.99	Morrisons

Gewurztraminer

These wines should be big, fat and spicy with relatively low acidity. They often have more than a touch of sweetness to enhance the fruit, although the drier the better for everyday drinking. Prices ranged from £2.79 to £9.49.

	Classic Gewurztraminer 1995 Posta Romana	£2.79	Co-operative

	Fairview 1996 Gewürztraminer	£3.99	Asda
Bronze	Preiss-Zimmer Gewurztraminer 1995 Vin d'Alsace Tradition	£5.29	Morrisons
Silver	Gewurztraminer Vin d'Alsace 1996 Cave des Vignerons Turckheim, Somerfield	£5.95	Somerfield

Italy

Not a great deal of fun here, but a considerable improvement on last year, when Italian whites were not worth including in their own right. Prices ranged from £2.19 to £6.75.

	Soave NV Venier	£2.67	Kwik Save
	Frascati Superiore 1995 Tuscolana Esportazioni, Co-op	£3.69	Co-op
	Orvieto Classico 1996 Cantina del Coppiere, St Michael	£3.99	M&S
Bronze	Trentino Chardonnay 1996 La Vis, Asda	£3.99	Asda
	Colli di Catone 1995 Frascati Superiore, Asda	£3.99	Asda
Bronze	Le Trulle 1996 Chardonnay	£4.39	Somerfield
Bronze	Colombara 1996 Soave Classico, Zenato	£4.95	Waitrose
	Bianco di Custoza 1996 La Casella, St Michael	£4.99	M&S

Medium Dry

This did not include Riesling, or indeed any German wines, but did encompass medium-dry wines that do not belong to any other white wine category and a Bordeaux simply because it tasted more medium than dry. A number of wines were flabby, but too many simply lacked freshness. See also Riesling (Medium-to-sweet style) and German style. Prices ranged from £2.75 to £4.49.

Bronze	Denbies 95 1995	£2.99	Kwik Save
Silver	Muscat Ottonel 1995 Nagyréde Estate	£2.99	Co-operative
Silver	Hungarian Pinot Gris NV Szölöskert Cooperative, Sainsbury's	£3.19	Sainsbury's

| Bronze | Australian Medium Dry NV Southcorp Wines, St Michael | £3.99 | **M&S** |
| Silver | TR2 Medium Dry White Wine 1995 Reserve, Wyndham Estate | £3.99 | **Morrisons** |

Muscadet

Generally there were more Muscadet of better quality, but none that reached the heights of last year's two silver medal winners. Prices ranged from £2.99 to £5.99.

	Muscadet 1996 Jean Michel	£2.79	**Kwik Save**
	Muscadet 1996 Les Celliers de la Sanguèze	£2.95	**Sainsbury's**
	Muscadet NV Les Celliers du Prieuré, Tesco	£3.99	**Tesco**
	Muscadet de Sèvre-et-Maine Sur Lie 1996 Pierre Guéry, Waitrose	£4.35	**Waitrose**
Bronze	Muscadet de Sèvre-et-Maine Sur Lie 1995 Domaine de la Haute Maillardière	£4.39	**Co-op**
	Muscadet de Sèvre-et-Maine Sur Lie 1995 Domaine Gautron	£4.49	**Asda**
	Muscadet de Sèvre-et-Maine Sur Lie 1995 Sainsbury's Classic Selection	£5.95	**Sainsbury's**

New Zealand

This antipodean wine-producing country is best known for Sauvignon Blanc, which it has propelled to superstar status, but New Zealand can also produce vibrant Chardonnay. Prices ranged from £3.39 to £8.99.

	Waimanu NV Premium Dry White Wine	£3.99	**Budgens**
Bronze	Cooks 1996 Sauvignon Blanc	£4.99	**Co-operative**
Silver	Kaituna Hills 1996 Chardonnay, St Michael	£5.50	**M&S**
Silver	Kaituna Hills 1996 Sauvignon Blanc, St Michael	£5.50	**M&S**

WHITE WINES

Gold	Villa Maria Private Bin 1996 Sauvignon Blanc	£6.49	**Booths**
Silver	Saints 1995 Chardonnay, St Michael	£6.99	**M&S**
Silver	Sacred Hill 1995 Whitecliff Sauvignon Blanc	£6.99	**Morrisons**
Gold	Coopers Creek 1996 Sauvignon Blanc	£7.49	**Somerfield**
Gold	Jackson Estate 1996 Sauvignon Blanc	£7.99	**Tesco**
Silver	The Millton Vineyard 1995 Chardonnay, Barrel Fermented	£7.99	**Safeway**
Gold	Lawson's Dry Hills 1996 Sauvignon Blanc	£7.99	**Waitrose**

Pinot Blanc

A generally disappointing category for what is one of the best-value Alsace varietals. Italy's Pinot Bianco invariably fails to hit the spot. Prices ranged from £3.29 to £4.99.

	Pinot Blanc 1996 Nagyréde Estate	£3.29	**Safeway**
Bronze	Pinot Blanc 1995 Vin d'Alsace, Cave Vinicole d'Ingersheim	£4.99	**Co-operative**

Pinot Gris

Another grape that is at its absolute best in Alsace, where it has a rich, heady, spicy character not normally found in Pinot Gris wines made elsewhere. Generally the spice is not so pungent as in Gewurztraminer, and hardly ever occurs, even in the mildest format, outside Alsace itself. To judge from the few samples submitted, the supermarkets do not appear to be interested in Pinot Gris. Prices ranged from £2.99 to £3.99

Silver	Bodega Jacques y Francois Lurton 1996 Pinot Gris	£3.99	**Waitrose**

Riesling

Dry style

After last year, when no German Dry Riesling deserved a medal, it's nice to see one getting the highest ranking in the category this time – but can we please have a few more submitted? Prices ranged from £2.99 to £6.99.

Silver	Kendermann 1995 Riesling Dry	£3.99	**Co-operative**
Bronze	Penfolds Rawson's Retreat Bin 202 1996 Riesling	£3.99	**Asda**
Bronze	Jacob's Creek 1996 Dry Riesling, Orlando	£4.59	**Co-operative**

Riesling

Medium-to-sweet style

In its medium-to-sweet style, the Riesling is supreme, but it's not often that you will find such supreme examples in a supermarket range. Prices ranged from £4.69 to the equivalent of £11.78.

Bronze	Scharzhofberger Riesling Kabinett 1995 Müller-Burggraef	£4.85	**Somerfield**
Bronze	Schloss Schönborn 1989 Geisenheimer Mäuerchen Riesling Spätlese	£5.95	**Waitrose**
Silver	Weingut Toni Jost 1994 Bacharacher Schloss Stahleck Riesling Kabinett	£6.95	**Waitrose**
Silver	Niederhäuser Hermannsberg Riesling Spätlese 1992 Staatliche Weinbaudomäne	£5.89	**Tesco**

Sauvignon Blanc

Most of the Sauvignon Blanc that did not survive the tasting assault course were French and primarily Loire, including a lot of Sancerre and Pouilly Fumé. New Zealand is now the king of Sauvignon, and whether French or Kiwi, the wine from this grape should be fresh and zesty.

232 WHITE WINES

New Zealand has the advantage of being able to ripen Sauvignon Blanc to a beautiful degree, yet retain refreshing acidity. Prices ranged from £2.95 to £8.99.

Bronze	Hungarian Sauvignon Blanc 1995 Private Reserve, Neszmély Winery	£3.29	Asda
Bronze	Chilean Sauvignon Blanc 1996 Vinicola Las Taguas, Asda	£3.49	Asda
Silver	Montagne Noire 1996 Sauvignon Blanc, Vin de Pays d'Oc, Asda	£3.49	Asda
Bronze	Sainsbury's Bordeaux Sauvignon NV Jean-Paul Jauffret	£3.49	Sainsbury's
Bronze	Sauvignon Blanc NV Bordeaux, Co-op	£3.49	Co-op
	Sauvignon Blanc NV Stowells of Chelsea	£14.59	Co-operative
	Castel Pujol 1996 Sauvignon Blanc	£3.99	Co-operative
Bronze	Chilean Sauvignon Blanc NV Sagrada Familia, Somerfield	£3.99	Somerfield
Bronze	Chilean Sauvignon Blanc 1996 Viña San Pedro, Safeway	£3.99	Safeway
Bronze	Chilean Sauvignon Blanc NV Sagrada Familia, Somerfield	£3.99	Somerfield
	Domaine Villeroy-Castellas 1996 Sauvignon Blanc, Vin de Pays des Sables du Golfe du Lion	£3.99	Budgens
Bronze	Fiuza 1995 Sauvignon	£3.99	Co-op
	Perdeberg Cellar 1996 Sauvignon Blanc, St Michael	£3.99	M&S
Bronze	Sauvignon Blanc 1996 Viña San Pedro, St Michael	£3.99	M&S
	Sauvignon Blanc 1996 Welmoed Winery	£3.99	Co-op
	Sauvignon Blanc Vin de Pays d'Oc NV Foncalieu, Co-op	£3.99	Co-op
Bronze	Touraine 1995 Sauvignon Blanc, BRL Hardy	£3.99	Safeway
	Château Lamothe Vincent 1996 Sauvignon	£4.19	Booths
	Sauvignon Blanc 1996 Welmoed Winery	£4.39	Booths
Bronze	Casablanca 1996 Sauvignon Blanc	£4.99	Co-op
Bronze	Cooks 1996 Sauvignon Blanc	£4.99	Co-operative
Silver	La Baume Sauvignon Blanc 1996 Vin de Pays d'Oc, Philippe de Baudin	£4.99	Safeway

Silver	Kaituna Hills 1996 Sauvignon Blanc, St Michael	£5.50	**M&S**
Gold	Villa Maria Private Bin 1996 Sauvignon Blanc	£6.49	**Booths**
Silver	Sacred Hill 1995 Whitecliff Sauvignon Blanc	£6.99	**Morrisons**
Gold	Coopers Creek 1996 Sauvignon Blanc	£7.49	**Somerfield**
Gold	Pouilly-Fumé 1996 Domaine J.M. Masson-Blondelet	£7.49	**Waitrose**
Gold	Jackson Estate 1996 Sauvignon Blanc	£7.99	**Tesco**
Gold	Lawson's Dry Hills 1996 Sauvignon Blanc	£7.99	**Waitrose**
Bronze	Thelema 1996 Sauvignon Blanc	£8.75	**Waitrose**
Gold	Katnook Estate 1996 Sauvignon Blanc	£8.99	**Booths**

Semillon

Pure and blended

The best dry Semillon wines are Australian, with their wonderful lime-fruit flavours. Although Sauvignon is Semillon's traditional blending partner, sometimes the cheaper Colombard performs a similar function, and there is a growing New World tendency to team this Bordeaux grape with Burgundy's Chardonnay. Prices ranged from £3.56 to £8.99.

Bronze	Barramundi NV Semillon/Chardonnay	£9.49	**Co-op**
Bronze	Southern Creek 1996 Semillon-Chardonnay, Hardys	£3.99	**Waitrose**
Silver	Barramundi NV Semillon/Colombard/Chardonnay	£4.29	**Booths**
Bronze	Peter Lehmann 1996 Semillon	£4.99	**Asda**
Bronze	Peter Lehmann 1996 Semillon	£4.99	**Safeway**
Bronze	Honey Tree Semillon Chardonnay 1996 Rosemount Estate, St Michael	£5.50	**M&S**
Bronze	Penfolds Barossa Valley 1996 Semillon-Chardonnay	£5.99	**Asda**
Silver	Penfolds 1994 Barrel Fermented Semillon	£5.99	**Waitrose**
Bronze	Peter Lehmann 1996 Semillon	£5.99	**Co-operative**
Silver	Leasingham Domaine 1993 Semillon	£6.49	**Co-op**

WHITE WINES

Bronze	Rosemount Estate 1996 Semillon Chardonnay	£6.49	Asda

Sweet or Dessert Wine Style

Anyone who steadfastly refuses to touch a sweet wine should buy the Lindemans and simply sniff it. Prices ranged from £2.59 to £19.50.

	Flamenco NV Spanish Sweet White	£2.59	Kwik Save
Bronze	Tamaioasa 1995 Pietroasa Estate	£3.89	Co-operative
Bronze	Monbazillac 1995 Les Caves Saint-Romain	£4.49	Co-operative
Bronze	Kirchheimer Schwarzerde Beerenauslese 1994 Zimmermann-Graeff	£3.99	Co-op
Bronze	Monbazillac Cuvée Prestige 1994 Domaine du Haut-Rauly	£3.99	Co-op
Gold	Lindemans 1994 Coonawarra Botrytis Riesling	£5.99	Somerfield
Silver	Brown Brothers 1995 Late Harvested Riesling	£6.99	Waitrose

Viognier

The Rhône Valley's very special and quite mysterious grape, Viognier is responsible for the Rhône's Condrieu, the best of which are highly perfumed, wonderfully fresh, with delicate, peachy fruit. None of these Viognier have the peachy character of the grape, but do share Condrieu's characteristic of being best drunk young; they make nice, floral-fresh alternatives to Chardonnay.

Bronze	Cuckoo Hill Viognier 1995 Vin de Pays d'Oc	£4.99	Co-operative
Silver	Cuckoo Hill Viognier NV Vin de Pays d'Oc	£4.99	Asda

ROSÉ WINES

Dry and Off-dry

Technically the most difficult style in which to produce something that stands out. Prices ranged from £2.59 to £4.99.

Bronze	Cabernet de Saumur Rosé NV Cave des Vignerons de Saumur, Tesco	£3.29	**Tesco**
Bronze	Winter Hill Rosé 1996 Vin de Pays de l'Aude	£3.29	**Waitrose**
Bronze	Chilean Cabernet Sauvignon Rosé NV Sainsbury's	£3.49	**Sainsbury's**
	Balbi Vineyard 1996 Syrah Rosé	£3.69	**Co-op**
	Hardys Grenache Shiraz 1996 Stamps of Australia	£4.49	**Co-operative**
Silver	Domaine de Sours 1996 Bordeaux Rosé	£4.99	**Sainsbury's**

Medium to Medium-sweet

Technically the easiest rosé style to produce, because the residual sugar hides mistakes, enhances the fruit and generally flatters the palate – although you wouldn't think so, considering how difficult it is to find anything drinkable, let alone interesting. Prices range from £3.19 to £4.29.

Bronze	Rosé d'Anjou NV Co-op	£3.19	**Co-op**
Bronze	Van Loveren 1996 Blanc de Noir Red Muscadel	£3.49	**Tesco**
Bronze	Blossom Hill Winery 1995 White Zinfandel	£4.29	**Londis**

SPARKLING WINES

Brut or Dry Sparkling Wine

Champagnes will always dominate this category, but it has been difficult for those used to drinking good-quality Champagne to find an alternative that satisfies them. Unfortunately, the quality of this year's Cava did not match that of last year's. Prices ranged from £3.99 to £22.99.

Bronze	Australian Sparking Wine NV Brut Reserve, Seppelt, Safeway	£4.99	Safeway
	Cava Brunet NV Brut Reserva	£4.99	Kwik Save
	Barramundi NV Brut	£5.49	Co-op
Bronze	Yaldara Rosé NV Reserve Brut	£5.75	Booths
	Codorníu Première Cuvée NV Brut Chardonnay	£6.49	Co-operative
	Seaview Rosé NV Brut	£6.49	Asda
	Seaview Rosé NV Brut	£6.49	Co-operative
Bronze	Chapel Down Epoch NV Brut	£6.99	Booths
Silver	Cranswick Pinot Chardonnay NV Brut	£6.99	Asda
Silver	Krone Borealis 1993 Brut	£6.99	Waitrose
	Lindauer NV Brut	£7.49	Booths
	Freixenet Cava NV Cordon Negro Brut	£7.69	Londis
Silver	Australian Chardonnay Blanc de Blancs 1994 Brut, Seppelt, St Michael	£7.99	M&S
Gold	Seaview Pinot Noir Chardonnay 1994 Brut	£8.49	Somerfield
Gold	Seaview Pinot Noir Chardonnay 1993 Brut	£8.49	Sainsbury's
	Yalumba Cuvée One Prestige NV Pinot Noir/Chardonnay	£8.49	Sainsbury's
Bronze	Yalumba Cuvée Two Prestige NV Cabernet Sauvignon	£8.49	Tesco
	Monastrell Xarel-lo NV Cava Brut, Freixenet	£8.99	Europa

Brut or Dry Sparkling Wine

Silver	Seppelt 1992 Sparkling Shiraz Bottle Fermented	£8.99	**Tesco**
	Gloria Ferrer Blanc de Noirs NV Freixenet Sonoma Caves	£9.49	**Europa**
Silver	Scharffenberger NV Brut	£9.49	**Asda**
Silver	Champagne André Simon NV Brut	£10.99	**Londis**
Silver	Champagne Paul Hérard NV Blanc de Noirs Brut	£11.39	**Morrisons**
Silver	Asda Champagne NV Brut Réserve, Cuvée Speciale	£11.99	**Asda**
	Champagne Prince William NV Brut Reserve	£11.99	**Somerfield**
	Sainsbury's Champagne NV Blanc de Noirs Brut	£11.99	**Sainsbury's**
Silver	Booths Champagne NV Brut	£12.69	**Booths**
Bronze	Sainsbury's Champagne NV Extra Dry, Duval-Leroy	£12.95	**Sainsbury's**
Bronze	Sainsbury's Champagne NV Brut Rosé, Beaumet	£13.95	**Sainsbury's**
Gold	Waitrose Champagne Blanc de Blancs NV Brut, NM-123	£13.95	**Waitrose**
	Champagne Veuve de Medts NV Brut Premier Cru, St Michael	£13.99	**M&S**
Silver	Tesco Champagne Blanc de Blancs NV Brut Cuvée Speciale	£13.99	**Tesco**
Gold	Quartet NV Brut	£14.95	**Waitrose**
Silver	Sainsbury's Vintage Champagne 1991 Blanc de Blancs Brut, UVCB	£14.95	**Sainsbury's**
Bronze	Champagne Prince William NV Blanc de Blancs Brut	£15.29	**Somerfield**
Gold	Champagne Prince William NV Rosé Brut	£15.29	**Somerfield**
	Champagne Jacquart NV Brut Tradition	£15.39	**Europa**
Gold	Champagne Chartogne-Taillet NV Brut, Cuvée Sainte-Anne	£15.99	**Safeway**
Silver	Champagne Lanson NV Black Label Brut	£18.49	**Co-operative**
Silver	Champagne Cuvée Orpale 1985 Blanc de Blancs Brut, St Michael	£22.50	**M&S**
Silver	Champagne Taittinger NV Brut Réserve	£22.99	**Budgens**

Sweet Sparkling Wine

These need to be as fresh, pure and fruity as possible, which means getting the wine off its yeast as soon as the fermentation is over and drinking it as quickly as possible. Prices ranged from £1.45 to £6.45.

Bronze	Lambrusco 4 NV GI SpA	£2.89	Kwik Save
Bronze	Asti NV Rialto	£4.29	Co-operative
	Asti Dolce NV Perlino, Safeway	£5.49	Safeway
	Sainsbury's Asti NV Casa Vinicola IVASS	£5.49	Sainsbury's
	Asti NV Tosti, St Michael	£5.99	M&S
Bronze	Comtesse de Die Tradition 1995 Clairette de Die, Première Cuvée	£6.45	Waitrose

FORTIFIED WINE

Port: Early-bottled Styles

This encompassed everything from cheap ruby through LBV and crusted to the most expensive vintage port. Although LBV stands for Late-Bottled Vintage, it's not out of place in the early-bottled category, as the emphasis is on vintage and vintage is an early-bottled style – so it's sort of late–early bottled! All early-bottled styles are ruby in colour and retain a fruitiness in bottle that tawny lack (although they have a smoothness and cask-matured complexity that early-bottled ports do not possess). There were no New World port-styles submitted for this edition, and the general quality of the ports entered was nowhere near as high as last year. Prices ranged from £4.99 to £14.95.

	Ruby Port NV Smith Woodhouse, Asda	£4.99	Asda
Silver	Finest Special Reserve Port NV Real Companhia, Tesco	£5.49	Tesco
Silver	Vintage Character Port NV Smith Woodhouse, Asda	£5.49	Asda
Gold	LBV Port 1990 Smith Woodhouse, Asda	£6.49	Asda
Bronze	Fine Vintage Character Port NV Smith Woodhouse, Co-op	£6.59	Co-op
Silver	Late Bottled Vintage Port 1991 Smith Woodhouse, Co-op	£6.99	Co-op
Silver	Rozès 1991 Late Bottled Vintage Port	£6.99	Morrisons
Bronze	Sainsbury's Vintage Character Port NV Taylor Fladgate & Yeatman	£6.99	Sainsbury's
Gold	Vintage Character Port NV Morgan Brothers, St Michael	£6.99	M&S
Bronze	The Navigators 1989 LBV Port, Somerfield	£7.15	Somerfield
Gold	LBV Port 1990 Smith Woodhouse, Tesco	£7.29	Tesco
Silver	Waitrose Late Bottled Vintage Port 1990 Bottled in 1996 by Smith Woodhouse	£7.85	Waitrose

Silver	Late Bottled Vintage Port 1988 Morgan Brothers, St Michael	£7.99	**M&S**
Bronze	Rozès 1992 Late Bottled Vintage Port	£7.99	**Budgens**
Silver	Sainsbury's LBV Port 1990 Temilobos	£7.99	**Sainsbury's**
Gold	Booths Finest Reserve Port NV Quinta da Rosa	£8.15	**Booths**
Bronze	Cockburn's Special Reserve Port NV	£8.99	**Asda**
Silver	Porto Souza 1991 L.B.V.	£8.99	**Co-operative**
Silver	Cockburn's Anno 1989 Late Bottled Vintage Port	£9.99	**Morrisons**
Gold	Graham's Late Bottled Vintage Port 1991	£9.99	**Asda**
Bronze	W.& J. Graham's Six Grapes Port NV	£11.99	**Tesco**
Bronze	Warre's 1982 Traditional Late Bottled Vintage Port	£13.95	**Waitrose**
Gold	Sainsbury's Vintage Port 1985 Quinta Dona Matilde	£14.95	**Sainsbury's**

Port: Late-bottled Styles

Essentially tawny ports. Cheap tawny ports are merely a blend of red and white ports: seldom exciting, but occasionally surprisingly good. Real tawny ports have a cask-aged colour, smoothness and complexity (often coffee-caramel) that can only be achieved through extended maturation in wood. The best tawnies are 10, 20 and 30 Year Old, but do not be mistaken: these are not the guaranteed minimum age. They merely represent a style of age that the wines must adhere to in an official blind tasting test. In theory, a 30 Year Old Tawny could be 12 months old, but in practice the composite age of most of these wines will be close to that indicated. Prices ranged from £4.99 to £13.45.

Gold	Yaldara Old Tawny NV Reserve	£5.99	**Co-operative**
Bronze	Tawny Port NV Morgan Brothers, St Michael	£6.99	**M&S**
Silver	10 Year Old Tawny Port NV Smith Woodhouse, Tesco	£9.99	**Tesco**
Silver	10 Years Old Port NV Morgan Brothers, St Michael	£9.99	**M&S**
Silver	Noval NV 10 Year Old Tawny Port	£13.45	**Waitrose**

Sherry

After last year's disappointing tasting, I'm happy to say that some very exciting Sherries were submitted this time, especially in the sweeter and more mature styles. Prices ranged from £3.59 to the equivalent of £19.90 a bottle.

Silver	Sainsbury's Oloroso NV Old Dry Sherry, Morgan Bros	£3.29	Sainsbury's
Silver	Amontillado Sherry NV Morrisons	£3.59	Morrisons
Bronze	Waitrose Oloroso Sherry NV Medium Sweet, Emilio Lustau	£4.65	Waitrose
Bronze	Cream Sherry NV Williams & Humbert, St Michael	£4.99	M&S
	Rich Cream Sherry NV Williams & Humbert, St Michael	£4.99	M&S
	Dry Oloroso Sherry NV Solera Jerezana, Waitrose	£5.25	Waitrose
Bronze	Rich Cream Sherry NV Solera Jerezana, Waitrose	£5.25	Waitrose
Bronze	Dry Amontillado Sherry NV Solera Jerezana, Waitrose	£5.25	Waitrose
Bronze	Dry Fly Medium Sherry NV Amontillado, Findlater's	£5.75	Waitrose
	Manzanilla Superior Sherry NV Sanchez Romate, Tesco	£3.35	Tesco
Bronze	Pedro Ximénez Cream of Cream NV Alvear, Sainsbury's	£3.95	Sainsbury's
Gold	Lustau Solera Reserva Fine Sherry NV Pedro Ximénez San Emilio	£10.99	Booths
Gold	Apostoles Palo Cortado Muy Viejo NV Gonzalez Byass	£9.95	Waitrose
Gold	Matusalem Oloroso Dulce Muy Viejo NV Gonzalez Byass	£9.95	Waitrose

Liqueur Muscat

Sweet, fortified Muscat is probably the oldest fortified wine style in the world and Spanish Moscatel must be one of the most ancient, yet cheap Valencia Moscatel is a modern wonder. So vivacious and fresh is it that it has eclipsed the quality of just a few years ago, and I sometimes wonder what competition judges might make of these wines if they were submitted into Sélection de Grains Nobles tastings at ten times their commercial price! Prices ranged from £2.99 to the equivalent of £11.98 per bottle.

Gold	Castillo de Liria NV Moscatel	£2.99	Kwik Save
Gold	Moscatel de Valencia NV Vicente Gandia, Somerfield	£3.39	Somerfield
Gold	Moscatel de Valencia 1995 Vicente Gandia, Safeway	£3.59	Safeway
Gold	Muscat de Frontignan Blanc 1996 Danie de Wet	£4.99	Asda
Bronze	Frontignan NV Vin de Liqueur	£5.49	Somerfield
Bronze	Dom Brial Muscat de Rivesaltes 1996	£3.99	Co-operative
Gold	Mick Morris Liqueur Muscat NV Rutherglen	£4.99	Sainsbury's
Bronze	Rothbury NV Museum Reserve Liqueur Muscat	£5.49	Co-op

BEER

Bitter or Traditional Ale Style

Without widgets

An English term for a well-hopped draught ale that is typically copper-coloured with ruddy glints and has a slight but distinctive bitter taste unspoilt by the fizziness of CO_2. It is unrealistic to expect the so-called bitter sold in a can or bottle to have any semblance of true draught bitter character, unless the residual gas is reduced to a minimal level and the consumer urged to pour the bitter from a great height. Most bitter is 3.75 to 4 per cent ABV, although Best or Special will be 4 to 4.75 per cent and some go as high as 5.5 per cent. Prices ranged from an equivalent of 47p per pint to £2.15.

Bronze	Aston Manor Best Bitter	£0.47	Kwik Save
	Parkin's Special Bitter Sainsbury's	£0.79	Sainsbury's
Bronze	York's Northern Bitter St Michael	£0.80	M&S
Bronze	IPA Draught Bitter Greene King	£0.85	Budgens
Bronze	Safeway Strong Bitter	£0.93	Safeway
	Tesco Strong Yorkshire Bitter	£0.98	Tesco
Bronze	John Smith's Bitter Tadcaster Brewery	£1.01	Londis
Gold	Ward's Classic Yorkshire Ale	£1.02	Booths
Bronze	Cains Formidable Ale	£1.13	Co-op
	Double Maxim Premium Vaux	£1.26	Co-op
Bronze	Caledonian 70/- Amber Ale Caledonian Brewery	£1.35	Co-op
	Ushers Founders Strong Ale	£1.42	Co-op
Silver	Bishops Finger Kentish Strong Ale Shepherd Neame	£1.42	Booths
Bronze	Black Douglas Broughton Ales	£1.42	Booths
Bronze	Two Pints Bitter Cropton Brewery	£1.42	Booths
Silver	Waggle Dance Traditional Honey Beer Vaux	£1.44	Booths
Bronze	Adnams Suffolk Strong Ale	£1.44	Sainsbury's
Bronze	Marston's Pedigree Bitter	£1.45	Booths

244 BEER

	Bombardier Premium Bitter Charles Wells	£1.47	Booths
Gold	Booth & Co. Ltd Anniversary Ale 1847–1997	£1.47	Booths
Gold	Daniels Hammer Strong Ale Thwaites	£1.47	Morrisons
Silver	Gentleman Jack Strong Ale Shepherd Neame, Asda	£1.47	Asda
Silver	Landlord Timothy Taylor's Strong Pale Ale	£1.47	Booths
Bronze	Master Brew Premium Ale Bottle Conditioned, Shepherd Neame	£1.47	Co-op
Bronze	Pendle Witches Brew Strong Lancashire Ale, Moorhouse's	£1.47	Booths
Bronze	Pendle Witches Brew Strong Lancashire Ale, Moorhouse's	£1.47	Morrisons
Silver	Traditional Premium Ale Caledonian, St Michael	£1.47	M&S
Silver	Bass Our Finest Ale	£1.49	Booths
Bronze	Marston's Pedigree Bitter	£1.49	Morrisons
Silver	Festive Ale Bottle Conditioned, King & Barnes	£1.50	Tesco
Silver	Coopers Sparkling Ale	£1.50	Safeway
Gold	Black Sheep Ale Paul Theakston's Black Sheep Brewery	£1.53	Co-op
Gold	Black Sheep Ale Paul Theakston's Black Sheep Brewery	£1.53	Tesco
Gold	Black Sheep Ale Paul Theakston's Black Sheep Brewery	£1.53	Morrisons
	Brewers Droop Marston Moor Brewery	£1.53	Morrisons
Bronze	Caledonian 80/- Export Ale Caledonian Brewery	£1.53	Co-op
Bronze	Cocker Hoop Golden Bitter Jennings Brothers	£1.53	Booths
	Greenmantle Ale Broughton Ales	£1.53	Co-op
Bronze	Master Brew Premium Ale Bottle Conditioned, Shepherd Neame	£1.53	Londis
Bronze	Old Fart Premium Strength Beer, Merrimans Brewery	£1.53	Morrisons
	Uncle Sams Bitter Cropton Brewery	£1.53	Booths
Bronze	Tennent's Robert Burns Scottish Ale	£1.54	Co-op

Bitter or Traditional Ale Style

Silver	Waggle Dance Traditional Honey Beer Vaux	£1.54	Co-op
Silver	Waggle Dance Traditional Honey Beer Vaux	£1.54	Morrisons
Silver	Waggle Dance Traditional Honey Beer Vaux	£1.54	Safeway
Gold	Ward's Classic Yorkshire Ale	£1.54	Co-op
Bronze	Marston's Pedigree Bitter	£1.55	Co-op
Silver	Backwoods Bitter Cropton Brewery	£1.58	Booths
Gold	Black Sheep Ale Paul Theakston's Black Sheep Brewery Paul Theakston	£1.58	Booths
Gold	Black Sheep Ale Paul Theakston's Black Sheep Brewery Paul Theakston	£1.58	Safeway
Gold	Bob's Gold Ruddles Character Ales	£1.58	Booths
	Cumberland Ale Jennings Brothers	£1.58	Co-op
	Cumberland Ale Jennings Brothers	£1.58	Morrisons
Bronze	Formidable Ale Cains	£1.58	Booths
Gold	Fuller's London Pride Premium Ale	£1.58	Booths
Silver	Monkmans Slaughter Bitter Cropton Brewery	£1.58	Booths
Silver	Spitfire Bottle Conditioned Ale Shepherd Neame	£1.58	Booths
	White Rabbit Premium Beer Mansfield Brewery	£1.58	Co-op
Silver	Bass Our Finest Ale	£1.59	Co-operative
Bronze	Marston's Pedigree Bitter	£1.59	Co-operative
Bronze	Tennent's Robert Burns Scottish Ale	£1.60	Safeway
Silver	Waggle Dance Traditional Honey Beer Vaux	£1.64	Co-operative
Silver	Waggle Dance Traditional Honey Beer Vaux	£1.64	Tesco
	Fuller's Refreshing Summer Ale	£1.65	Safeway
Bronze	Merlin's Ale Broughton Ales	£1.65	Co-op
Bronze	Old Jock Ale Broughton Ales	£1.65	Co-op
Silver	Waitrose Scottish Ale Caledonian Brewery	£1.65	Waitrose
Silver	CH'TI Bière de Garde en Nord Amber Beer	£1.66	Safeway
Silver	6X Export Wadworth	£1.69	Co-operative
Silver	6X Export Wadworth	£1.69	Safeway
Silver	6X Export Wadworth	£1.69	Europa

BEER

Silver	Bishops Finger Kentish Strong Ale Shepherd Neame	£1.69	**Budgens**
	Bombardier Premium Bitter Charles Wells	£1.69	**Co-op**
Bronze	Cocker Hoop Golden Bitter Jennings Brothers	£1.69	**Co-op**
Silver	Exmoor Gold Gold Hill Brewery	£1.69	**Tesco**
	Fargo Charles Wells	£1.69	**Kwik Save**
Gold	Fuller's London Pride Premium Ale	£1.69	**Co-operative**
Silver	Hobgoblin Extra Strong Ale Wychwood Brewery	£1.69	**Morrisons**
Bronze	Pendle Witches Brew Strong Lancashire Ale, Moorhouse's	£1.69	**Co-op**
Bronze	Sneck Lifter Jennings Brothers	£1.69	**Morrisons**
Silver	Spitfire Bottle Conditioned Ale Shepherd Neame	£1.69	**Budgens**
	Tangle Foot Strong Ale Badger Brewery	£1.69	**Morrisons**
Silver	Bishops Finger Kentish Strong Ale Shepherd Neame	£1.70	**Europa**
Silver	Spitfire Bottle Conditioned Ale Shepherd Neame	£1.70	**Europa**
Silver	Bishops Finger Kentish Strong Ale Shepherd Neame	£1.76	**Co-op**
Gold	Fuller's London Pride Premium Ale	£1.76	**Co-op**
Gold	Fuller's London Pride Premium Ale	£1.76	**Safeway**
Bronze	Golden Promise Organic Ale Caledonian Brewery	£1.76	**Co-op**
Silver	Hobgoblin Extra Strong Ale Wychwood Brewery	£1.76	**Safeway**
Gold	Riggwelter Strong Yorkshire Ale Black Sheep Brewery	£1.76	**Booths**
Gold	Riggwelter Strong Yorkshire Ale Black Sheep Brewery	£1.76	**Morrisons**
	Sneck Lifter Jennings Brothers	£1.76	**Co-op**
Silver	Spitfire Bottle Conditioned Ale Shepherd Neame	£1.76	**Co-op**
Silver	Spitfire Bottle Conditioned Bitter Shepherd Neame	£1.76	**Morrisons**
	Tangle Foot Strong Ale Badger Brewery	£1.76	**Safeway**
	Young's Ram Rod Strong Ale	£1.76	**Tesco**
Silver	6X Export Wadworth	£1.81	**Budgens**

Bitter or Traditional Ale Style

Gold	Batemans XXXB Classic Bitter	£1.81	**Tesco**
Silver	Bishops Finger Kentish Strong Ale Shepherd Neame	£1.81	**Londis**
Bronze	Fuller's ESB Export Extra Special Bitter	£1.81	**Co-operative**
Bronze	Fuller's London Pride Premium Ale	£1.81	**Budgens**
Silver	Hobgoblin Extra Strong Ale Wychwood Brewery	£1.81	**Tesco**
Silver	Old Speckled Hen Strong Fine Ale, Morland	£1.81	**Co-operative**
Silver	Old Speckled Hen Strong Fine Ale, Morland	£1.81	**Co-op**
Silver	Old Speckled Hen Strong Fine Ale, Morland	£1.81	**Safeway**
Silver	Old Speckled Hen Morland	£1.81	**Europa**
Gold	Riggwelter Strong Yorkshire Ale Black Sheep Brewery	£1.81	**Sainsbury's**
	Sneck Lifter Jennings Brothers	£1.81	**Tesco**
Silver	Spitfire Bottle Conditioned Ale Shepherd Neame	£1.81	**Londis**
Silver	Spitfire Bottle Conditioned Ale Shepherd Neame	£1.81	**Tesco**
Gold	Worthington's White Shield Fine Strong Ale	£1.84	**Booths**
	Daredevil A Very Strong Traditional Ale, Everards	£1.92	**Co-op**
Silver	Fuller's 1845 Bottle Conditioned Celebration Strong Ale	£1.92	**Co-operative**
Bronze	Fuller's ESB Export Extra Special Bitter	£1.92	**Budgens**
Silver	Fuller's Old Winter Ale	£1.92	**Budgens**
Silver	Monkey Wrench Strong Ale Daleside Brewery	£1.92	**Tesco**
Silver	Old Hooky Premium Ale Hook Norton Brewery	£1.92	**Budgens**
Silver	St Peter's Golden Ale St Peter's Brewery	£1.92	**Tesco**
Silver	Fuller's 1845 Bottle Conditioned Celebration Strong Ale	£1.99	**Tesco**
Silver	Old Speckled Hen Strong Fine Ale, Morland	£1.99	**Budgens**
Silver	Fuller's 1845 Bottle Conditioned Celebration Strong Ale	£2.03	**Budgens**

Bitter or Traditional Ale Style

With widgets

Widgetized bitter is nowhere near as successful as widgetized stout, for the simple reason that the head on a pint of traditional pulled real ale is air, not nitrogen. You could put a widget in an air-flushed can or bottle of bitter containing little CO_2, but the beer would go off before it reached the shelf. These products should not be regarded as bitters but judged as a completely separate category of smooth, creamy beer (which many people like, judging by the Caffrey's phenomenon). In which case, they should not bear the same name as the brew you can get by the pint or bottle. Even so, the brewers are still missing out on a large group of consumers who would bridge the gap between those who are happily hooked on creamy widget beers and those who would not touch the stuff with a barge pole. There are many beer drinkers who would drink a widgetized beer if it had some real bitterness coming through.

Bitterness in beers – all beers, including lagers, stouts etc – is measured in EBUs, and it strikes me that the brewers should have 30–50 per cent more EBU in a widgetized beer to get a similar taste coming through the creamy mask of nitrogen bubbles. Prices ranged from the equivalent of 80p per pint to £1.91.

	Keoghan's Ale Draught, Federation Brewery	£0.96	Morrisons
	Ruddles Draught Best Bitter Rutland Brewery	£1.29	Budgens
Bronze	Banks's Draught Smoothpour	£1.35	Co-operative
Bronze	Boddingtons Draught	£1.38	Co-operative
Silver	John Smith's Extra Smooth Bitter	£1.42	Co-operative
Bronze	Kilkenny Irish Beer Draught St Francis Abbey Brewery, Guinness	£1.45	Budgens
Silver	Boddingtons Manchester Gold	£1.54	Londis
Gold	Beamish Red Irish Ale	£1.55	Safeway
Silver	Boddingtons Manchester Gold	£1.55	Morrisons
Gold	Fuggles Imperial Strong Ale Castle Eden Brewery	£1.58	Kwik Save
Bronze	Caffrey's Draught Irish Ale	£1.61	Safeway
Bronze	Caffrey's Draught Irish Ale	£1.61	Tesco

Bronze	Kilkenny Irish Beer Draught St Francis Abbey Brewery, Guinness	£1.61	Co-operative
Bronze	Kilkenny Irish Beer Draught St Francis Abbey Brewery, Guinness	£1.61	Tesco
Bronze	Kilkenny Irish Beer Draught St Francis Abbey Brewery, Guinness	£1.61	Morrisons
Bronze	Kilkenny Irish Beer Draught St Francis Abbey Brewery, Guinness	£1.61	Safeway
Bronze	Kilkenny Irish Beer Draught St Francis Abbey Brewery, Guinness	£1.67	Londis
Gold	Fuggles Imperial Strong Ale Castle Eden Brewery	£1.69	Co-operative
Gold	Fuggles Imperial Strong Ale Castle Eden Brewery	£1.69	Co-op
Bronze	Caffrey's Draught Irish Ale	£1.71	Co-operative
Bronze	Caffrey's Draught Irish Ale	£1.74	Budgens
Gold	Fuggles Imperial Strong Ale Castle Eden Brewery	£1.76	Safeway
Gold	Fuggles Imperial Strong Ale Castle Eden Brewery	£1.81	Budgens

Dark Beers

Milds, stouts and porters: without widgets

Most mild is dark brown, although lighter examples do exist. It should be a soft-tasting ale with a sweetness that devotees enjoy for its lingering quality – although most bitter drinkers would find this cloying. Classic stout is bitter stout, and Guinness, Murphy's and Beamish are all first-rate examples; they are all Irish, of course, whereas stout is a derivative of old English Porter. A plethora of English and Scottish stouts and porters have emerged in the last few years. Mild is 2.7 to 3.2 per cent AVB, porter around 5 per cent and stout 4.5 to 5 per cent, although bottled versions exported to the tropics can be as high as 8 per cent. Prices ranged from an equivalent of 90p per pint to £2.18.

Bronze	Brady's Original Irish Stout Kwik Save	£0.90	Kwik Save
Bronze	Guinness Original Stout	£1.04	Londis
Bronze	Guinness Original Stout	£1.18	Tesco
Bronze	Guinness Original Stout	£1.29	Budgens

Bronze	Guinness Original Stout	£1.37	Budgens
Bronze	Guinness Original Stout	£1.42	Safeway
Bronze	Guinness Original Stout	£1.42	Co-operative
Bronze	Whitechapel Porter Shepherd Neame, Asda	£1.47	Asda
Bronze	Rusty Rivet Authentic Brown Ale, Shepherd Neame, Asda	£1.47	Asda
Bronze	Pete's Wicked Ale	£1.74	Morrisons
	Tesco Porter Select Ales Marston Thompson & Evershed	£1.58	Tesco
	Marston's Oyster Stout Bottle Conditioned	£1.69	Co-op
	Marston's Oyster Stout Bottle Conditioned	£1.69	Booths
	Marston's Oyster Stout Bottle Conditioned	£1.69	Morrisons
Gold	The Famous Taddy Porter Samuel Smith	£1.70	Co-op
Gold	The Famous Taddy Porter Samuel Smith	£1.75	Tesco
Silver	The Celebrated Oatmeal Stout Samuel Smith	£1.75	Co-operative
Silver	Original Porter Strong Dark Ale Shepherd Neame	£1.76	Co-op
Bronze	Sainsbury's Blackfriars Porter	£1.76	Sainsbury's
Bronze	Old Growler Nethergate Brewery	£1.92	Tesco
Gold	Guinness Foreign Extra Stout	£2.05	Co-operative
	Staropramen Dark Lager Prague Breweries	£2.05	Sainsbury's
Gold	Guinness Foreign Extra Stout	£2.15	Booths
Bronze	Dragon Stout Desnoes & Geddes	£2.18	Kwik Save

Dark Beers

Stouts: with widgets

This could and should include widgetized porters and mild, but no brewery has made the former and Sainsbury's widgetized mild was very disappointing. The startling difference between bitter bottled stout and creamy draught stout is due to gas: the bottled version, like all bottled beers, contains CO_2, which is coarse on the tongue and accentuates the extreme bitter character of a stout, whereas the head on the draught version is principally nitrogen, an inert gas that is smooth on the tongue, and the creamy effect this provides subdues the bitter elements. Most beer writers are very sniffy about the widget, but without it draught stout drinkers would go thirsty at home. The widget in a can replicates the creamy effect by pushing nitrogen and beer through a tiny hole to create millions of minuscule, long-lasting bubbles. Draught stout is about 4 to 4.5 per cent ABV. Prices ranged from the equivalent of 96p to £1.76.

Bronze	Safeway Irish Stout Draught	£0.96	Safeway
Bronze	Beamish Draught Irish Stout	£1.38	Co-operative
Bronze	Beamish Draught Irish Stout	£1.38	Morrisons
Bronze	Murphy's Draught Irish Stout	£1.42	Tesco
Bronze	Murphy's Draught Irish Stout	£1.42	Morrisons
Bronze	Murphy's Draught Irish Stout	£1.45	Budgens
Gold	Draught Guinness	£1.48	Co-operative
Gold	Draught Guinness	£1.48	Morrisons
Silver	Gillespie's Draught Malt Stout Scottish & Newcastle Breweries	£1.51	Morrisons
Silver	Gillespie's Draught Malt Stout Scottish & Newcastle Breweries	£1.51	Safeway
Gold	Draught Guinness	£1.54	Londis
Gold	Draught Guinness	£1.57	Budgens
Gold	Murphy's Draught Irish Stout	£1.69	Co-operative
Gold	Murphy's Draught Irish Stout	£1.69	Morrisons
Gold	Murphy's Draught Irish Stout	£1.69	Budgens
Gold	Draught Guinness	£1.74	Europa
Gold	Murphy's Draught Irish Stout	£1.76	Safeway

Lager and Pilsner Styles

Without widgets

The name Lager comes from the German *Lager*, or storehouse, as this beer should be aged for up to six months at a very cold temperature to precipitate the finest suspended matter, rendering the Lager star-bright. Most commercial brews of Lager will, however, be aged for fewer than six weeks. Pils, Pilsener and Pilsner are all much-abused designations that are now applied to lager-type beers of any strength, quality or age, although they were originally restricted to lagers brewed in the Czech town of Pilsen. As Pilsener caught on, the name of the Czech town was used for any top-quality, well-hopped lager of at least 5 per cent ABV brewed from Pilsener malt to give the very long and delicate, almost floral-perfumed, flavour for which this beer was justifiably famous. Only one Ice Beer made the cut. From my notes there is nothing to suggest that Ice Beer is any better than ordinary lager styles. If anything, it is less distinctive and just more expensive. Prices ranged from an equivalent of 48p per pint to £2.22.

	Blonderbraü Pils	£0.68	**Budgens**
	Sainsbury's Bière des Flandres French Lager	£0.68	**Sainsbury's**
	Waitrose Strong Lager	£0.90	**Waitrose**
Bronze	Sainsbury's Bière d'Alsace French Lager	£0.91	**Sainsbury's**
Bronze	Ceres Royal Export	£1.01	**Co-op**
Bronze	Flanders Bier Asda	£1.02	**Asda**
Bronze	Holland Bier Asda	£1.02	**Asda**
Silver	Sainsbury's Stolz Pilsner Authentic German Beer	£1.02	**Sainsbury's**
Bronze	Saaz Pils French Premium Lager Beer	£1.13	**Co-op**
Bronze	Safeway Bière d'Alsace French Lager	£1.13	**Safeway**
Bronze	Sainsbury's Cerveza de España Premium Spanish Lager	£1.13	**Sainsbury's**
Bronze	Waitrose French Lager	£1.13	**Waitrose**
Silver	German Pilsener Bier Tesco	£1.14	**Tesco**
Silver	Gilde Pilsener	£1.14	**Kwik Save**
Silver	Sainsbury's German Pilsener Premium Lager	£1.16	**Sainsbury's**
Bronze	San Miguel Export Cerveza Especial	£1.18	**Kwik Save**
Bronze	Drewrys Genuine Imported American Beer Private Liquor Brands UK	£1.20	**Co-op**
	Grolsch Premium Lager	£1.22	**Kwik Save**
Silver	Premium Original Pilsener Lager St Michael	£1.22	**M&S**
Bronze	Waitrose Czech Lager	£1.24	**Waitrose**
Bronze	Biere d'Alsace Premium French Lager Fischer, St Michael	£1.25	**M&S**
Bronze	Kronenbourg 1664 Courage Ltd	£1.28	**Londis**
Gold	Asda German Pilsener	£1.29	**Asda**

Lager and Pilsner Styles

	Italian Birra Export Premium Lager, Asda	£1.29	Asda
	Waitrose Westphalian Lager	£1.29	Waitrose
Bronze	Castle Lager SA Breweries	£1.31	Tesco
Bronze	Vratislav Lager Tesco	£1.31	Tesco
	Beck's	£1.32	Europa
Gold	Budweiser Budvar	£1.35	Booths
Gold	Budweiser Budvar	£1.35	Morrisons
Bronze	Kronenbourg 1664 Courage Ltd	£1.38	Tesco
Silver	DAB Original German Beer Dortmunder Actien-Brauerei	£1.40	Co-op
Bronze	Nastro Azzurro Premium Beer, Peroni	£1.46	Morrisons
	Budweiser Budvar	£1.47	Budgens
Gold	Budweiser Budvar	£1.53	Safeway
	Foster's Ice Beer Courage Limited	£1.54	Londis
Gold	Budweiser Budvar	£1.58	Tesco
Silver	Hürlimann Premium Swiss Lager Shepherd Neame	£1.58	Booths
	Amstel Bier	£1.63	Co-operative
Silver	Black Fort Premium Lager Som's	£1.64	Co-op
	Atlanta Ice St Michael	£1.66	M&S
Gold	Budweiser Budvar	£1.67	Co-operative
	Stella Artois Premium Lager Beer	£1.69	Co-operative
	Bud Ice Anheuser-Busch Inc.	£1.70	Budgens
Silver	Carlsberg Ice Beer	£1.70	Safeway
Bronze	König-Pilsener	£1.70	Europa
Bronze	Moretti Birra Friulana	£1.70	Tesco
Gold	Pilsner Urquell	£1.70	Morrisons
Gold	Pilsner Urquell	£1.70	Safeway
	Bud Ice Anheuser-Busch Inc.	£1.72	Londis
	San Miguel Premium Export Lager	£1.72	Co-operative
	Stella Artois Dry Export Strength Premium Beer, Whitbread	£1.72	Safeway
Bronze	Fischer Tradition Bière Blonde Spéciale d'Alsace	£1.74	Tesco
	Bud Ice Anheuser-Busch Inc.	£1.80	Co-operative
	Bud Ice Anheuser-Busch Inc.	£1.80	Tesco
	Foster's Ice Beer Courage Limited	£1.81	Budgens
Bronze	Cobra Indian Lager Mysore Breweries	£1.88	Europa
Gold	Grolsch Premium Lager	£1.88	Morrisons
Bronze	Staropramen Prague Breweries	£1.98	Morrisons

	Beck's	£1.99	Co-operative
Bronze	Staropramen Prague Breweries	£2.05	Co-operative
Bronze	Staropramen Prague Breweries	£2.05	Co-op
Bronze	Staropramen Prague Breweries	£2.05	Tesco
Bronze	Staropramen Prague Breweries	£2.05	Safeway
	Staropramen Dark Lager Prague Breweries	£2.05	Tesco
Gold	Grolsch Premium Lager	£2.06	Co-operative
Gold	Grolsch Premium Lager	£2.08	Safeway
	Beck's	£2.12	Budgens
Gold	Grolsch Premium Lager	£2.21	Budgens
Silver	Carlsberg Elephant Strong Imported Beer	£2.38	Co-operative
Silver	Carlsberg Elephant Strong Imported Beer	£2.38	Morrisons
Silver	Carlsberg Elephant Strong Imported Beer	£2.38	Tesco
Silver	Carlsberg Elephant Strong Imported Beer	£2.41	Europa
Gold	Grolsch Premium Lager	£2.46	Europa
Silver	Duvel Brouwerij Moortgat	£2.56	Co-op

Lager and Pilsner Styles

With widgets

The widget seems even less successful when applied to lager styles than it does when applied to bitter ales. Prices ranged from the equivalent of £1.19 to £1.29.

Boston Beer Whitbread	£1.55	Co-op
Boston Beer Whitbread	£1.55	Safeway
Boston Beer Whitbread	£1.61	Co-operative
Boston Beer Whitbread	£1.61	Londis

Pale Ale

Pale Ale is the name applied to a particular bottled version of draught bitter. First brewed in London in the mid-eighteenth century, it did not become famous until Bass produced this style of beer at its Burton-on-Trent brewery, since when Burton has become synonymous with Pale Ale. This is because the Burton water contains gypsum, which precipitates the most ultra-fine sediments suspended in a beer, giving it a much paler colour: hence Pale Ale, thus Burton Pale Ale. Prices ranged from an equivalent of 75p per pint to £2.03.

Silver	Theakston Lightfoot Traditional Pale Beer	£1.50	Booths
Silver	Theakston Lightfoot Traditional Pale Beer	£1.54	Co-op
Silver	Tesco Select Ales India Pale Ale Bottle Conditioned, Marston Thompson & Evershed	£1.58	Tesco
Bronze	Wallace IPA Maclay & Co. Thistle Brewery	£1.58	Co-op
Silver	Theakston Lightfoot Traditional Pale Beer	£1.64	Co-operative
Bronze	Deuchars IPA Export Strength, Caledonian Brewery	£1.65	Co-op
Silver	Samuel Smith's Old Brewery Pale Ale	£1.70	Co-op
Silver	India Pale Ale Original Export Shepherd Neame	£1.76	Co-op
Silver	Marston's India Export Pale Ale Head Brewers Choice	£1.76	Co-op
Silver	Marston's India Export Pale Ale Head Brewers Choice	£1.76	Morrisons
Gold	Marston's Burton S.P.A.	£1.81	Tesco
Gold	Marston's Burton S.P.A.	£1.81	Morrisons

Prices

Prices were correct at the time of tasting. You should expect some changes due to exchange-rate fluctuations, prices rising at source, possible increases in VAT and other variables, but these should be within reason, and the historical price in this book will help you to spot any excessive increases.

Please note that prices were not adjusted prior to publication because all the wines and beers were tasted within their own price category; to change that would be to make a mockery of the blind tasting, the notes made and the medals awarded.

Different Vintages

Wines recommended in this book are specific to the vintages indicated. Follow-on vintages *might* be of a similar quality and character, but are likely to be either better or worse. Wines of real interest are seldom exactly the same from one year to the next. Cheap fruity wines, whether white or red, are often better the younger they are, and the difference between vintages is generally less important for bulk wines produced in hotter countries, but even these will vary in some vintages. The difference in vintage is usually most noticeable for individually crafted wines produced the world over. Don't be put off a wine because it is of a different vintage, as you could be missing an even greater treat, but do try a bottle before laying out on a case or two.

Is a £3 Gold Medal as good as a £6 Gold Medal?

It is possible, but unlikely. It should be remembered that a medal is awarded for the category, which includes price as well as style. If this were not so, and medals were awarded purely on quality, regardless of price, then the world's most expensive wines would have to be the yardsticks, and a £20 wine would be hard pushed to qualify for a bronze, let alone a £3 wine earning a gold. The best-value £3 gold medal wine might match up to, say, a £4 gold medal wine, but you cannot realistically expect it to compare with a £6 gold medal wine.

SPIRIT PRICE GUIDE

Although *SuperBooze* does not taste spirits, it does provide a price comparison of own-label and common major brands, which illustrates what the street price is and reveals how much over the odds you may be paying.

Spirit prices are subject to almost continuous change, as supermarkets try to maintain a competitive edge, thus, this price guide can only be regarded as a snapshot of the market at one particular point in time, in this case July 1997. Although this yo-yo effect prevents the price guide from being used daily on a shop-by-shop basis, it does provide the reader with the means to save a considerable amount of money when purchasing spirits. For although the supermarkets claim to keep their spirit prices competitive, this snapshot proves that many do not or are caught out when others drop their prices. The cheapest figures, highlighted in bold, indicate the going street price, while the column on the right reveals how much you could be paying over the odds.

Comparing prices for own-label spirits can result in misleading differentials, as you will not necessarily be comparing like with like, but the table demonstrates that it pays to shop around. Note that not every supermarket stocks every product.

SPIRIT PRICE GUIDE

	Asda	Booth's	Budgens	Co-op	Co-operative	Europa	Kwik Save
Brandy							
Own-Brand Armagnac	–	–	–	–	–	–	–
Own-Brand Cognac	**11.69**	15.29	–	–	12.99	–	–
Own-Brand Grape	7.99	8.13	7.99	–	8.29	8.69	**7.29**
Asbach German	–	15.49	–	14.99	16.29	**14.75**	–
Courvoisier ***	17.39	17.69	17.43	17.69	17.69	17.99	–
Janneau Armagnac	–	–	15.69	16.19	**14.73**	15.49	–
Martell ***	17.99	17.99	17.99	**17.69**	**17.69**	17.99	17.95
Metaxa Greek	–	**14.69**	–	14.89	–	–	–
Rémy Martin VSOP	25.79	**24.15**	25.33	25.99	–	25.69	–
Three Barrels	11.99	11.99	11.99	**11.49**	11.99	11.99	11.95
Gin							
Own Brand	7.99	7.75	8.74	8.49	8.19	8.29	**7.39**
Beefeater	–	12.73	–	**11.69**	12.69	12.69	12.59
Gordons	10.99	**9.49**	9.99	10.99	10.99	10.99	9.89
White Satin	9.75	9.75	9.75	9.99	9.75	9.75	**9.69**
Rum							
Own-Brand White	7.95	7.69	–	8.59	7.99	8.35	**7.19**
Own-Brand Dark	8.19	7.73	–	8.59	8.19	8.35	**7.69**
Bacardi	11.69	11.79	11.69	11.79	11.69	11.69	**11.65**
Captain Morgan Black	**11.69**	–	11.95	11.95	11.95	11.95	11.89
Lambs Navy	10.99	12.29	11.73	11.69	11.99	11.99	**10.95**
Woods Navy 100°	–	–	–	–	16.99	16.99	–
Vodka							
Own-Brand	7.45	7.59	7.64	7.69	7.45	7.95	**5.89**
Smirnoff Blue	**13.69**	13.89	–	13.89	–	13.79	–
Smirnoff Red	10.59	10.59	10.59	10.69	10.59	10.59	10.45
Stolichnaya	–	**12.29**	–	–	–	–	–
Vladivar	–	9.99	**8.49**	9.29	9.49	9.49	8.95
Whisky							
Own-Brand Scotch	8.99	8.99	9.15	8.25	8.99	8.99	**6.39**
Jim Beam Bourbon	–	–	–	15.49	15.49	15.49	–
Bells	11.99	11.99	**11.73**	11.99	11.99	11.99	11.95

Brandy/Rum/Gin/Vodka/Whisky

Londis	M&S	Morrisons	Safeway	Sainsbury's	Somerfield	Tesco	Waitrose	Max. Difference
–	–	–	–	15.49	–	**14.65**	14.95	0.84
–	–	**11.69**	12.99	13.49	12.99	11.99	13.45	3.60
8.25	12.99	8.05	–	–	9.49	9.53	9.59	5.70
–	–	–	–	–	–	–	17.65	2.90
17.99	–	17.69	17.69	17.69	17.69	17.49	**16.65**	1.34
–	–	15.23	–	–	–	–	–	0.96
17.99	–	17.99	17.99	17.99	17.99	17.99	17.95	0.30
–	–	–	–	–	–	14.89	–	0.20
–	–	24.99	25.75	25.75	–	25.79	25.75	1.84
11.99	–	11.99	11.99	11.99	11.99	11.99	–	0.50
7.75	9.99	8.19	8.99	7.45	8.95	7.99	8.99	2.60
12.69	–	–	12.99	12.69	12.99	12.69	12.65	1.30
10.99	–	10.99	10.99	10.99	10.99	9.99	10.99	1.50
9.89	–	9.75	9.75	9.75	9.75	9.75	9.75	0.30
8.79	–	8.05	8.99	8.99	8.35	7.95	8.99	1.80
8.49	–	8.25	9.99	9.99	9.35	8.19	9.99	2.30
11.59	–	11.69	11.69	11.69	11.69	11.69	11.69	0.14
11.99	–	11.95	11.99	**11.69**	11.95	**11.69**	–	0.30
11.99	–	11.99	10.99	11.99	11.99	10.99	10.99	1.34
–	–	**16.65**	–	–	16.99	16.99	–	0.34
7.75	9.50	7.45	7.75	7.45	7.45	7.45	7.95	3.61
–	–	–	13.89	13.79	13.79	13.79	–	0.20
10.69	–	10.45	10.59	10.59	**9.99**	10.59	10.59	0.70
–	–	–	12.69	12.49	–	12.49	12.49	0.40
8.49	–	8.99	9.49	9.49	9.49	9.49	–	1.50
8.39	12.99	8.99	8.99	8.99	9.03	8.99	8.99	6.60
14.99	–	15.49	15.49	15.49	15.79	15.49	15.45	0.80
11.99	–	11.99	11.99	11.99	11.99	11.99	11.99	0.26

SPIRIT PRICE GUIDE

	Asda	Booth's	Budgens	Co-op	Co-operative	Europa	Kwik Save
Canadian Club	**13.69**	13.99	–	13.99	–	13.99	–
Chivas Regal	–	24.69	–	–	**24.25**	–	–
Claymore	9.65	9.69	9.99	9.99	8.99	9.99	**8.95**
Jack Daniels Bourbon	16.99	16.99	–	16.99	16.99	16.99	**16.39**
Famous Grouse	12.29	12.39	12.13	12.29	12.29	12.29	**11.69**
Glenfiddich	19.99	19.99	19.23	19.49	19.99	19.99	18.95
Glenlivet	19.99	20.49	–	19.99	19.99	19.99	–
Glenmorangie	21.19	22.99	19.99	21.49	21.99	21.99	**19.79**
Grants	11.39	11.49	11.29	11.49	11.19	11.29	10.95
J&B Rare	–	14.69	**14.45**	14.69	–	14.99	–
Jameson Irish	13.69	13.49	11.99	13.69	13.69	13.69	**11.89**
Macallan	22.49	22.49	–	**21.99**	22.49	22.49	–
Mackinlay	–	–	–	–	–	–	–
Teachers	11.49	11.79	11.69	11.69	11.39	11.49	**10.95**
Vat 69	9.59	–	9.99	**9.49**	9.99	9.99	9.69
Johnnie Walker Black	18.99	18.99	18.99	18.69	**17.49**	18.99	–
White Horse	10.95	10.99	10.99	10.99	**10.29**	10.99	10.95
Whyte & Mackay	**10.95**	11.49	10.99	11.29	11.29	11.79	**10.95**
Liqueurs etc							
Baileys Irish Cream	**11.49**	11.99	11.79	11.79	11.79	11.79	**11.49**
Cadburys Cream	–	**10.99**	–	**10.99**	–	–	–
Carolans Irish Cream	**7.29**	7.49	–	7.59	–	6.99	–
Cointreau	15.99	16.15	15.99	15.99	15.99	15.99	**14.29**
Drambuie (50cl)	13.99	13.69	**12.49**	–	12.49	12.99	–
Grand Marnier	–	18.99	18.29	18.95	–	**13.99**	–
Malibu	10.99	11.19	10.99	10.99	10.99	10.99	10.69
Pernod	13.99	**12.75**	13.99	13.89	13.99	13.99	13.29
Southern Comfort	14.99	15.49	14.99	14.99	14.99	14.99	**14.69**
Terry's Orange Chocolate	–	11.75	–	9.99	–	–	–
Tia Maria	13.89	14.29	–	13.99	13.99	13.99	**13.49**
Warninks Advocaat	9.89	9.99	–	9.89	9.89	9.89	**9.25**

Note All prices for 70cl unless otherwise stated.

Brandy/Rum/Gin/Vodka/Whisky

Londis	M&S	Morrisons	Safeway	Sainsbury's	Somerfield	Tesco	Waitrose	Max. Difference
13.79	–	**13.69**	13.99	–	13.99	13.99	13.95	0.30
–	–	–	–	–	–	24.64	–	0.44
9.49	–	9.69	9.49	9.99	9.99	9.99	–	1.04
16.99	–	**16.39**	16.99	16.99	16.99	16.99	16.95	0.60
12.29	–	12.29	12.29	12.29	11.79	12.29	11.79	0.60
18.49	–	19.19	19.99	19.99	19.99	19.19	19.95	1.04
–	–	19.99	19.99	19.99	20.08	19.99	**17.95**	2.54
22.49	–	21.49	21.99	21.99	21.99	21.99	19.95	3.20
11.29	–	11.19	11.19	11.19	11.19	**10.49**	**10.49**	1.00
14.99	–	–	–	–	**14.45**	–	–	0.24
13.39	–	–	13.69	13.69	13.69	13.69	11.95	1.80
–	–	22.49	22.49	22.49	22.95	22.49	22.45	0.96
–	–	–	–	–	–	10.68	–	–
11.39	–	11.39	11.39	11.39	11.39	11.39	11.39	0.84
–	–	9.69	9.99	9.99	9.99	9.99	9.99	0.50
18.99	–	18.39	18.99	18.99	18.99	18.99	–	1.50
10.79	–	10.99	10.99	10.99	10.99	10.99	10.99	0.70
11.49	–	10.99	10.99	11.29	10.99	10.99	10.99	0.54
11.99	–	11.55	11.79	11.55	11.79	11.55	11.79	0.50
–	–	–	–	–	11.19	**10.99**	–	0.20
–	–	7.99	7.99	–	–	7.99	–	0.70
16.49	–	14.39	15.99	15.99	15.99	15.99	15.95	2.20
–	–	13.75	13.99	13.99	–	–	13.95	1.50
–	–	–	–	**13.99**	–	19.03	–	5.04
10.99	–	10.79	10.99	10.99	**9.99**	10.99	10.99	1.20
13.49	–	13.99	13.99	13.99	13.89	13.99	13.95	1.24
14.99	–	**14.69**	14.99	14.99	14.99	15.19	14.95	0.80
–	–	–	10.75	–	–	**7.79**	–	3.96
14.29	–	13.99	13.99	13.99	13.99	13.99	13.95	0.80
–	–	9.35	9.89	9.89	9.58	9.89	9.89	0.74

GLOSSARY OF TECHNICAL AND TASTING TERMS

I have tried to make the descriptions self-evident wherever possible, but every subject from house-building to fly-fishing has developed its own jargon to express concepts more precisely, and booze is no exception. I hope the following will clarify the meaning of terms the reader may not be familiar with.

ABC This stands for 'Anything But Chardonnay' or 'Anything But Cabernet' and is used by those elements of the trade, the public and the critics who are fed up with the endless proliferation of these two grapes, and who seek quality wines made from almost any other grape.

ABV This stands for Alcohol By Volume and is expressed in percentage terms. For those who remember the Degrees Proof system, a typical spirit of 70% Proof would be equal to 40 per cent ABV.

Accessible Literally means that the wine is easy to approach, with no great barriers of tannin, acidity or undeveloped extract to prevent enjoyment and drinkability. This term is often used for young, fine-quality wine where the tannin is supple and thus approachable, although it will undoubtedly improve with age.

Acidity Essential for the life and vitality of all wines. Too much will make wine too sharp (not sour – that's a fault), but not enough will make it taste flat and dull, and the flavour will not last in the mouth.

Aftertaste The flavour and aroma left in the mouth after the wine has been swallowed. When attractive, this adds a pleasurable dimension to a wine, and could be the reason why you prefer it to a similar wine with no aftertaste as such.

Ages gracefully A wine that retains finesse as it matures, and sometimes even increases in finesse.

Aggressive The opposite of soft and smooth.

Alcohol It may sound obvious, but alcohol is essential to the flavour and body of alcoholic products. Because wines contain a greater percentage of alcohol than beers, a de-alcoholized wine is intrinsically more difficult to perfect than a de-alcoholized beer.

Glossary of Technical and Tasting Terms 263

Aldehyde The midway stage between an alcohol and an acid, formed during the oxidation of an alcohol. Acetaldehyde is the most important of the common wine aldehydes, forming as wine alcohol oxidizes into acetic acid (vinegar). Small amounts of acetaldehyde add to the complexity of a wine, but too much will make a table wine smell like sherry.

AOC *Appellation d'Origine Contrôlée* is the top rung in the French wine classification system, although in practice it includes everything from the greatest French wines to the absolute pits. If I have learned anything, it is that it is better to buy an expensive *vin de pays* than a cheap AOC. A £4.99 white Burgundy can be rubbish, but a £4.99 *vin de pays* Chardonnay will often be delicious.

Appellation Literally 'name', this usually refers to an official, geographically based designation for a wine.

Aroma This term should really be confined to the fresh and fruity smells reminiscent of grapes, rather than the more winey or bottle-mature complexities of bouquet; but it is not always possible to use this word in its purest form, hence aroma and bouquet may be read as synonymous.

Attack A wine with good attack is one that is complete and readily presents its full armament of taste characteristics to the palate. The wine is likely to be youthful rather than mature, and its attack augurs well for its future.

Balance Refers to the harmonious relationship between acids, alcohol, fruit, tannin and other natural elements. If you have two similar wines but you definitely prefer one of them, its balance is likely to be one of the two determining factors (length being the other).

Big vintage, year Terms usually applied to great years in which the exceptional weather conditions produce bigger (i.e. fuller, richer) wines than normal. May also be used literally, to describe a year with a big crop.

Big wine A full-bodied wine with an exceptionally rich flavour.

Bio-dynamic Wines or beers produced bio-dynamically are made from raw materials (grapes, barley, hops etc.) grown without the aid of chemical or synthetic sprays or fertilizers, and are vinified with natural yeast and the minimum use of filtration, SO_2 and chaptalization.

Biscuity A desirable aspect of bouquet found in some Champagnes, particularly a well-matured Pinot Noir-dominated blend (Chardonnay-dominated Champagnes tend to go toasty).

Bite A very definite qualification of grip. Usually a desirable characteristic, but an unpleasant bite is possible.

Bitterness Can be good or bad! (1) An unpleasant aspect of a poorly made wine. (2) An expected characteristic of an as yet undeveloped concentration of flavours that should, with maturity, become rich and delicious.

Blanc de Blancs Literally 'white of whites', a white wine made from white grapes; a term often, but not exclusively, used for sparkling wines.

Blanc de Noirs Literally 'white of blacks', a white wine made from black grapes; a term often, but not exclusively, used for sparkling wines. In the New World the wines usually have a tinge of pink, often no different from that of a fully fledged rosé, but a classic *blanc de noirs* should be as white as possible without using artificial means.

Blind, blind tasting An objective tasting where the identity of wines is unknown to the taster until after he or she has made notes and given scores. All competitive tastings are blind.

Blowzy An overblown, exaggerated fruity aroma, such as fruit jam, that may be attractive in a cheap wine, but would indicate a lack of finesse in a more expensive product.

Blush An Americanism conjured up to sell rosé wines to people who think that rosé is cheap and nasty. Zinfandel is the most popular blush wine style and there is even such a thing as Blush Chardonnay!

Body The extract of fruit (in a wine) or malt (in a beer) and alcoholic strength that together give an impression of weight in the mouth.

Botrytis Literally 'rot', which is usually an unwanted disorder of the vine. But *botrytis cinerea* or 'noble rot' is necessary for the production of the finest quality of sweet wines and, perhaps confusingly, is commonly contracted to 'botrytis' or 'botrytized grapes' when discussing such wines.

Bottle-age The length of time a wine or beer spends in bottle before it is consumed. A wine that has good bottle-age is one that has had sufficient time to mature properly. Bottle-ageing has a mellowing effect.

Bouquet This should really be applied to the combination of smells directly attributable to a wine's maturity in bottle – thus, aroma for grape and bouquet for bottle. But it is not always possible to use these words in their purest form, hence aroma and bouquet may be read as synonymous.

Bourgeois growth A Bordeaux château classification beneath *cru classé*.

Breathing Term used to describe the interaction between a wine and the air after a bottle has been opened and before it is drunk.

Breed The finesse of a wine that is due to the intrinsic quality of grape and *terroir* combined with the skill and experience of a great winemaker.

Breezy A fruitiness that is so fresh that it feels and tastes not just lifted, but as if the very freshness is actually breezing around the mouth

Brut Normally reserved for sparkling wines, this literally means raw or bone-dry, but in practice there is always some sweetness and so the wine can at the most only be termed dry.

Buttery Normally a rich, fat and positively delicious character found in many white wines, particularly if produced in a great vintage or a warm country.

Carbon gas This is naturally produced in the fermentation process, when the sugar is converted into almost equal parts of alcohol and carbon dioxide or carbonic gas. Carbonic gas is normally allowed to escape during fermentation, although a tiny amount will always be present in its dissolved form in any wine, even a still one, otherwise it would taste dull, flat and lifeless. If the gas is prevented from escaping, the wine becomes sparkling.

Chaptalization The practice of adding sugar to fresh grape juice to raise a wine's alcoholic potential. The term is named after Antoine Chaptal, a brilliant chemist and technocrat who served Napoleon as Minister of the Interior from 1800 to 1805 and instructed wine-growers on the advantages of adding sugar at the time of pressing.

Charm A subjective term: if a wine charms, it appeals without blatantly attracting in an obvious fashion.

Chewy An extreme qualification of meaty.

Citrus 'Citrussy' indicates aromas and flavours of far greater complexity than mere 'lemony' can suggest.

Clean A straightforward term applied to any wine devoid of unwanted or unnatural undertones of aroma and flavour.

Closed Refers to the nose or palate of a wine that fails to open or show much character. It also implies that the wine has some qualities, even if they are 'hidden' – these should open up as the wine develops in bottle.

Cloying The sickly, sticky characteristic of a poor sweet wine, where the finish is heavy and often unclean.

Coarse A term that should be applied to a 'rough and ready' wine; not necessarily unpleasant, but certainly not fine.

Coconut An attractive if very obvious characteristic that almost invariably applies to American oak, particularly if it is part of the bouquet as well as the palate, although a certain coconutty character can develop from honeyed, bottle-aged aromas of fruit on the finish or aftertaste of a wine.

Commercial A diplomatic way for experts to say 'I don't like this, but I expect the masses will!' A commercial wine is blended to a widely acceptable formula: at its worst it may be bland and inoffensive, at its best it is probably fruity, quaffable and uncomplicated.

Complete A wine that has everything (fruit, tannin, acidity, depth, length, etc) and, thus, feels satisfying in the mouth.

Complexity An overworked word that implies a wine has many different nuances of smell or taste. Great wines in their youth may have a certain complexity, but it is only with maturity in bottle that a wine will eventually achieve full potential in terms of complexity.

Concoction Usually a derogatory term, but when found in a guide to exclusively exciting wines or beers like this, it will at the very least be tongue in cheek (if you will excuse the pun). I might be referring to a literal concoction of component parts (as in a cocktail wine) or to what tastes like a medley of fruits or flavours in a less expensive wine.

Cool-fermented An obviously cool-fermented wine is very fresh, with simple aromas of apples, pears and bananas.

Corked This does not imply that there is anything inherently wrong with the wine, but that there is a penicillin infection inside the cork which gives an unpleasant musty character, spoiling an otherwise good wine. It should be highly improbable to find two consecutive corked bottles of the same wine, but every day scientists are discovering 'corky'-smelling compounds that have nothing to do with the cork, so it is quite possible for entire batches of wine to smell or taste corked. No wine buyer should, however, put such wines on the shelf.

Correct A wine with all the correct characteristics for its type and origin. Not necessarily an exciting wine, therefore no wine in *SuperBooze* should be merely correct.

Creamy A subjective term used to describe a creamy flavour that may be indicative of the variety of grape or the method of vinification. I tend to use this word in connection with the fruitiness or oakiness of a wine.

Crémant Traditionally ascribed to a Champagne with a low pressure and a soft, creamy mousse, this term has now been phased out in Champagne owing to its use for other French *Méthode Champenoise* appellations such as Crémant de Bourgogne and Crémant d'Alsace.

Crisp A clean wine, with good acidity showing on the finish, yielding a fresh, clean taste.

Cru Literally a 'growth', *cru* usually refers to a single named vineyard that has been defined and delimited over the centuries by one or more elements of *terroir* that are markedly different from those of the surrounding vineyards. This forms the basis of official classifications, such as the *grands crus* of Burgundy and the *crus classés* of Bordeaux.

Cru Bourgeois An official Bordeaux classification ranking below the *cru classé* system.

Cru classé An official classification in Bordeaux, established in 1855, whereby the best châteaux are graded in a five-tier hierarchical system from *premier cru classé*, or first growth, down to *cinquième cru classé*, or fifth growth.

Cuvée Originally the wine of one *cuve* or vat, but now refers to a specific blend or product which, in current commercial practice, will be from several vats.

Definition A wine with good definition is one that is not just clean with a correct balance, but also has a positive expression of its grape variety and/or origin.

Delicate Describes the quieter characteristics of quality that give a wine charm.

Demi-sec Literally 'semi-dry' but actually tastes quite sweet.

Depth Refers first to a wine's depth of flavour and secondly to its depth of interest.

Disgorgement This is part of the process of making a bottle-fermented sparkling wine such as Champagne. After fermentation the yeast forms a deposit which must be removed. To do this the bottles are inverted in freezing brine just long enough for the sediment to form a semi-frozen slush that adheres to the neck of the bottle. This enables the bottle to be returned to an upright position without disturbing the wine. The temporary cap used to seal the bottle is removed and the

268 SUPERBOOZE

internal pressure is sufficient to eject or disgorge the slush of
sediment without losing very much wine at all. The wine is then
topped up and a traditional Champagne cork used to seal the bottle.

Distinctive A wine with a positive character. All fine wines are
distinctive to some degree, but not all distinctive wines are necessarily
fine.

DO This stands for Spain's *Denominación de Origen*, which is
theoretically the equivalent of the French AOC. See **AOC**.

DOC Confusingly, this stands both for Italy's *Denominazione di Origine
Controllata* and for Portugal's *Denominaçao de Origem Controlada*,
which are theoretically the equivalent of the French AOC. See **AOC**.
It also stands for Spain's *Denominación de Origen Calificada*, which is
the equivalent of the Italian DOCG. See **DOCG**.

DOCG Italy's *Denominazione di Origine Controllata e Garantita* is
theoretically one step above the French AOC. Ideally it should be
similar to, say, a *premier* or *grand cru* in Burgundy or a *cru classé* in
Bordeaux, but in reality it is almost as big a sop as Italy's DOC itself.

Dosage When the sediment is removed from a sparkling wine, a little
sugar dissolved in wine is added to balance the acidity, which would
taste harsh otherwise, as all bubbly must be made from relatively
high-acid wines.

Easy Synonymous to a certain extent with accessible, but probably
implies a cheaper, value-for-money wine, whereas accessible often
applies to finer wines.

EBU This stands for European Bitterness Unit, a standard measure of
bitterness used for beers – all beers, including lagers, stouts, etc.
Sometimes referred to as IBU or International Bitterness Unit.

Elegant A subjective term applied to wines that may be described as
stylish or possessing finesse.

Expansive A wine that is big, but open and accessible.

Expressive A wine true to its grape variety and area of origin.

Extract The term covers all the solids in a wine or beer that literally
give the drink its body.

Fat A wine full in body and extract.

Fermentation All beers and wines are the result of fermentation,
where yeast cells convert sugar (or maltose in the case of beer) into
alcohol and carbonic gas.

Filter, filtration There are various methods of filtration, which essentially involve the passing of wine or beer through a medium that removes particles of a certain size.

Finesse That elusive, indescribable quality that separates a fine wine from those of lesser quality.

Fine wine Quality wines, representing only a small percentage of all wines produced.

Finish The quality and enjoyment of a wine's aftertaste.

Firm Refers to a certain amount of grip. A firm wine is one of good constitution, held up by a certain amount of tannin and acidity.

Flabby The opposite of crisp: a wine lacking in acidity and consequently dull, weak and short.

Flat (1) A sparkling wine that has lost all its mousse. (2) A term interchangeable with flabby, especially when referring to a lack of acidity on the finish.

Fleshy Refers to a wine with plenty of fruit and extract and with a certain underlying firmness.

Flor A scum-like yeast film that occurs naturally and floats on the surface of some sherries as they mature in part-filled wooden butts. It is the *flor* that gives Fino Sherry its inimitable character.

Flying winemaker The concept of the flying winemaker was born in Australia, where consultants like Brian Croser (now Petaluma) and Tony Jordan (now Green Point) would hop by plane from harvest to harvest practising their skills across the entire Australian continent. Riding on the success of Australian wines in the UK market, other Oz wine wizards began to stretch their wings, flying in and out of everywhere from Southern Italy to Moldova, usually at the behest of British supermarkets. Like the spread of Chardonnay and Cabernet, the flying winemakers were at first welcomed by the wine press, then turned upon for standardizing wine wherever they went. The truth is that before the arrival of international grapes and international winemakers, the peasant co-operatives in these countries had no idea that they could even produce wines to compete on the international market. Now that they have established a certain standard with known grape varieties and modern technology, they are beginning to turn to their roots, to see whether indigenous varieties might have the potential to produce more expressive wines. But for the ubiquitous international grapes and winemakers, they would still be producing dross in wineries not fit to hold a party in.

Fresh Wines that are clean and still vital with youth.

Fruit Wine is made from grapes and must therefore be 100 per cent fruit, yet it will not have a fruity flavour unless the grapes used have the correct combination of ripeness and acidity.

Full Usually refers to body, e.g. full-bodied. But a wine can be light in body yet full in flavour.

Fût A wooden cask, usually made of oak, in which some wines are aged, or fermented and aged.

Generic A wine, usually blended, of a general appellation.

Generous A generous wine gives its fruit freely on the palate, while an ungenerous one is likely to have little or no fruit and, probably, an excess of tannin. All wines should have some degree of generosity.

Gluggy Easy to guzzle.

Grande Marque Literally a great or famous brand; in the world of wine, the term *grande marque* is specific to Champagne and applies to members of the Syndicat de Grandes Marques, which includes of course all the most famous names.

Grand vin Normally used in Bordeaux, this applies to the main wine sold under the château's famous name, and will have been produced from only the finest barrels. Wines excluded during this process go into second, third and sometimes fourth wines that are sold under different labels.

Grapy Applied to the aroma and flavour of a wine that are reminiscent of grapes rather than overtly winey.

Green Unripe

Grip Applied to a firm wine with a positive finish. A wine showing grip on the finish indicates a certain bite of acidity or, if red, tannin.

Gutsy A wine full in body, fruit, extract and, usually, alcohol. Normally applied to ordinary-quality wines.

Guzzly Synonymous with gluggy.

Hollow A wine that appears to lack any real flavour in the mouth compared with the promise shown on the nose. Usually due to a lack of body, fruit or acidity.

Honest Applied to any wine, but usually those of a fairly basic quality, 'honest' implies it is true in character and typical of its type and origin. It also infers that the wine does not seem to have been souped up or mucked about in any unlawful way. The use of the word is,

Glossary of Technical and Tasting Terms

however, a way of damning with faint praise, for it does not suggest a wine of any special or memorable quality.

Hops The flower of the hop, either dried or in the form of a concentrate, is widely used to flavour – or to be more precise, season – a beer during the brewing process.

Jammy Literally tastes of jam, and there is good and less good – probably more cloying – jamminess, although the term 'preserve' might be used if the jam has a particular finesse. Everything is relative, so whereas jammy is generally a derogatory term, it is possible to find a really enjoyable jamminess, especially if the wine is inexpensive. As all the wines in *SuperBooze* are very strongly recommended (because those that do not make the grade are excluded), jammy will be used in a positive sense nine times out of ten in this book.

Landed-age Most Champagnes of old had good landed-age, a period of ageing in the importer's cellar prior to releasing the wine on to the market, and it is during this time that the toasty and biscuity post-disgorgement bottle-aromas begin to emerge. Few importers today bother or can afford to give Champagne any sort of regimented ageing, thus, when the term is applied to current wines, the landed-age will almost always be inadvertent: either the importer has not actually sold the stock or it has stuck on the retailer's shelf.

Lees The sediment that accumulates in the bottom of a vat during the fermentation of a wine.

Length Indicates that the flavour of a wine lingers in the mouth for a long time after swallowing. If two wines taste the same, yet you definitely prefer one but do not understand why, it is probably because the one you prefer has a greater length.

Light vintage, year A year that produces relatively light wines. Not a great vintage, but not necessarily a bad one either.

Lingering Normally applied to the finish of a wine: an aftertaste that literally lingers.

Liquorous Liqueur-like or *liquoreux* in French, this term is often applied to dessert wines of a certain viscosity and unctuous quality.

Liveliness A term that usually implies a certain youthful freshness of fruit owing to good acidity and a touch of carbonic gas.

Longevity Potentially long-lived wines may owe their longevity to a significant content of one or more of the following: tannin, acidity, alcohol and sugar.

Maceration A term usually applied to the period during the vinification process when the fermenting juice is in contact with the grape skins. This traditionally applies in red wine making, but it is on the increase for white wines utilizing pre-fermentation maceration techniques.

Macération carbonique **or maceration style** Generic terms for several similar methods of initially vinifying wine under the pressure of carbonic gas, and identifiable by an aroma of peardrops, bubblegum or nail-varnish. Beaujolais Nouveau is the archetypal *macération carbonique* wine.

Malt and malting Malt is the biscuity-smelling germinated grain of cereal (usually barley), and malting is the application of warmth and moisture that germinates the grain.

Mellow A wine that is round and nearing its peak of maturity.

Méthode Champenoise Process whereby an effervescence is induced through secondary fermentation in bottle, used for Champagne and other good-quality sparkling wines.

Mid-palate (1) The centre-top of your tongue. (2) A subjective term to describe the middle of the taste sensation when taking a mouthful of wine. Could be hollow if the wine is thin and lacking, or full if the wine is rich and satisfying.

Must Unfermented or partly fermenting grape juice.

Nose The smell or odour of a wine, encompassing both aroma and bouquet.

Oak Many wines are fermented or aged in wooden casks, for which the most commonly used wood is oak. There are two main categories of oak, French and American, and they are both used the world over. The French always use French oak, and the greatest California wines are also usually made in French oak barrels. American oak is traditional in Spain, particularly Rioja, and Australia, although both these countries make increasing use of French oak. Oak often gives a vanilla taste to wine because it contains a substance called vanillin, which also gives vanilla pods their aroma. French oak, however, is perceived to be finer and more refined (guess who started that one), while American oak is generally considered to have a more upfront, obvious character. The reason for this is not because one is French and the other American (although the latter grows quicker and has a bigger grain, which does have some influence), but because French oak is traditionally weathered in the open for several years, which leaches out the most volatile aromatics, and is split, not sawn, whereas American oak is kiln-dried, thus, not leached, and sawn, which ruptures the grain, exposing the wine to the most volatile elements in a relatively short time. If French oak were to be kiln-dried and sawn, and American weathered and split, I suspect our perception of the two forms of oak might well be reversed. American oak is charred in the construction of a barrel (wine makers can order it lightly toasted, medium toast, or highly charred), and this too has an effect, adding caramel, toffee and smoky-toasty aromas to a wine. The toastiness in oak is different from the toastiness derived from the grape itself (usually Chardonnay). Strangely, oak can have a cedary taste, although this is probably confined to older wood and spicy red grape varieties. If you get a very strong impression of coconut, it's a good bet that the oak used was American. Oak barrels are very expensive to buy and labour-intensive to work with, so if you find a very cheap wine with obvious oak character, it will inevitably be due to the use of oak chips or shavings, which are chucked into a huge, gleaming stainless-steel vat of wine. Cheating maybe, but legal, and if people like the taste of oak-aged wine but cannot afford to pay very much for a bottle, why not?

Off vintage, year A year in which many poor wines are produced owing to adverse climatic conditions, such as insufficient sunshine during the summer, which can result in unripe grapes, or rain or humid heat at the harvest, which can result in rot. Generally a vintage to be avoided, but approach any opportunity to taste the wines with an open mind because there are always good wines made in every vintage, however poor, and they have to be sold at bargain prices because of the vintage's bad reputation.

Open-knit An open and enjoyable nose or palate; usually a modest wine, not capable of much development.

Opulent Suggestive of a rather luxurious varietal aroma, very rich but not quite blowzy.

Overtone A dominating element of nose and palate, often one that is not directly attributable to the grape or wine.

Oxidative A wine that openly demonstrates the character of maturation on the nose or palate. An extremely oxidative wine will have a sherry-like aroma.

Palate The flavour or taste of a wine.

Peacock's tail Evocative term used to describe the elegant fanning out of flavours on the finish of a wine. This often occurs in wines with a tightly focused concentration of mid-palate fruit, which leads the taster to expect an intense finish, but surprisingly unfolds into a medley of different flavours, possibly indicating the potential complexity the wine may possess if aged a little longer.

Peak The so-called peak in the maturity of a wine depends upon the preferences of the consumer. Those liking fresher, crisper wines will perceive an earlier peak (in the same wine) than 'golden oldie' drinkers. A rule of thumb that applies to all extremes of taste is that a wine will remain at its peak for as long as it took to reach it.

Peardrop See *Macération carbonique*.

Pétillant A wine with enough carbonic gas to create a light sparkle.

Petit château Literally small château, this term is applied to any wine château that is neither a *cru classé* nor a *cru bourgeois*.

Phylloxera A native American bug that wiped out European vineyards in the late nineteenth century. The remedy was (and still is, because phylloxera still exists in almost every vineyard) to graft vines on to native American rootstocks, which have a natural resistance. There are, however, a few tiny plots dotted here and there where phylloxera failed to penetrate and the vines are still grown on their own rootstock. These are usually referred to as pre-phylloxera vines and the wines they produce are highly prized.

QbA Germany's *Qualitätswein bestimmter Anbaugebiete* is theoretically the equivalent of the French AOC. See **AOC**.

Reserve Wine Still wines from previous vintages that are blended with the wines of one principal year to produce a balanced, non-vintage Champagne.

Reticent Suggests that the wine is holding back on its nose or palate, perhaps through youth, and may well develop with a little more maturity.

Glossary of Technical and Tasting Terms

Rich, richness A balanced wealth of fruit and depth on the palate and finish.

Ripe Grapes ripen, wines mature. The term ripe should refer to richness that only ripe grapes can give, although a certain amount of residual sugar can fool even an experienced taster into mistaking sweetness for ripeness.

Ripe acidity The main acidity in ripe grapes (tartaric acid) tastes refreshing and fruity, even in large proportions, whereas the main acidity in unripe grapes (malic acid) tastes hard and unpleasant.

Robust A milder form of aggressive, which may often be applied to a mature product, i.e. the wine is robust by nature, not aggressive through youth.

Sassy A less cringing version of the cheeky, audacious character found in a wine with bold, brash, but not necessarily big, flavour.

Sharp In wine, this term applies to acidity, whereas bitterness applies to tannin and, sometimes, other natural solids. An immature wine might be sharp, but this term, if used by professional tasters, is usually a derogatory one. Good acidity is usually described as ripe acidity, which can make the fruit refreshingly tangy.

Sherbetty A subjective term to indicate the ultra-fresh fruit found in some wines.

Sherry-like Undesirable in low-strength or unfortified wines, this refers to the odour of wine in an advanced state of oxidation.

Short Refers to a wine that may have a good nose and initial flavour, but falls short on the finish, its taste quickly disappearing after the wine has been swallowed.

Skin-contact The maceration of grape skins in must or fermenting wine can extract varying amounts of colouring pigments, tannin and various aromatic compounds.

Sleepy-hop aroma The powerful, resinous aroma reminiscent of hop-pillows.

Smooth The opposite of aggressive and more extreme than round.

Soapy A very fresh characteristic often (but not solely) found in Riesling, soapiness wears off after time in bottle and usually indicates a degree of potential finesse in a wine.

Soft Interchangeable with smooth, although it usually refers to the fruit on the palate, whereas smooth is more often applied to the finish. Soft is very desirable, but 'extremely soft' may be derogatory, inferring a weak and flabby wine.

SO_2 Chemical formula for sulphur dioxide. See **Sulphur dioxide**.

Solera A system of continually refreshing an established blend with a small amount of new wine (equivalent to the amount extracted from the solera) to effect a wine of consistent quality and character. Some soleras were laid down in the nineteenth century and whereas it would be true to say that every bottle sold now contains a little of that first vintage, it would not even be a teaspoon. You would have to measure it in molecules, but there would also be infinitesimal amounts of each and every vintage from the date of inception to the year before bottling.

Soupy or Souped-up Implies a wine has been blended with something richer or more robust. A wine may well be legitimately souped-up, or it could mean that the wine has been played around with. The wine might not be correct, but it could still be very enjoyable.

Spicy A varietal characteristic of certain grapes such as Gewürztraminer. The Tokay-Pinot Gris and Auxerrois also definitely have some spiciness.

Spritz or spritzig Synonymous with *pétillant*.

Structure The structure of a wine is literally composed of its solids (tannin, acidity, sugar, and extract or density of fruit flavour) in balance with the alcohol, and how positive is its form and feel in the mouth.

Stylish Wines possessing all the subjective qualities of charm, elegance and finesse. Wines might have the 'style' of a certain region or type, but a wine is either stylish or it is not. It defies definition.

Subtle Although this should mean a significant yet understated characteristic, it is often employed by wine snobs and frauds who taste a wine with a famous label and know that it should be special, but cannot detect anything exceptional, and need an ambiguous word to talk their way out of the hole they have dug for themselves.

Suck-a-stone A note of freshness detected in Sauvignon Blanc that is reminiscent of the effect of sucking a smooth pebble (for anyone old and poor enough to remember – or for anyone who done any survival training); the suck-a-stone quality can usually be picked up on the nose as well as the palate and is an indication of the wine's finesse.

Sulphur dioxide This is added to help prevent oxidation and bacterial spoilage. Sulphur should not be noticeable in the finished product,

Glossary of Technical and Tasting Terms

but for various reasons a whiff may be detected on recently bottled wines, which a good swirl in the glass or a vigorous decanting should remove. With a few months in bottle this whiff ought to disappear. The acrid odour of sulphur in a wine should, if detected, be akin to the smell of a recently extinguished match. If it has a rotten egg aroma the wine should be returned to the retailer, as this means the sulphur has reduced to hydrogen sulphide. All good winemakers try to use as little sulphur as possible, but some people worry about its use in wine when there are far higher concentrations in orange juice, packets of ham and virtually any preserved commodity which many of the same people consume without thought, let alone worry, on a daily basis.

Supple Indicates a wine easy to drink, not necessarily soft, but suggesting more ease than simply 'round' does. With age, the tannin in wine becomes supple.

Supple tannins Tannins are generally perceived to be harsh and mouth-puckering, but the tannins in a ripe grape are supple, whereas those in an unripe grape are not.

Tank sample A trade sample drawn from the tank and probably not stabilized, so it's a case of if it's good, then fine, but if it's not, then it's wise to reserve your opinion.

Tannin Generic term for various substances found naturally in wine from the skin, pips and stalks of grapes. It can also be picked up from wooden casks. The tannins in unripe grapes are not water-soluble and will remain harsh no matter how old the wine is, whereas the tannins in ripe grapes are water-soluble and drop out as the wine matures. Ripe grape tannin softens with age, is indispensable in the structure of a serious red wine, and is useful when matching food and wine. Tannin is also essential for the preservation of red wines.

Tart Refers to a noticeable acidity, coming somewhere between sharp and piquant.

Terroir Literally 'soil' in French, but in a viticultural sense *terroir* refers to the complete growing environment, which also includes altitude, aspect, climate and any other factor that may affect the life of a vine.

Thin A wine lacking in body, fruit and other properties.

Tight A firm wine of good extract and possibly significant tannin that seems to be under tension, like a wound spring waiting to be released. Its potential is far more obvious than that of reticent or closed wines.

Toasty A bottle-induced aroma commonly associated with the Chardonnay grape and/or oak.

Typical An over-used and less than honest form of 'honest'.

Typicity A wine that shows good typicity is one that accurately reflects its grape and soil.

Undertone Subtle and supporting, not dominating like an overtone. In a fine wine, a strong and simple overtone of youth can evolve into a delicate undertone with maturity, adding to a vast array of other nuances that give it complexity.

Ungenerous A wine that lacks generosity has little or no fruit and far too much tannin (if red) or acidity for a correct and harmonious balance.

Upfront Suggests an attractive, simple quality immediately recognized, which says it all. The wine may initially be interesting, but there would be no further development and the last glass would say nothing more than the first.

Vanillin An aldehyde with a vanilla aroma found naturally in oak to some degree or another.

Varietal, varietal character The character of a single grape variety as expressed in the wine it produces.

Vinification Far more than simply fermentation, this involves the entire process of making wine, from the moment the grapes are picked to the point it is bottled.

Vin ordinaire Literally an ordinary wine, this term is synonymous with the derogatory meaning of table wine.

Vintage (1) A wine of one year. (2) Synonymous with harvest.

Vivid The fruit in some wines can be so fresh, ripe, clean-cut and expressive that it quickly gives a vivid impression of complete character in the mouth.

Warm, warmth Suggestive of a good-flavoured red wine with a high alcoholic content or, if used with cedary or creamy, well matured in oak.

Weight, weighty Refers to the body of a wine.

Widget Nickname employed by Boddingtons for their version of the Draughtflow system developed by Guinness to replicate the creamy head of a draught stout. Guinness may have invented this simple but clever plastic device, but the widget was unknown before cult comedian Jack Dee sang the immortal words, 'It's got a widget, a widget it has got.'

Yield There are two forms of yield: how much fruit is produced from a given area of land, and how much juice you press from it. Confusingly, wine people in Europe tend to talk about hectolitres per hectare (hl/ha), which is literally how much juice has been squeezed from an area of land. This is more than a bit daft and open to abuse, but generally white wines can benefit from a higher yield than red wines, although sweet wines should be the lowest of all yields. Sparkling wines can get away with relatively high yields. For example, Sauternes averages 25hl/ha, Bordeaux 50hl/ha, and Champagne 80hl/ha.

Zesty A lively characteristic that suggests a zippy, tactile impression combined, maybe, with a hint of citrussy aroma.

Zing, zingy, zip, zippy Terms all indicative of something refreshing, lively and vital, resulting from a high balance of ripe fruit acidity.

INDEX

This index is to the wines and beers as found in the Supermarket Directory, not the Wine & Beer Rankings.

6X Export, Wadworth, *37, 70, 78, 142*
10 Year Old Tawny Port NV Smith Woodhouse, Tesco, *178*
10 Years Old Port NV Morgan Brothers, St Michael, *114*

A

Adnams Suffolk Strong Ale, *154*
Agramont 1995 Viura Chardonnay, *192*
Amazon NV Brazilian Cabernet Sauvignon, *117*
Amontillado Sherry NV Morrisons, *122*
Amstel Bier, *69*
Apostoles Palo Cortado Muy Viejo NV Gonzalez Byass, *197*
Argentine Dry Red NV Bright Brothers, *59*
Artadi 1994 Viñas de Gain, Rioja, *18*
Asda Champagne NV Brut Réserve, Cuvée Speciale, *11*
Asda German Pilsener, *13*
Asti Dolce NV Perlino, Safeway, *139*
Asti NV Rialto, *65*
Asti NV Tosti, St Michael, *112*
Aston Manor Best Bitter, *94*
Atlanta Ice, St Michael, *115*
Australian Chardonnay Blanc de Blancs 1994 Brut, Seppelt, St Michael, *112*
Australian Chardonnay NV Somerfield, *163*
Australian Dry Red Wine NV D.W.L., *59*
Australian Marsanne 1996 Murchison Vineyard, Safeway, *138*
Australian Medium Dry NV Southcorp Wines, St Michael, *109*
Australian Shiraz Cabernet NV Sainsbury's, *146*
Australian Sparkling Wine NV Brut Reserve, Seppelt, Safeway, *138*
Avignonesi 1993 Pinot Nero di Valdicapraia, *190*
Avignonesi 1993 Vino Nobile di Montepulciano, *32, 189*

B

Backwoods Bitter, Crtopton Brewery, *26*
Badger Hill 1994 Chardonnay Oak Barrel Fermented, *62*
Balbi Vineyard 1995 Malbec Syrah, *90*
Balbi Vineyard 1996 Malbec, *133*
Balbi Vineyard 1996 Syrah Rosé, *48*
Banks's Draught, Smoothpour, *67*

INDEX

Bankside Shiraz 1994 Hardys, *5*
Banrock Station 1996 Mataro Grenache Shiraz, Hardys, *147*
Barolo 1992 Cantina Terre del Barolo, *44*
Barolo 1992 Cantine Gemma, *173*
Barolo 1992 Giacosa Fratelli, *173*
Baron d'Arignac 1996 Vin de Pays de l'Aude, *29*
Baron de Ley 1991 Rioja Reserva, *5*
Barramundi NV Brut, *49*
Barramundi NV Semillon/Chardonnay, *45*
Barramundi NV Semillon/Colombard/Chardonnay, *20*
Bass, Our Finest Ale, *25, 68*
Batemans XXXB Classic Bitter, *182*
La Baume Sauvignon Blanc 1996 Vin de Pays d'Oc, Philippe de Baudin, *137*
La Baume Syrah Grenache 1995 Vin de Pays d'Oc, *60*
Beamish Draught Irish Stout, *67, 123*
Beaumes de Venise 1994 Côtes-du-Rhône-Villages, Carte Noire, *172*
Beck's, *38, 71, 78*
Belondrade y Lurton 1994 Rueda, *195*
Beyers Truter NV Pinotage, Tesco, *170*
Bianco di Custoza 1996 La Casella, St Michael, *110*
Bière d'Alsace Premium French Lager, Fischer, St Michael, *114*
Big Frank's Red 1995 Minervois, *118*
Bin 444 Cabernet Sauvignon 1994 Wyndham Estate, *119*
Bishops Finger Kentish Strong Ale, Shepherd Neame, *23, 36, 55, 78, 102*
Bisquertt 1995 Merlot, *60*
Black Douglas, Broughton Ales, *23*
Black Fort Premium Lager, Som's, *53*
Black Sheep Ale, Paul Theakston's Black Sheep Brewery, *25, 51, 125, 141, 180*
Blonderbraü Pils, *34*
Blossom Hill Winery 1995 White Zinfandel, *99*
Bob's Gold, Ruddles Character Ales, *26*
Boddingtons Draught, *67*
Boddingtons Manchester Gold, *101, 125*
Bombardier Premium Bitter, Charles Wells, *54, 24*
Bonarda NV Picajuan Peak, *169*
Booth & Co. Ltd Anniversary Ale, 1847–1997, *24*
Booths Champagne NV Brut, *22*
Booths Finest Reserve Port NV Quinta da Rosa, *22*
Booths Oak Aged Vintage Claret 1994 Bordeaux Supérieur, *17*
Bordeaux Blanc Sec 1995 Aged in Oak, Safeway, *136*
Boston Beer, Whitbread, *52, 68, 101, 141*
Bourgogne Chardonnay 1996 Charles Viénot, *33*
Bourgogne Hautes-Côtes-de-Beaune 1995 Tête de Cuvée, Les Caves des Hautes-Côtes, *188*
Bourgogne Pinot Noir 1995 Charles Viénot, *31*
Bovlei Winery 1995 Merlot, *118*

Index

Brady's Original Irish Stout, Kwik Save, *94*
Breakaway 1995 Grenache Shiraz, *134*
Brewers Droop, Marston Moor Brewery, *125*
Bright Brothers 1994 Old Vines, *3*
Brouilly 1995 Georges Duboeuf, *61*
Brown Brothers 1995 Late Harvested Riesling, *195*
Browns of Padthaway 1995 Shiraz T-Trellis, *189*
Bud Ice, Anheuser-Busch Inc., *36, 71, 102, 182*
Budweiser Budvar, *23, 35, 69, 123, 140, 180*
Bulgarian Cabernet Sauvignon 1991 Reserve, Vini, Safeway, *134*
Bulgarian Cabernet Sauvignon 1992 Barrel Matured, Vinprom, Safeway, *133*
Bulgarian Country Wine NV Cabernet Sauvignon & Merlot, Domaine Boyar, *88*
Bulgarian Merlot & Cabernet Sauvignon 1995 Domaine Boyar, *88*
Bulgarian Merlot Reserve 1992 Domaine Boyar, *89*
Bulgarian Vintage Blend 1995 Chardonnay & Sauvignon Blanc, Domaine Boyar, *32*
The Bulgarian Vintners' NV Cabernet Sauvignon & Merlot, *116*
Bush Vine Grenache 1995 Limited Edition, *147*

C

Cabernet de Saumur Rosé NV Cave des Vignerons de Saumur, Tesco, *176*
Cabernet Sauvignon 1995 Angove's, Co-op, *42*
Cabernet Sauvignon 1995 Campo dos Frades, *169*
Cabernet Sauvignon Vin de Pays d'Oc NV Les Vignerons du Val d'Orbieu, Somerfield, *158*
Cabernet Sauvignon/Shiraz 1996 Du Toitskloof Wine Cellar, *186*
Cadet Claret 1995 Baron Philippe de Rothschild, *31*
Caffrey's Draught Irish Ale, *37, 70, 141, 181*
Cains Formidable Ale, *50*
Caledonian 70/- Amber Ale, Caledonian Brewery, *50*
Caledonian 80/- Export Ale, Caledonian Brewery, *51*
Canfera 1994 Single Vineyard, St Michael, *107*
Le Canne 1995 Boscaini Bardolino Classico Riserva, *43*
Canyon Road 1994 Cabernet Sauvignon, St Michael, *106*
Cape Afrika 1992 Pinotage, *43*
Cape Afrika 1996 Rhine Riesling, *46*
Cape Cinsaut NV Tesco, *169*
Carlsberg Elephant, Strong Imported Beer, *72, 79, 128, 184*
Carlsberg Ice Beer, *142*
Carmen 1995 Grande Vidure Cabernet Reserve, *18*
Casa di Giovanni 1994 Oak Aged, Safeway, *134*
Casa Leona 1995 Reserve Cabernet

284 INDEX

Sauvignon, St Michael, *105*
Casa Leona 1996 Chardonnay, St Michael, *109*
Casa Leona 1996 Reserve Merlot, St Michael, *105*
Casa Porta 1995 Cabernet Sauvignon, *97*
Casablanca 1996 Sauvignon Blanc, *47*
Castel Pujol 1994 Tannat, *59*
Castel Pujol 1996 Sauvignon Blanc, *63*
Castelgreve 1995 Chianti Classico, *61*
Castillo de Liria NV Moscatel, *94*
Castle Lager, SA Breweries, *179*
Cava Brunet NV Brut Reserva, *93*
The Celebrated Oatmeal Stout, Samuel Smith, *71*
Ceres Royal Export, *49*
CH'TI Bière de Garde en Nord, Amber Beer, *142*
Chablis 1994 Les Maîtres Goustiers, SA L.R., *99*
Chablis 1995 C.V.C., St Michael, *111*
Chablis NV Guy Mothe, Asda, *10*
Chablis Premier Cru Fourchaume 1994 Domaine du Colombier, *10*
Chablis Premier Cru Fourchaume 1995 Domaine du Colombier, *10*
Chablis, Sainsbury's Classic Selection 1995 Domaine Sainte Celine, *150*
Champagne André Simon NV Brut, *100*
Champagne Chartogne-Taillet NV Brut, Cuvée Sainte-Anne, *139*
Champagne Cuvée Orpale 1985 Blanc de Blancs Brut, St Michael, *112*
Champagne Jacquart NV Brut Tradition, *78*
Champagne Lanson NV Black Label Brut, *66*
Champagne Paul Hérard NV Blanc de Noirs Brut, *122*
Champagne Prince William NV Blanc de Blancs Brut, *165*
Champagne Prince William NV Brut Reserve, *165*
Champagne Prince William NV Rosé Brut, *165*
Champagne Taittinger NV Brut Réserve, *34*
Champagne Veuve de Medts NV Brut Premier Cru, St Michael, *112*
Chapel Down Epoch NV Brut, *21*
Chapel Hill NV Cabernet Sauvignon, *41*, *97*
Chapel Hill NV Irsai Oliver, *63*
Chardonnay 1995 Jidvei Winery, *33*
Chardonnay Bin 65 1996 Lindemans, St Michael, *110*
Chardonnay Colombard 1996 Wingara, Safeway, *137*
Chardonnay Oaked 1996 Mátra Mountain, *136*
Chardonnay par Yves Grassa 1996 Barrel Fermented, Vin de Pays des Côtes-de-Gascogne, *8*
Chardonnay Viognier 1996 Juanico, St Michael, *111*
La Chasse du Pape Réserve 1995 Côtes-du-Rhône, *135*
Château de Parenchère 1995 Bordeaux Supérieur, *5*

Index

Château du Bluizard 1995
Beaujolais-Villages, *170*

Château du Plantier 1995 Entre-
Deux-Mers, *137*

Château Fourtanet 1993 Côtes-de-
Castillon, *43*

Château la Brunette 1995 Bordeaux,
17

Château La Lagune 1993 Haut-
Médoc, *191*

Château La Vieille Cure 1990
Sainsbury's Selected Vintage, *148*

Château Lamothe Vincent 1996
Sauvignon, *20*

Château Malijay 1995 Fontanilles,
Côtes-du-Rhône, *31*

Château Monlot Capet 1993 St.-
Emilion Grand Cru, *45*

Château Pierrousselle 1995
Bordeaux, Co-op, *42*

Château Pierrousselle 1995 Entre-
Deux-Mers, Co-op, *46*

Château Reynella 1994 Basket
Pressed Cabernet Merlot, *6*

Château Reynella 1995 Chardonnay,
10

Château Saint Auriol 1994
Corbières, *187*

Château Saint Galier 1995 Graves,
118

Château Saint Robert 1993 Graves,
161

Château Saint-Maurice 1995 Côtes-
du-Rhône, *187*

Château Sénéjac 1993 Haut-Médoc,
189

Château Tahbilk 1996 Marsanne
Unwooded, *65*

Château Terres Douces 1995 Cuvée
Prestige, *193*

Château Valoussière 1995 Coteaux-
du-Languedoc, Brut de Cuve,
160

Châteauneuf-du-Pape 1994 Cellier
des Princes, *45*

Châteauneuf-du-Pape 1994
Domaine du Vieux Lazaret, *119*

Châteauneuf-du-Pape 1995
Domaine de la Solitude, *162*

Châteauneuf-du-Pape 1995 Le
Chemin des Mulets, *174*

Châteauneuf-du-Pape 1996 S.A.
V.J.Q., Tesco, *173*

Chenin Blanc 1996 Barrel
Fermented, Ryland's Grove, *175*

Chenin Blanc NV Vin de Pays du
Jardin de la France, Tesco, *174*

Chianti 1995 Piccini, Co-op, *42*

Chianti Classico 1994 Ampelos,
Tesco, *170*

Chianti Classico 1995 Basilica
Cafaggio, St Michael, *106*

Chianti Classico 1995 Montecchio,
161

Chianti Classico, Villa Primavera
1995 Conti Serristori,
Somerfield, *161*

Chianti Rufina 1995 Fratelli Grati,
Tesco, *170*

Chilean Cabernet Merlot 1995
Vinicola Las Taguas, Asda, *3*

Chilean Cabernet Sauvignon 1995
Viña Cornellana, Somerfield, *159*

Chilean Cabernet Sauvignon 1996
Viña San Pedro, Safeway, *134*

Chilean Cabernet Sauvignon Rosé
NV Sainsbury's, *150*

Chilean Long Slim Red 1994

Cabernet Merlot, Co-op, *41*
Chilean Long Slim White 1996 Chardonnay Semillon, Co-op, *45*
Chilean Sauvignon Blanc 1996 Viña San Pedro, Safeway, *137*
Chilean Sauvignon Blanc 1996 Vinicola Las Taguas, Asda, *6*
Chilean Sauvignon Blanc NV Sagrada Familia, Somerfield, *163*
Chimango NV Tempranillo Malbec, Tesco, *169*
Church Road Reserve 1994 Cabernet Sauvignon Merlot, *191*
Churchill's White Port NV, *22*
Claret Bordeaux NV Co-op, *41*
Claret NV Cuvee Prestige, Sainsbury's, *147*
Claret NV Paul Barbe, Asda, *2*
Claret NV Yvon Mau, Tesco, *169*
Claret Réserve NV Yvon Mau, Tesco, *170*
Classic Gewurztraminer 1995 Posta Romana, *62*
Classic Pinot Noir 1993 Posta Romana, *97*
Clos Malverne 1995 Auret, *173*
Clos Malverne 1996 Pinotage, *188*
Clos Saint Michel 1995 Châteauneuf-du-Pape, *190*
Cobra Indian Lager, Mysore Breweries, *79*
Cockburn's Anno 1989 Late Bottled Vintage Port, *123*
Cockburn's Special Reserve Port NV, *12*
Cocker Hoop Golden Bitter, Jennings Brothers, *54, 25*
Codorníu Première Cuvée NV Brut Chardonnay, *66*
Colli di Catone 1995 Frascati Superiore, Asda, *7*
Colombara 1996 Soave Classico, Zenato, *192*
Colombard Chardonnay NV, *93*
Comtesse de Die Tradition 1995 Clairette de Die, Première Cuvée, *195*
Concha y Toro 1996 Merlot, *187*
Cono Sur 1995 Cabernet Sauvignon, Selection Reserve, *61*
Cooks 1996 Sauvignon Blanc, *64*
Coopers Creek 1996 Sauvignon Blanc, *164*
Coopers Sparkling Ale, *140*
Corbans 1994 Marlborough Pinot Noir Private Bin, *190*
Cornas 1994 M. Chapoutier, *191*
Cosme Palacio y Hermanos 1995 Rioja, *188*
Costières de Nîmes 1995 Les Garrigues, Sainsbury's, *146*
Côte-de-Beaune-Villages 1995 Jules Vignon, Co-op, *43*
Côtes-du-Brulhois 1990 Cave de Donzac, *17*
Côtes-du-Lubéron 1995 Rhône Valley Red Wine, Pol Romain, *117*
Côtes-du-Rhône 1993 Domaine de Pauline, *170*
Côtes-du-Rhône 1996 Aged in Oak, Roger Bernoin, *3*
Côtes-du-Rhône NV Co-op, *41*
Côtes-du-Rhône NV F. Dubessy, *89*
Côtes-du-Rhône NV Gabriel Meffre, Morrisons, *117*
Côtes-du-Roussillon NV Foncalieu, Morrisons, *120*

Index

Côtes-du-Ventoux 1995 La Falaise, *16*
La Coume de Peyre 1996 Vin de Pays des Côtes-de-Gascogne, *136*
Cranswick Estate 1995 Shiraz, *118*
Cranswick Pinot Chardonnay NV Brut, *11*
Cream Sherry NV Williams & Humbert, St Michael, *113*
Crozes-Hermitage 1994 Cave de Tain l'Hermitage, *119*
Crozes-Hermitage 1994 Quinson, *31*
Crozes-Hermitage 1995 Groupe Jean-Paul Selles, *160*
Cuckoo Hill Oak Barrel Chardonnay 1995 Vin de Pays d'Oc, *64*
Cuckoo Hill Viognier 1995 Vin de Pays d'Oc, *64*
Cuckoo Hill Viognier NV Vin de Pays d'Oc, *8*
Cumberland Ale, Jennings Brothers, *53, 126*
Cune 1994 Rioja, *76*
Currawong Creek 1996 Chardonnay, *192*
La Cuvée Mythique 1994 Vin de Pays d'Oc, *135*

D

DAB Original German Beer, Dortmunder Actien-Brauerei, *51*
Daniels Hammer Strong Ale, Thwaites, *124*
Dão 1994 Co-op, *42*
Daredevil, A Very Strong Traditional Ale, Everards, *57*
Deep Pacific 1996 Merlot-Cabernet Sauvignon, *89*
Denbies 95 1995, *92*

Deuchars IPA, Export Strength, Caledonian Brewery, *53*
Diego de Almagro 1993 Felix Solis, *29*
Diemersdal 1996 Merlot, *172*
Diemersdal 1996 Pinotage, *188*
Diemersdal 1996 Syrah, *172*
Dom Brial Muscat de Rivesaltes 1996, *66*
Domaine Bordeneuve 1996 Vin de Pays des Côtes-de-Gascogne, *162*
Domaine de Conroy 1994 Brouilly, *172*
Domaine de Grangeneuve 1995 Coteaux-du-Tricastin, Cuvée Tradition, *4*
Domaine de Jouclary 1993 Cabardès, *170*
Domaine de l'Hortus 1994 Classique, *18*
Domaine de Planterieu 1996 Vin de Pays des Côtes-de-Gascogne, Maïté Dubuc-Grassa, *191*
Domaine de Saubagnère 1995 Sauvignon Colombard, Vin de Pays des Côtes-de-Gascogne, *175*
Domaine de Sours 1996 Bordeaux Rosé, *151*
Domaine des Bruyères 1995 Côtes-de-Malepère, *90*
Domaine Georges Bertrand 1994 Corbières, Cuvée Spéciale, *171*
Domaine Jeune 1996 Cépage Counoise, Vin de Pays du Gard, St Michael, *105*
Domaine L'Argentier 1995 Terret, Vin de Pays des Côtes-de-Thau, *32*

288 INDEX

Domaine La Tuque Bel-Air 1994 Côtes-de-Castillon, *160*
Domaine Mandeville Chardonnay 1996 Vin de Pays d'Oc, St Michael, *110*
Domaine Saubagnère 1995 Vin de Pays des Côtes-de-Gascogne, Les Domaines, Tesco, *175*
Domaine Villeroy-Castellas 1996 Sauvignon Blanc, Vin de Pays des Sables du Golfe du Lion, *32*
La Domeque, Tête de Cuvée 1995 Vieilles Vignes Syrah, Vin de Pays d'Oc, *4*
La Domeque, Tête de Cuvée 1996 Vieilles Vignes Blanc, Vin de Pays d'Oc, *9*
Dornfelder 1994 Gustav Adolf Schmitt, *30*
Double Maxim Premium, Vaux, *50*
Dragon Stout, Desnoes & Geddes, *95*
Draught Guinness, *35, 68, 79, 101, 124*
Drewrys Genuine Imported American Beer, Private Liquor Brands UK, *50*
Dry Amontillado Sherry NV Solera Jerezana, Waitrose, *196*
Dry Fly Medium Sherry NV Amontillado, Findlater's, *197*
Dry Oloroso Sherry NV Solera Jerezana, Waitrose, *196*
Duque de Viseu 1992 Dão, *43*
Duvel, Brouwerij Moortgat, *57*

E

Elhovo 1992 Cabernet Sauvignon Reserve, Domaine Boyar, *89*
Enate Tinto 1995 Cabernet Sauvignon Merlot, *187*
Ermitage du Pic St.-Loup 1996 Coteaux du Languedoc, Maurel Vedeau, Waitrose, *187*
Esk Valley 1995 Merlot Cabernet Sauvignon, *190*
Espiga 1995 Vinho Tinto, *17*
Etchart 1996 Cafayate Torrontes, *63*
Exmoor Gold, Gold Hill Brewery, *181*

F

Fairview 1996 Chenin Blanc, *192*
Fairview 1996 Gewürztraminer, *7*
Falcoaria 1994 Almeirim, *188*
The Famous Taddy Porter, Samuel Smith, *55, 181*
Fargo, Charles Wells, *95*
La Falleras 1996 St Michael, *104, 108*
Faugères 1994 Gilbert Alquier, *18*
Faustino V 1991 Rioja Reserva, *98*
Festive Ale, Bottle Conditioned, King & Barnes, *180*
Fetzer Valley Oaks 1994 Cabernet Sauvignon, *188*
Fine Vintage Character Port NV Smith Woodhouse, Co-op, *49*
Finest Madeira NV Madeira Wine Company, Tesco, *178*
Finest Special Reserve Port NV Real Companhia, Tesco, *177*
Fischer Tradition, Bière Blonde Spéciale d'Alsace, *181*
Fitou Oak Aged 1995 Baron de la Tour, *171*
Fiuza 1995 Chardonnay, *47*
Fiuza 1995 Sauvignon, *46*

Index

Fixin 1994 Les Vins Pierre Leduc, 44
Flamenco NV Spanish Full Red, 88
Flamenco NV Spanish Sweet White, 91
Flanders Bier, Asda, 12
Fleurie 1995 Clos de la Chapelle des Bois, 5
Fleurie 1995 Paul Boutinot, 19
Floral Vinho Tinto Reserva 1994 Caves Aliança, 16
Formidable Ale, Cains, 26
La Fortuna 1996 Merlot, 97
Foster's Ice Beer, Courage Limited, 37, 101
Four Rivers 1995 Cabernet Sauvignon, 42
Frascati Superiore 1995 Tuscolana Esportazioni, Co-op, 46
Freixenet Cava NV Cordon Negro Brut, 99
French Dry White Wine NV Bouey, Tesco, 174
Frontier Island Merlot 1994 Hungarian Country Wine, 75
Frontignan NV Vin de Liqueur, 166
Fuggles Imperial Strong Ale, Castle Eden Brewery, 37, 54, 70, 95, 143
Fuller's 1845, Bottle Conditioned Celebration Strong Ale, 38, 71, 183
Fuller's ESB Export, Extra Special Bitter, 37, 71
Fuller's London Pride, Premium Ale, 26, 37, 56, 69, 143
Fuller's Old Winter Ale, 38
Fuller's Refreshing Summer Ale, 141

G

Gabbia d'Oro NV Vino Rosso, 87
Galet Vineyards 1996 Roussanne Barrel Reserve, Sainsbury's, 150
Gentil 'Hugel' 1995 Alsace, 149
Gentleman Jack Strong Ale, Shepherd Neame, Asda, 13
German Pilsener Bier, Tesco, 178
Gewurztraminer Vin d'Alsace 1996 Cave des Vignerons Turckheim, Somerfield, 164
Gigondas 1995 Domaine de la Mourielle, 61
Gigondas 1995 Fleuron des Vignes, 43
Gilde Pilsener, 94
Gillespie's Draught Malt Stout, Scottish & Newcastle Breweries, 124, 140
Gloria Ferrer Blanc de Noirs NV Freixenet Sonoma Caves, 77
Golden Promise Organic Ale, Caledonian Brewery, 55
Graham's Late Bottled Vintage Port 1991, 12
Gran Condal 1990 Rioja Reserva, 44
Grande Cuvée Chardonnay 1995 Laroche, Vin de Pays d'Oc, 33
Great with Fish 1996 Vin de Pays de l'Aude, Tesco, 175
Great with Steak 1995 Merlot, Vin de Pays d'Oc, Tesco, 169
Greenmantle Ale, Broughton Ales, 51
Grolsch Premium Lager, 39, 67, 80, 95, 128, 144
Guelbenzu 1995 Jardin, 18
Guinness Foreign Extra Stout, 28, 72

INDEX

Guinness Original Stout, 35, 68, 100, 140, 179

H

Haan 1996 Barossa Valley Chardonnay, St Michael, 111
Hanwood 1995 Cabernet Sauvignon, McWilliams, 118
Hardys 1994 Cabernet Sauvignon, 136
Hardys Grenache Shiraz 1996 Stamps of Australia, 65
Hidden River NV Ruby Cabernet, 76
Hobgoblin Extra Strong Ale, Wychwood Brewery, 126, 143, 182
Hock 1996 Deutscher Tafelwein Rhein, St Michael, 108
Hock 1996 K. Linden, Kwik Save, 91
Hock Deutscher Tafelwein NV Zeller Barl Kellerei, Londis, 98
Hock NV Maas Nathan, Tesco, 174
Hock NV Peter Bott, 91
Hoegaarden White Beer, Bottle Conditioned, 55, 142
Holland Bier, Asda, 13
Honey Tree Semillon Chardonnay 1996 Rosemount Estate, St Michael, 110
Honey Tree Shiraz Cabernet 1996 Rosemount Estate, St Michael, 106
Hoya de Cadenas 1989 Reserva, 60
Hungarian Chardonnay 1996 Private Reserve, Neszmély Winery, 6
Hungarian Country White NV Stowells of Chelsea, 62
Hungarian Pinot Gris NV Szölöskert Cooperative, Sainsbury's, 149
Hungarian Sauvignon Blanc 1995 Private Reserve, Neszmély Winery, 6
Hürlimann Premium Swiss Lager, Shepherd Neame, 25

I

Impala 1996 Cape White, 92
Impala 1996 Pinotage, 90
India Pale Ale Original Export, Shepherd Neame, 56
IPA Draught Bitter, Greene King, 34
Italian Birra, Export Premium Lager, Asda, 13

J

Jacana 1995 Pinotage Reserve, 136
Jacana 1996 Chardonnay, 164
Jackson Estate 1996 Sauvignon Blanc, 176
Jacob's Creek 1996 Dry Riesling, Orlando, 64
Jade Peaks 1996 Chenin Blanc, 91
James Herrick 1995 Chardonnay, Vin de Pays d'Oc, 77
James Herrick 1995 Cuvée Simone, Vin de Pays d'Oc, 160, 171, 187
James Herrick 1996 Chardonnay, Vin de Pays d'Oc, 163
Jamiesons Run 1996 Chardonnay, 164
Jennsberg 1995 Cabernet Sauvignon Merlot, 171
Jennsberg 1996 Pinot Noir, Asda, 4

Index

John Smith's Bitter, Tadcaster Brewery, *100*
John Smith's Extra Smooth Bitter, *67*
José Neiva 1994 Oak Aged, *16, 19*

K

Kaituna Hills 1996 Chardonnay, St Michael, *110*
Kaituna Hills 1996 Sauvignon Blanc, St Michael, *110*
Katnook Estate 1996 Sauvignon Blanc, *21*
Kendermann 1995 Riesling Dry, *64*
Keoghan's Ale, Draught, Federation Brewery, *123*
Kilkenny Irish Beer Draught, St Francis Abbey Brewery, Guinness, *35, 68, 102, 126, 141, 180*
Kingston 1995 Grenache, *59*
Kingston 1996 Shiraz Mataro, *42*
Kirchheimer Schwarzerde Beerenauslese 1994 Zimmermann-Graeff, *48*
König-Pilsener, *78*
Kourtaki NV Retsina of Attica, *92*
Krone Borealis 1993 Brut, *195*
Kronenbourg 1664, Courage Ltd, *100, 179*

L

L de La Louvière 1994 Pessac-Léognan, *190*
Lambrusco 4 NV GI SpA, *93*
Landlord, Timothy Taylor's Strong Pale Ale, *24*
Landskroon 1996 Cinsaut Shiraz, *134*
Langenbach Kabinett 1995 Binger St.-Rochuskapelle, *63*
Late Bottled Vintage Port 1988 Morgan Brothers, St Michael, *113*
Late Bottled Vintage Port 1991 Smith Woodhouse, Co-op, *49*
Lawson's Dry Hills 1996 Sauvignon Blanc, *194*
LBV Port 1990 Smith Woodhouse, Asda, *12*
LBV Port 1990 Smith Woodhouse, Tesco, *178*
Leasingham Domain 1994 Cabernet Sauvignon Malbec, *44*
Leasingham Domaine 1993 Semillon, *48*
Libertas 1994 Merlot, *76*
Liebfraumilch 1996 Rheinhessen, St Michael, *108*
Lindauer NV Brut, *22*
Lindemans 1994 Coonawarra Botrytis Riesling, *165*
Lindemans Bin 50 1995 Shiraz, *61*
Lindemans Padthaway 1995 Pinot Noir, *148*
Long Mountain 1995 Chenin Blanc, *99*
Long Mountain 1995 Shiraz, *187*
Lurton, Bodega Jacques y François, 1996 Pinot Gris, *192*
Lustau Solera Reserva Fine Sherry NV Pedro Ximénez San Emilio, *22*

M

Macabeo Chardonnay 1996 Concavins & Hugh Ryman, St Michael, *109*

292 INDEX

Mâcon-Igé 1996 Les Vignerons d'Igé, *33*

Mamre Brook 1995 Chardonnay, *194*

Manzanilla Superior Sherry NV Sanchez Romate, Tesco, *177*

Marble Mountain 1995 St.-George Cabernet Sauvignon, Asda, *3*

Marqués de Cacérès 1992 Rioja, *61*

Marqués de Monistrol 1993 Merlot, *42*

Marqués de Murrieta Ygay 1989 Rioja Reserva Especial, *190*

Marston's Burton S.P.A., *128, 183*

Marston's India Export Pale Ale, Head Brewer's Choice, *56, 127*

Marston's Oyster Stout, Bottle Conditioned, *27, 54, 126*

Marston's Pedigree Bitter, *52*

Marston's Pedigree Bitter, *24, 68, 124*

Mas de Daumas Gassac 1995 Vin de Pays de l'Hérault, *21*

Master Brew Premium Ale, Bottle Conditioned, Shepherd Neame, *51, 101*

Matusalem Oloroso Dulce Muy Viejo NV Gonzalez Byass, *197*

McLaren Vale Shiraz 1994 Maglieri, Tesco, *173*

Merlin's Ale, Broughton Ales, *53*

Merlot Vin de Pays d'Oc 1996 Baron Philippe de Rothschild, *76*

Mick Morris Liqueur Muscat NV Rutherglen, *153*

The Million Vineyard 1995 Chardonnay, Barrel Fermented, *138*

Minervois 1995 Domaine Roche Vue, *134*

Monastrell Xarel-lo NV Cava Brut, Freixenet, *77*

Monbazillac 1995 Les Caves Saint-Romain, *65*

Monbazillac Cuvée Prestige 1994 Domaine du Haut-Rauly, *48*

Monkey Wrench Strong Ale, Daleside Brewery, *183*

Monkmans Slaughter Bitter, Cropton Brewery, *27*

Mont-Marçal 1991 Cabernet Sauvignon Reserva, *18*

Montagne Noire 1996 Sauvignon Blanc, Vin de Pays d'Oc, Asda, *7*

Montagne Noire Chardonnay 1996 Vin de Pays d'Oc, Asda, *7*

Montagne Noire Red NV Vin de Pays de l'Aude, Asda, *2*

Montagny Premier Cru 1995 Les Vignes de la Croix, St Michael, *111*

Montepulciano d'Abruzzo 1995 Bianchi, *159*

Montepulciano d'Abruzzo 1995 Umani Ronchi, *186*

Moretti, Birra Friulana, *181*

Morgon, Les Charmes 1994 Domaine Brisson, *44*

Moscatel de Valencia 1995 Vicente Gandia, Safeway, *139*

Moscatel de Valencia NV Vicente Gandia, Somerfield, *166*

Mosel Deutscher Tafelwein NV St.-Urbanus Weinkellerei, Co-op, *45*

Mount Hurtle 1995 Grenache Shiraz, *4*

Mouton Cadet Réserve 1994 Baron Philippe de Rothschild, *31*

Index

Murphy's Draught Irish Stout, 35–36, 70, 123, 126, 143, 179
Muscadet 1996 Jean Michel, 91
Muscadet 1996 Les Celliers de la Sanguèze, 149
Muscadet de Sèvre-et-Maine Sur Lie 1995 Domaine de la Haute Maillardière, 47, 8, 150
Muscadet de Sèvre-et-Maine Sur Lie 1996 Pierre Guéry, Waitrose, 192
Muscadet NV Les Celliers du Prieuré, Tesco, 175
Muscat de Frontignan Blanc 1996 Danie de Wet, 11
Muscat Ottonel 1995 Nagyréde Estate, 63

N

Nastro Azzurro, Premium Beer, Peroni, 124
The Navigators 1989 LBV Port, Somerfield, 166
Nexus 1994 San Simone, 31
Niederhäuser Hermannsberg Riesling Spätlese 1992 Staatliche Weinbaudomäne, 176
Niersteiner Gutes Domtal NV Zeller Barl Kellerei, Londis, 98
Ninth Island 1996 Chardonnay, 21
Noval NV 10 Year Old Tawny Port, 197

O

Oaked Cabernet Sauvignon 1996 Thomas Hardy, Safeway, 135
Oaked Chardonnay 1996 Thomas Hardy, Safeway, 138
Oaked Shiraz NV Thomas Hardy, Safeway, 135
Ochoa 1995 Tempranillo-Garnacha, 76
Old Fart, Premium Strength Beer, Merrimans Brewery, 125
Old Growler, Nethergate Brewery, 183
Old Hooky Premium Ale, Hook Norton Brewery, 38
Old Jock Ale, Broughton Ales, 53
Old Speckled Hen, Morland, 79
Old Speckled Hen, Strong Fine Ale, Morland, 38, 56, 71, 144
Les Oliviers NV Vin de Table Blanc, 90
Les Oliviers NV Vin de Table Rouge, 87
Original Porter Strong Dark Ale, Shepherd Neame, 56
Orobio Rioja Reserva 1990 Artadi, Sainsbury's Selected Vintage, 148
Orvieto Classico 1996 Cantina del Coppiere, St Michael, 109

P

Pago de Carraovejas 1994 Ribera del Duero, 19
Palacio de la Vega 1993 Navarra, 31
Palmeras Estate 1995 Oak Aged Cabernet Sauvignon, 17
Parducci 1994 Petite Sirah, 119
Parkin's Special Bitter, Sainsbury's, 154
Parras Valley 1994 Cabernet Sauvignon-Merlot, St Michael, 104
Paul Masson NV California Red Wine, 90

Pedro Ximénez Cream of Cream NV Alvear, Sainsbury's, *152*
Pelican Bay NV Australian Chardonnay, Kwik Save, *93*
Pelican Bay NV Australian Red Wine, Kwik Save, *89*
Pelican Bay NV Australian Shiraz-Cabernet, *90*
Pendle Witches Brew, Strong Lancashire Ale, Moorhouse's, *24, 54, 124*
Penfolds 1994 Barrel Fermented Semillon, *193*
Penfolds Barossa Valley 1996 Semillon-Chardonnay, *9*
Penfolds Bin 128 1994 Shiraz, *162*
Penfolds Kalimna Bin 28 1993 Shiraz, *6*
Penfolds Kalimna Bin 28 1994 Shiraz, *62*
Penfolds Koonunga Hill 1996 Chardonnay, *193*
Penfolds Rawson's Retreat Bin 35 1995 Cabernet Sauvignon-Shiraz-Ruby Cabernet, *97*
Penfolds Rawson's Retreat Bin 202 1996 Riesling, *7*
Penfolds The Valleys 1995 Chardonnay, *164*
Pepperwood Grove 1995 Cabernet Franc, *30*
Perdeberg Cellar 1996 Sauvignon Blanc, St Michael, *109*
Pete's Wicked Ale, *127*
Peter Lehmann 1995 Cabernet Sauvignon, *135*
Peter Lehmann 1996 Semillon, *9, 65, 138*
Petit Chablis 1996 C.V.C., St Michael, *111*
Piesporter Michelsberg 1996 K. Linden, *92*
Pilsner Urquell, *127, 142*
Pinot Blanc 1995 Vin d'Alsace, Cave Vinicole d'Ingersheim, *64*
Pinot Blanc 1996 Nagyréde Estate, *136*
Pinot Noir 1995 River Route Selection, *2*
Pinotage 1995 Bovlei Winery, *60*
Plantagenet 1994 Shiraz, *19*
Poggio A'Frati 1991 Rocca di Castagnoli, Chianti Classico Riserva, *189*
Porto Souza 1991 L.B.V., *67*
Pouilly-Fumé 1996 Domaine J.M. Masson-Blondelet, *194*
Preiss-Zimmer Gewurztraminer 1995 Vin d'Alsace Tradition, *121*
Premium Original Pilsener Lager, St Michael, *114*
Prestige Oak-Aged Claret 1994 Saint Vincent Baron, *60*
Prunotto Fiulot 1995 Barbera d'Alba, *188*

Q

Quartet NV Brut, *196*
Quinta de Pancas 1995 Cabernet Sauvignon, *160*

R

Rawson's NV Ruby Cabernet Merlot, *159*
Redwood Trail Chardonnay 1994 By Sterling Vineyards, *99*
Redwood Trail Pinot Noir 1995 Coastal Vintners, *97*

Index

Réserve Chardonnay 1995 Vin de Pays d'Oc, Vignobles James Herrick, *176*

Rich Cream Sherry NV Solera Jerezana, Waitrose, *197*

Rich Cream Sherry NV Williams & Humbert, St Michael, *113*

The Ridge Wines 1995 Coonawarra Cabernet, St Michael, *107*

Riddoch 1994 Chardonnay, *21*

Ridgewood 1996 Mataro–Grenache, *186*

Riggwelter Strong Yorkshire Ale, Black Sheep Brewery, *27, 127, 155*

Rioja Barrel Fermented 1995 Almenar, Somerfield, *163*

Rioja NV Almaraz, Somerfield, *159*

Rioja Tempranillo 1994 Bodegas Age, St Michael, *106*

Riverview 1995 Chardonnay–Pinot Gris, *137*

Robertson 1996 Merlot, *42*

Romanian Country Wine NV Vinvico, *45*

Romanian Merlot 1996 Kwik Save, *88*

Romanian Pinot Noir 1993 Special Reserve, Rovit SA, Safeway, *133*

Rosé d'Anjou NV Co-op, *48*

Rosemount 1993 Orange Vineyard Cabernet Sauvignon, St Michael, *107*

Rosemount 1995 Orange Vineyard Chardonnay, St Michael, *112*

Rosemount Estate 1995 Cabernet Sauvignon, *76*

Rosemount Estate 1995 Chardonnay Show Reserve, *194*

Rosemount Estate 1995 Chardonnay, St Michael, *111*

Rosemount Estate 1996 Chardonnay, *33*

Rosemount Estate 1996 Semillon Chardonnay, *10*

Rosemount Estate 1996 Shiraz Cabernet, *61*

Rosenview 1996 Cabernet Sauvignon, *135*

Rosenview 1996 Cinsaut, *133*

Roseral 1994 Rioja, St Michael, *106*

Rothbury NV Museum Reserve Liqueur Muscat, *49*

Rouge de France NV Sélection Cuvée VE, Celliers de la Comtesse, *88*

Rowan Brook Cabernet Sauvignon 1994 Winemaker's Reserve Oak Aged, Asda, *4*

Rowan Brook Chardonnay 1996 Winemaker's Reserve Oak Aged, Asda, *8*

Rozès 1991 Late Bottled Vintage Port, *122*

Rozès 1992 Late Bottled Vintage Port, *34*

Rozzano 1995 Villa Pigna, *4*

Ruby Port NV Smith Woodhouse, Asda, *11*

Ruddles Draught Best Bitter, Rutland Brewery, *35*

La Rural 1996 Malbec, *4*

Rusty Rivet, Authentic Brown Ale, Shepherd Neame, Asda, *13*

S

Saaz Pils, French Premium Lager Beer, *50*

296 INDEX

Sacred Hill 1995 Whitecliff Sauvignon Blanc, *122*

Safeway Bière d'Alsace, French Lager, *140*

Safeway Irish Stout, Draught, *139*

Safeway Strong Bitter, *139*

Sainsbury's Asti NV Casa Vinicola IVASS, *151*

Sainsbury's Australian Shiraz 1995 Austral Wines, *147*

Sainsbury's Bière d'Alsace, French Lager, *154*

Sainsbury's Bière des Flandres, French Lager, *153*

Sainsbury's Blackfriars Porter, *154*

Sainsbury's Bordeaux Sauvignon NV Jean-Paul Jauffret, *149*

Sainsbury's Burgundy NV Guichard Potheret, *148*

Sainsbury's Cabernet Sauvignon 1995 Fiuza & Bright, *146*

Sainsbury's Cerveza de España, Premium Spanish Lager, *154*

Sainsbury's Champagne NV Blanc de Noirs Brut, *151*

Sainsbury's Champagne NV Brut Rosé, Beaumet, *152*

Sainsbury's Champagne NV Extra Dry, Duval-Leroy, *151*

Sainsbury's El Conde NV Vino de Mesa Tinto, *146*

Sainsbury's German Pilsener, Premium Lager, *154*

Sainsbury's LBV Port 1990 Temilobos, *152*

Sainsbury's Madeira NV Cossart Gordon, *153*

Sainsbury's Madeira NV Dry Sercial 5 Year Old, *153*

Sainsbury's Mosel NV Ehemalig Kurfürstliche Weinkellerei, *149*

Sainsbury's Oloroso NV Old Dry Sherry, Morgan Bros, *152*

Sainsbury's Sangiovese NV Bodegas Peñaflor, *146*

Sainsbury's Stolz Pilsner, Authentic German Beer, *154*

Sainsbury's Tempranillo NV Bodegas Peñaflor, *147*

Sainsbury's Vintage Champagne 1991 Blanc de Blancs Brut, UVCB, *152*

Sainsbury's Vintage Character Port NV Taylor Fladgate & Yeatman, *152*

Sainsbury's Vintage Port 1985 Quinta Dona Matilde, *153*

Sainsbury's White Burgundy NV Guichard Potheret, *150*

Saint-Denis Fine White Burgundy NV Chardonnay, *121*

Saint-Véran 1996 Domaine des Deux Roches, *10*

Saints 1994 Cabernet Merlot, St Michael, *106*

Saints 1995 Chardonnay, St Michael, *111*

Samuel Smith's Old Brewery Pale Ale, *55*

San Miguel Export, Cerveza Especial, *94*

San Miguel, Premium Export Lager, *70*

Sangiovese NV Picajuan Peak, *169*

Santa Lucia 1995 Lightly Oaked Viura, *19*

Santara 1995 Chardonnay, *20, 46*

Santara Tempranillo 1996 Conca de

Index

Barberà, *159*
Sauvignon Blanc 1996 Viña San Pedro, St Michael, *110*
Sauvignon Blanc 1996 Welmoed Winery, *20, 47*
Sauvignon Blanc NV Bordeaux, Co-op, *45*
Sauvignon Blanc NV Stowells of Chelsea, *63*
Sauvignon Blanc Vin de Pays d'Oc NV Foncalieu, Co-op, *47*
Scharffenberger NV Brut, *11*
Scharzhofberger Riesling Kabinett 1995 Müller-Burggraef, *163*
Schloss Schönborn 1989 Geisenheimer Mäuerchen Riesling Spätlese, *193*
Schoone Gevel 1995 Merlot, *171*
Schoone Gevel 1996 Chardonnay Reserve, *176*
Seaview Pinot Noir Chardonnay 1993 Brut, *151*
Seaview Pinot Noir Chardonnay 1994 Brut, *165*
Seaview Rosé NV Brut, *11, 66*
Seppelt 1992 Sparkling Shiraz Bottle Fermented, *177*
Shiraz 1994 Baileys, *44*
Shiraz 1995 Coonawarra Winegrowers, St Michael, *107*
Shiraz 1995 Oak Matured, St Michael, *106*
Shiraz 1996 McWilliam's, Safeway, *134*
Siglo Reserva 1988 Rioja, *62*
Skylark Hill Syrah 1995 Vin de Pays d'Oc, *89*
Skylark Hill Very Special White NV Vin de Pays d'Oc, Kwik Save, *92*
Sneck Lifter, Jennings Brothers, *55, 126, 182*
Soave NV Venier, *91*
Solana 1994 Torrontés & Treixadura, *121*
Soltero 1994 Rosso di Sicilia, Settesoli, *160*
La Source 1994 Cabernet Sauvignon, Vin de Pays d'Oc, *117*
South African Dry White NV W1226, Somerfield, *162*
South African Pinotage NV Clear Mountain, *30*
South African Premium Shiraz 1995 Tesco, *173*
South African Red NV Wonderfully Fruity, Morrisons, *117*
South Australia Chardonnay 1995 W1226, Asda, *7*
South Bay Vineyards NV American Pinot Noir, Sainsbury's, *148*
Southbrook Farms NV Canadian Cassis, *12*
Southern Creek 1996 Semillon-Chardonnay, Hardys, *192*
Spitfire Bottle Conditioned Ale, Shepherd Neame, *26, 36, 56, 79, 102, 127, 182*
St Peter's Golden Ale, St Peter's Brewery, *183*
St.-Julien 1993 Raoul Johnston, Tesco, *174*
St.-Laurens 1996 QbA Pfalz, *92*
Staropramen Dark Lager, Prague Breweries, *155, 184*
Staropramen, Prague Breweries, *57, 72, 128, 144, 184*
Stella Artois Dry, Export Strength

Premium Beer, Whitbread, *142*
Stella Artois, Premium Lager Beer, *69*
Sutter Home 1994 Zinfandel, *30*
Syrah 1996 Vin de Pays d'Oc, Paul Sapin, St Michael, *105*

T

Tamaioasa 1995 Pietroasa Estate, *63*
Tangle Foot Strong Ale, Badger Brewery, *127, 143*
Tannat Matured in Oak 1996 Juanico, St Michael, *105*
Tatachilla 1995 Merlot, Clarendon Vineyard, *189*
Tawny Port NV Morgan Brothers, St Michael, *113*
Temple Ruins Greek Red Wine 1995 Asda, *2*
Tempranillo NV Stowells of Chelsea, *59*
Tempranillo Oak Aged NV Co-op, *41*
Tennent's Robert Burns, Scottish Ale, *52, 141*
Tesco Champagne Blanc de Blancs NV Brut Cuvée Speciale, *177*
Tesco Porter Select Ales, Marston Thompson & Evershed, *180*
Tesco Select Ales India Pale Ale, Bottle Conditioned, Marston Thompson & Evershed, *180*
Tesco Strong Yorkshire Bitter, *178*
Theakston Lightfoot, Traditional Pale Beer, *25, 52, 69*
Thelema 1996 Sauvignon Blanc, *194*
Tocornal NV Cabernet-Malbec, *134*
Top 40 Chardonnay NV Vin de Pays d'Oc, Foncalieu, *193*
Touraine 1995 Sauvignon Blanc, BRL Hardy, *137*
TR2 Medium Dry White Wine 1995 Reserve, Wyndham Estate, *120*
Traditional Premium Ale, Caledonian, St Michael, *115*
Tramontane 1996 Syrah, Vin de Pays d'Oc, Asda, *3*
Trentino Chardonnay 1996 La Vis, Asda, *7*
Trentino Pinot Nero 1995 La Vis, Asda, *3*
Le Trulle 1994 Primitivo del Salento, *170*
Le Trulle 1996 Chardonnay, *163*
Two Pints Bitter, Cropton Brewery, *23*

U

Uggiano 1994 Chianti dei Colli Fiorentini, *118*
Uggiano 1995 Chianti Classico, *119*
Uncle Sams Bitter, Cropton Brewery, *25*
Ushers Founders Strong Ale, *51*

V

Vacqueyras 1995 Cuvée du Marquis de Fonseguille, *43*
Valblanc 1995 Colombard, Vin de Pays du Gers, *32*
Valdezaro 1996 Chilean Cabernet Sauvignon, *117*
Valdivieso 1996 Chardonnay, *9, 193*
Valdivieso 1996 Malbec, *5*
Valle de Vistalba 1995 Barbera, Casa Nieto & Senetiner, *17*
Valle de Vistalba 1995 Malbec, Casa Nieto & Senetiner, *60*

Index

Van Loveren 1996 Blanc de Noir Red Muscadel, *176*
Vergelegen 1995 Chardonnay, *138*
La Vieille Ferme 1994 Côtes-du-Rhône Réserve, *171*
Vignetti Casterna 1994 Valpolicella, Pasqua, *159*
Villa Maria Private Bin 1996 Sauvignon Blanc, *20*
Villa Montes 1994 Merlot Oak Aged Reserve, *135*
Vin de Pays de l'Aude White NV Foncalieu, Morrisons, *120*
Vin de Pays de Vaucluse 1996 Du Peloux, Safeway, *133*
Vin de Pays des Côtes-de-Gascogne 1995 DG 32800, Somerfield, *162*
Vin de Pays des Côtes-de-Gascogne 1996 Asda, *6, 109*
Vin de Pays du Gers 1996 St Michael, *108*
Vin Rouge NV Vin de Table Français, Chantovent, *87*
Viña Alarba 1995 Calatayud, *16*
Viña Caña Reserva 1987 Rioja, Somerfield, *161*
Viña Mara 1990 Rioja Reserva, Tesco, *172*
Viñas del Vero 1994 Merlot, *76*
Vine Vale Shiraz 1995 Peter Lehmann, *61*
Vine Vale Vineyard 1996 Chardonnay, St Michael, *112*
Vinha Nova NV Vinho de Mesa Tinto, *16*
Vintage Character Port NV Morgan Brothers, St Michael, *113*
Vintage Character Port NV Smith Woodhouse, Asda, *12*
Vintage Claret Aged in New Oak 1995 Yvon Mau, Tesco, *172*
Vionta 1995 Albariño, *77*
Virginie 1994 Cabernet Sauvignon, Vin de Pays d'Oc, *17*
Virginie 1995 Vermentino, Vin de Pays d'Oc, *20*
Vouvray 1996 Hand Picked, Denis Marchais, *9*
Vratislav Lager, Tesco, *179*

W

W.& J. Graham's Six Grapes Port NV, *178*
Waggle Dance Traditional Honey Beer, Vaux, *24, 52, 69, 125, 140, 181*
Waimanu NV Premium Dry Red Wine, *30*
Waimanu NV Premium Dry White Wine, *32*
Waitrose Champagne Blanc de Blancs NV Brut, NM-123, *196*
Waitrose Czech Lager, *198*
Waitrose French Lager, *198*
Waitrose Late Bottled Vintage Port 1990 Bottled in 1996 by Smith Woodhouse, *197*
Waitrose Oloroso Sherry NV Medium Sweet, Emilio Lustau, *196*
Waitrose Scottish Ale, Caledonian Brewery, *198*
Waitrose Strong Lager, *198*
Waitrose Westphalian Lager, *198*
Wallace IPA, Maclay & Co. Thistle Brewery, *53*
Ward's Classic Yorkshire Ale, *23, 52*
Warre's 1982 Traditional Late

Bottled Vintage Port, *197*
Warwick Estate 1993 Cabernet Franc, *189*
Weingut Toni Jost 1994 Bacharacher Schloss Stahleck Riesling Kabinett, *193*
Western Cape Shiraz/Cabernet Sauvignon 1995 Tesco, *172*
White Rabbit Premium Beer, Mansfield Brewery, *53*
Whitechapel Porter, Shepherd Neame, Asda, *13*
Winter Hill Rosé 1996 Vin de Pays de l'Aude, *195*
Wolf Blass Cabernet Sauvignon 1995 Yellow Label, *98, 161*
Wolf Blass Chardonnay Barrel Fermented 1996 , *99*
Wolf Blass Chardonnay Semillon 1996 , *99*
Wolf Blass Shiraz Cabernet Sauvignon 1995 Red Label, *98*
Worthington's White Shield, Fine Strong Ale, *27*
Wyndham Estate 1995 Oak Cask Chardonnay, *121*

Y

Yaldara Old Tawny NV Reserve, *66*
Yaldara Rosé NV Reserve Brut, *21*
Yalumba Cuvée One Prestige NV Pinot Noir/Chardonnay, *151*
Yalumba Cuvée Two Prestige NV Cabernet Sauvignon, *177*
York's Northern Bitter, St Michael, *114*
Young Vatted Cabernet Sauvignon 1995 Pietroasa Vineyards, *30*
Young's Ram Rod, Strong Ale, *182*

Z

Zagara 1995 Nero d'Avola, *134*
Zimmermann NV Rivaner, *120*